Pytho

the life and work of

Margaret Lumley Brown

Pythoness

the life and work of

Margaret Lumley Brown

As told and Edited by
GARETH KNIGHT

Thoth Publications
Loughborough, Leicestershire

Copyright 2006 Thoth Publications

NowickiAll rights reserved. No reproduction, copy or transmission of this publication may be made without written permission. No paragraph of this publication may be reproduced, copied or transmitted in any form or by any means, electronic or mechanical without the written permission from the Publisher, or in accordance with the provision of the Copyright Act 1956 (as amended). Any person who does any unauthorised act in relation to this publication may be liable for criminal prosecution and civil claims for damages.

The Moral Rights of the Author have been asserted.

A CIP catalogue record for this book is available from the British Library.

Cover design by Helen Surman

Published by Thoth Publications
64, Leopold Street, Loughborough, LE11 5DN

ISBN 978 1 870450 75 1
Web address www.thoth.co.uk
email: enquiries@thoth.co.uk

In Memoriam
Henry and Edward
Priests of Pasht

CONTENTS

INTRODUCTION	Page 1
Chapter One Haunting Experiences	Page 19
Chpater Two Psychic Encounters	Page 68
Chapter Three Communications	Page 123
Chapter Four Poetics	Page 212
Index	Page 247

INTRODUCTION

"Probably the finest medium and psychic of the twentieth Century"

The Society of the Inner Light, one of the leading esoteric schools of our day, is closely associated in the public mind with its founder Dion Fortune. What is less known is the importance of her colleague Margaret Lumley Brown, who took over many of Dion Fortune's functions after the latter's death in 1946.

Of Margaret Lumley Brown, Dion Fortune's biographers Fielding and Collins, in *The Story of Dion Fortune*, have this to say:

> Margaret Lumley Brown was probably the finest medium and psychic of this century, although the public never knew her. She raised the arts of psychism and mediumship to an entirely new level and the high quality of communication that came through her has not been equalled.

These are high claims, but from personal acquaintance and direct experience of her work, I would certainly not disagree with this opinion. Some of the evidence for its validity is to be found in Part Three of this book, which contains the record of a number of her trance addresses.

After Dion Fortune's death the ongoing work of the Society of the Inner Light was largely inspired and sustained by her remarkable abilities. She was, in title and in function, its Arch Pythoness. That is to say, the principal receiver of inner plane communications, whether private advice and instruction to those responsible for running the Society, or more publicly to the membership at various meetings.

She continued in this role until the early 1960's when the Society underwent a change of direction, with a greater

Christian emphasis, buttressed by various techniques of psychological and spiritual self assessment, Margaret Lumley Brown, now in her seventies, was relegated to a much diminished role.

I resigned from the Society in 1965 feeling that the way it was going was not that in which I wished to proceed, although Margaret Lumley Brown remained a member for the rest of her life.

I got to know Margaret Lumley Brown quite well in my capacity as editor of *New Dimensions*, a small esoteric magazine of the time, for which she wrote a number of articles. My wife and I retain a vivid memory of entertaining her to dinner, when she transported us with a fund of tales of other-worldly creatures she had observed through second sight. The stories generally had to be coaxed out of her, and were delivered in a matter of fact, slightly apologetic manner, of one who realised that all this must seem rather odd to those not gifted with her unusual faculties.

There was a certain invocatory power about her stories that was not merely subjective, for when we returned to the room after she had gone, there was a strange stillness in the air, and all the candle flames were standing straight to a remarkable height. Nothing weird, but certainly impressive, and a fitting end to a memorable evening.

Another somewhat startling impression came when we walked her down to the tube station. I knew from previous conversation that she suffered some distress when crossing a busy street because she was sensitive to the traffic rushing through her aura. However, this seemed to have a positive side to it, for she walked straight out into the maelstrom of traffic at a busy junction, looking neither to right nor to left, yet arrived unscathed and unperturbed at the other side, waving airily to us like some ancient goddess as she disappeared into the bowels of the earth, on this occasion courtesy of London Transport.

It was more than a decade before we met again, and this the result of a highly unlikely coincidence. My wife and daughter were shopping in the small country town in which we now lived when someone collapsed on the pavement just front of them. My wife caught the old lady as she staggered and fell, and was amazed to find that it was Margaret Lumley Brown she was holding in her arms!

It turned out that she was no longer resident at the Society of the Light's headquarters, and whilst looking for a place to live, was staying with a niece who lived nearby. We were delighted to greet her as a temporary neighbour and invited her to dine once more. There were no more candle phenomena but she delighted us with the priceless remark, said in all seriousness, that she quite liked the town, (which was situated on an ancient Roman crossroads), but sometimes found it rather hard to sleep on account of the noise of the marching legions.

In a bare account such as this it may well appear that she must have been a rather scatty creature after the mode of Noel Coward's hilarious spiritualist medium Madame Arcati in *Blithe Spirit*. She was, on the contrary, a very clear headed and articulate person with a formidable historical knowledge. It would seem that she was particularly sensitive to 'place memories' in the psychic atmosphere – an awareness that amounted to a curse rather than a blessing when it first opened.

Towards the end of her stay, she arrived on the doorstep and presented me with a little bundle. It contained a black plaster statue of a goddess of extremely primitive aspect, and a somewhat inefficient but very evocative brass thurible ornamented with swans and roses. Along with these artefacts were a number of letters and press cuttings, an old sketchbook of psychic impressions, and three little printed books, two of which she had written herself. Thrusting all this into my hands she declared that she was appointing me her literary executor.

Soon afterwards she moved away, having been offered accommodation in the house of a friend, and within a year or so she had died. She was probably aged about eighty-six, although when I last saw her she gaily professed to being 'nearly ninety!'

The small books were all published in 1918 or 19, the two of them by herself under the pen name of Irene Hay. One was a volume of poems called *The Litany of the Sun*, the other, *Both Sides of the Door – a Psychological Sketch*, which was a hair raising account of the first opening up of her psychism. Some of the contents are reproduced in Parts Four and One of this book.

Although rendered as a fictional account, *Both Sides of the Door* is a detailed record, with minor name changes, of her remarkable experiences in January 1913 at a haunted house near Marble Arch in London's west end. The earlier part also provides a useful potted biography of her early years, which were also unusual in many respects, and which we here relate.

She describes her father as a Northamptonshire squire with an unusual temperament. A man with exceptional ability of which he had made no use, being cursed with indolence and a swindling solicitor who finally lost him most of his money. He was naturally just and generous, but his gifts had festered into melancholy, religious bigotry, and a passionate hatred of everything post George III, in whose reign he had of course never lived. However, the feeling for that period gave him, besides an unfortunate lack of humour, a profound love of horses, wine and the Classics.

His wife was sweet and gentle, but being Victorian rather than Georgian, had little in common with him. She, like everyone else in the house, was completely dominated by his eccentric through not unkindly personality. He never lost his temper with her, but treated her invariably with an affectionate but pitiful courtesy, commiserating her with uncynical solicitude upon the feebleness of her health, understanding and sex.

He brought up his children consistently, his greatest regret being that all the old women in the village were too decadent to be able to teach his daughters how to spin. He consoled himself for this by teaching them to read from primers with long s's and children's books in vogue from seventy to a hundred years before.

Little boys and girls in these books, unless related, did not use the indelicate Christian name in addressing each other. They called each other Miss Snooks and Master Brooks, and their parents Sir and Ma'am. Their passion for obtaining suitable information was only equalled by the parents' passion for imparting it. It was only a very wicked child that ever refused to listen to the flow of its elders' knowledge, and then it died or became a permanent invalid. Good children not only profited by information, but were themselves able to improve each other by introducing into all conversation some apt quotation from the Scriptures.

There was also a tale of two children who were apparently on thorns to learn about a spider's anatomy. One said to the other: 'Pray, Maria, let us learn together the history of insects. Papa says it is what all girls should do for their amusement.'

The sound principles of this type of literature were perhaps undermined by Ovid, to whom at the age of eight each child was introduced with the accompaniment of a huge dictionary, dated 1715, and a grammar conscientiously written almost entirely in Latin and much battered from contact with the heads of several preceding generations in the family, who had all begun Latin at the same age and from the same books.

Their father insisted that the Elizabethan woman was the best feminine type, for she had the virtues of a man and the graces of a women, besides being excellently versed in the Classics and cooking!

When her father died Margaret was twelve and her sister a few years older. Money affairs were so bad that the house had to be sold. What was over when the debts were settled bought their mother a small annuity. A great-aunt sent Margaret to a boarding school, where she arrived with the best 18th century manners, which appeared to be of use only in the dancing class.

Their mother, though a semi-invalid, had a sense of the ridiculous if not of humour, and was now able to develop a rather obliterated taste for modernity and dress, insofar as her infinitesimal means allowed, and to pass a not too cheerless existence in various cheap apartments in England and abroad.

The children had nothing in common with their mother intellectually, but had a real affection for her. All three were in unusual harmony. They called her by her Christian name in preference to 'Mother' and the relationship on both sides was more as between ordinary friends than between parent and children. They never interfered with each other and took for granted that their mother had other friends, possibly nearer and dearer than they were. She did the same by them, often joking about the curious fact of their being her children, and joining with them in mutual marvel at their late father whom, in her gentle way, she regretted having married.

Margaret lived with her mother after leaving school. She had grown up a voracious reader of all sorts and conditions of books. Her mother gave her freedom and sympathy, and she was not unhappy. At this time she wrote several articles which were mostly rejected and received three offers of marriage which she herself rejected. When she was twenty-two her mother suddenly died while on a visit to some relations.

The relations offered Margaret a home but were obviously grateful to her for refusing it. Her mother had only possessed an annuity, but the previous year a great-aunt had left £120 a year to be divided equally between the sisters. With her share of this Margaret went to London to await her sister and events. She took up her abode in a Bayswater boarding house which agreed to keep the soul in the body for 15 shillings a week.

She was anxious to set about getting some work and went to various agencies where she was informed that training was absolutely necessary for any good post. They suggested that perhaps she might try a shop or an office but finally intimated that there was really no place at all for 'fine ladies'. She was however too sensitive and shy to be sure that she was even a human being, let alone a member of any special 'class'.

At last she succeeded in obtaining a post in an insurance office but had to leave within the week as the unusual life made her feel ill. She was disappointed, for the girls in the office had been kind, the work was perfectly easy, and the hours short. After recuperating, she ventured on to another office in the City with the same results, except that the girls were unkind and the manager too kind. Then she decided it would be better to do no more till her sister arrived.

The boarding house was getting more and more on her nerves, but as there were few as cheap she was reluctant to leave. The type of humanity there was new to her. She had been welcomed in as an insignificant girl who would be properly awed by the confidences of the landlady, who apparently had the vocation of performing the office of midwife to some long suffering beings whom she described as 'titled ladies'. She would lead conversation into the intricacies of her profession when not confiding her experiences as a woman who possessed the fatal gift of attraction to members of the opposite sex, with all the inconveniences and annoyances that bought.

Having borne as much of these revelations as she could stand without being sick, Margaret found some furnished rooms near Notting Hill Gate. There she met the young apprentice dress maker who features as Ruth in the events described in *Both Sides of the Door*. She seemed to keep house there but after three weeks confided that she had been coerced into being a virtual servant and did not dare quarrel openly with the owners because it was the only roof she had. The proprietors turned out to be systematic petty thieves and exploiters of vulnerable tenants and Margaret and the girl, after a somewhat distressing confrontation, succeeded in moving out together into a small unfurnished flat in Maida Vale for £40 a year.

Here, having been introduced to the facilities of the pawnbroker's trade she was able to raise enough cash on her bits of jewellery to put down the deposit on some hire purchase furniture. They were joined two weeks later by her elder sister, who had been on the continent, and then detained in hospital with scarlet fever on the way home. Here they lived for two years until the events related in *Both Sides of the Door* and, although relatively impecunious, contrived to move in fashionable literary and bohemian circles.

The writer Algernon Blackwood was a close friend, and his initials and a personal dedication in the poetic style of the day, complete with green ink, appears in one of the books she gave me. Alas, however, I have been informed by Mike Ashley, Blackwood's biographer, that it is not in his handwriting!

To Irene Hay
with a little book

Dreamer of delicate dreams
Above the town
All veiled in shimmery green
your home looks down
Like some enchanted bower,
All agleam,
Of some remote sweet princess
Of a dream.

INTRODUCTION

Your home? – Beyond the streams
Beyond the years,
Beyond the misty ramparts
Of the hills,
Beyond all music, and the salt of tears
In that Scots faeryland that ever thrills
Through the wide earth on which her children roam –
With pride and dreams of honour and romance
(Oh heritance!)
There is your home.

A.B. 18/10/19

The book is a little volume of the poems of Anyte of Tegea and Sappho, translated from the ancient Greek.

Her own poetry appeared in various literary journals of the time, and *The Litany of the Sun* is a collection of them, published in 1918 by Erskine Macdonald for two shillings and sixpence. This received encouraging reviews in *The Scotsman, The Times Literary Supplement, The Publishers' Circular, Library World, The Glasgow Herald, The Financial Chronicle* and *The Spectator*, and some are reproduced in Part Four.

Not surprisingly, some of them reflect her longstanding interests. She was strongly attracted to the Stuart cause, and at a later stage of her esoteric career she learned that in a recent incarnation she had, as a young boy, been hanged for taking part in the 1745 rebellion. She also felt a strong affinity for the ancient Babylonian civilisation; and in particular for the goddess Ishtar. In her early years she had written some *Babylonian Fragments* that almost wrote themselves under pressure, rather than being laboriously composed, and these excited particular favourable comment amongst reviewers.

Whether it was a feeling of affiliation to a Babylonian goddess of Venus or her early introduction to Ovid that encouraged her liberal views, in the 1920's she came into contact and worked with Dr. Marie Stopes, the campaigner for sex education and birth control facilities for women of the working classes – victims of a social repression that seems bizarre or even ludicrous now but which was a great afflication at the time.

Somewhere along the line she also developed a strong interest in the legend of the lost continent of Atlantis. Indeed, within the papers that she left is some correspondence with the explorer Col. P.H.Fawcett, who in 1925, at the age of 61, set out to try to discover evidence of the lost continent in the Amazon jungle, a quest in which he was encouraged by the famous writer of romantic adventure fiction Rider Haggard.

It was in response to a couple of articles that Colonel Fawcett had written in *The Occult Review* that she contacted him, asking if he could give her advice on joining an esoteric society. He was not particularly helpful about this but in a brief but courteous note of 30th November 1923 replied:

> *Re your question – There is no actual "Lodge" in England, of the kind you seek. The term as applied to Headquarters of cults or Societies is of course of no importance in an occult sense. There are however many Messengers and Members of the Occult Communities to be met if you can recognise them! The "Lodges" of the Occult Hierarchy are such an extremely lofty organisation – even though physical – as to be beyond ones ability to contact.*
>
> *There is however a `focussing point`, if one may term it so, upon which a spiritual current is specially directed (as there are others scattered over the world) in these Isles. It was used by the first reformers, also known to, utilised by and perverted by the monks who built Glastonbury. Hence perhaps the fall of that magnificent building.*
>
> *If sensitive you may feel at Glastonbury what you will feel nowhere else in Britain. The Caucasus was the*

location in pre-war times of one of the Great Lodges, but it was withdrawn about the commencement of this century for obvious reasons. There may be some "Community" there still but I cannot say for certain. I imagine it doubtful as it is a coming centre of much unrest.

Yours truly, P.H.Fawcett.

Within a year however Margaret Lumley Brown wrote to him again, evidently asking him about an Atlantean vision or dream she had had. He responded by return, on 9th September 1924 at somewhat greater length.

Your query suggests that you have been getting communications purporting to be of an Atlantean nature. Such is not impossible as Atlantis is very much `in the air` just now. Such communication might certainly come through sensitives; that is to say waves of released information are picked up, or a deliberate plan is being developed. Are you by any chance getting strange characters? I happen to know a good many of these, albeit I am only aware of the meaning of very few. Such evidence would be very interesting, a good deal more so than general statements. If you are not, try to get them.

To attempt to get into communication with an Occult Community depends so absolutely upon the Hierarchy of the latter as to be very improbable. You could never be quite sure that you were not being deluded without other proof of some kind. It might however occur if conditions were suitable and a purpose were being served – for mere curiosity probably not.

Most, but not all, in the less backward of us were once members of the Atlantean race in its multitudinous branches, and those who held responsible positions are undoubtedly bound up with it consciously or unconsciously. We cannot shake off historical influences, and there are very interesting circumstances in the working out of occult law which throw us up against old associations again and again.

Psychics may give very genuine information, but it has to be carefully sifted as there are so many cross currents, particularly when not in trance. Time of course they know nothing about. In fact it is subject to acceleration and retardation by laws they know nothing about.

I may be in London before long and if you are in touch with anything Atlantean might possibly be able to help you.

Yours very truly, P.H.Fawcett

She obviously responded to this and made some remarks related to the occult significance of sonics, probably those that derived from her 1913 experiences. This time she received a long letter hand written letter in reply, dated 12th October 1924.

Your experiences are interesting, though it is difficult to fathom a purpose. I should be inclined to suggest that being sensitive to this particular range of world memory, and having some particular association with an Atlantean experience, as yet incompleted, you are being drawn once more into the chain of 'correspondences' which lead to some special purpose. The potency of words is little understood. It is rather the sound or intonation which is important, the word may be meaningless – like the potency of the 'Om' or 'Ohm'. All ritual was originally based upon this knowledge, and it is quite possible today to invoke the aid of very powerful influences by calling upon certain names a definite number of times. I have known of very curious cases of cure of cobra bite by *the recitation of a certain formula, itself puerile to a degree, but setting up a condition antagonistic to the poison when accompanied by a definite motion of hands and posture of body. `Science` would of course call this absurd. But the art of healing is extremely crude, and the germ theory, the knife, inoculation, the vitamin hypotheses will all in time share the fate of the `leech`.*

He continued with some thoughts about possible styles of Atlantean dress and of possible impending catastrophe if the world does not mend its ways and suggested a reputable psychic in London to whom she might turn for advice, concluding:

There is no need to doubt the reality of psychic vision – the process is easily explicable – but it is so often vitiated by personal consciousness, cross currents, and the perpetual bombardment of noises, smells, segments of the myriads of whirling thoughts to which we are subjected by day and to a lesser degree by night. That is why trance clairvoyance is so much more reliable. You will find Vont Peters goes into trance or rapidly intermittent trance, and is very highly efficient, if you are in sympathy with him. No psychic is any good if there is disharmony, and the poorer qualities of human nature do not assist these higher faculties – that is why the statesmen, financiers, judges and business men of all kinds who, under the rose, consult psychics so freely, get relatively little from them and that often in an enigmatical way.

I will let you know when I am in London. I shall probably [be] there sometime.

Yours sincerely, P.H.Fawcett.

> *By the way I am neither a spiritualist nor a Theosophist in the accepted sense – merely an interested enquirer with perhaps exceptional experience as enquirers go. It is far better not to adopt any cult whatever, but remain independent. They all mislead in one way or another – valuable as they may be in some ways.*
>
> *Glastonbury is one of those scarce and privileged points upon which certain spiritual forces impinge with particular strength. Hence probably the choice of site for the original chapel. There is also a triangle of adverse influences of about two million square miles and one of beneficial influences, which are respectively accumulating their respective effects.*
>
> *I might be able to bring you into touch with Mr. Bligh Bond – of Glastonbury fame – if your experiences suggest it. He is an old friend of mine and an exceedingly clever man – whom the gods have also tried in the fire of misfortune, as they do all [who] recognise them.*

Oddly enough, it is just at the time of this correspondence that Dion Fortune in Glastonbury was, in the process of trance clairvoyance, getting the beginnings of the material that led to the establishment of her esoteric fraternity. On at least one of these occasions Bligh Bond had been present, and a good deal of the material she subsequently received related to Atlantis. However it was another twenty years before Margaret Lumley Brown found her way to the Society of the Inner Light.

In the meantime she closely followed the fate of Colonel Fawcett and retained a number of press cuttings of his adventures. He sailed for Rio de Janeiro in 1925 as the culmination of the best part of eighteen years exploration in the South American jungles, in which he felt he had gone far to prove the existence of a majestic civilisation perhaps 10,000 years old, ante-dating Egypt, that held the secret of a mysterious light, possibly based on knowledge of atomic energy, and familiar with astronomy. The expedition was sanctioned by the Royal Geographical Society and the American Geographical Society despite its hazardous and spectacular nature. It had to contend with tribes of desperate ferocity and all but impenetrable jungle. On previous occasions Colonel Fawcett had seen men impaled by Indian arrows and a mule crushed by a fifty foot anaconda. He took only two men with him, his son John, 21 years old, and a family friend Raleigh Rimell, aged 23. A previous large expedition had been annihilated by pestilence and Indians, but with only three men, and speaking the language of the tribes, Fawcett felt he had an excellent chance. On a previous expedition he had saved his life with an electric torch, which led the Indians to endow him with certain godlike propensities. Facing the likelihood of a repetition of this experience he had some special lights made which could be adjusted on his head to appear as great, bulbous, flashing eyes.

With his two young companions Colonel Fawcett disappeared into the jungle in 1925 but never returned. A relief expedition mounted in 1928 concluded that the Fawcett party must have been wiped out by Indians.

In the *Sunday Dispatch* for September 11th 1932 however, the explorer's wife, Mrs. Nina Fawcett, put her name to an article that announced that she was convinced her husband was still alive. Almost continually during his absence, she had received what she considered reliable telepathic messages from him assuring her of his safety

The messages were not received directly by Mrs. Fawcett herself, but through four clairvoyants living as far apart as New Zealand, San Francisco, Tunis and Exeter, who had been specially chosen by Colonel Fawcett before his departure as a means of possible communication.

She said telepathic communications concerning her husband began early in 1925 and continued fairly regularly until late in 1928. Sometimes weeks would elapse in silence but then she would suddenly get messages from all four quarters giving the same information and even tallying in the dates given – to within a day or two. Since 1928 they had come less frequently and had seemed more like 'television experiences' to those in communication. She believed, as a consequence of these messages, that he had penetrated to a ruined ancient city inhabited by a white skinned fraternity marvellously versed in the powers of thought transference, and that the three explorers had remained there to be initiated into these telepathic powers.

She also mentioned an incident in the autumn of 1927. A European traveller had declared seeing Colonel Fawcett and although the sighting subsequently proved false, at the time Mrs. Fawcett had been prepared to go out to Brazil with her son Brian to accompany a rescue expedition. She had, however, received a letter 'from a woman in England – not one of our regular 'correspondents" dated October 12th which read in part:

> *'I am writing to tell you that I had a telepathic message from the colonel last night. He told me to tell you not to worry, that everything was coming out right, and on no account were you and Brian to [go] out to him, as he might need you to be waiting for him, if possible in November, but in case of trouble, in February, he hoped...'*

It is tempting to wonder whether this unknown correspondent was Margaret Lumley Brown. She certainly maintained sufficient interest in the Colonel's expedition to keep a file of press cuttings, she had a very strong and long standing interest in the subject of his expedition, and she certainly had remarkable psychic abilities.

INTRODUCTION

Many years later I recall her intense interest in a book by the spiritualist medium Geraldine Cummins entitled *The Fate of Colonel Fawcett* which seemed to contain further communications from this source. Geraldine Cummins was a spiritualist medium almost in a class of her own, of such integrity that she rarely made any claims as to the validity of communications she received. As far as physical evidence is concerned, however, the last word on the fate of the Colonel rests with his son Brian's book *Exploration Fawcett* that contains much of his father's papers and an account of the various alleged sightings and attempted rescue expeditions.

Our main story concerns however the fate of Margaret Lumley Brown and until she turns up as a member of the Society of the Inner Light in 1944 we know almost nothing more about her. Her sister, upon whom she relied quite heavily, had apparently recently died, and Dion Fortune offered her accommodation at her headquarters in Queensborough Terrace. Whether this was an act of altruistic kindness on Dion Fortune's part or whether she had an eye to her potential gifts, we do not know.

Within two years however Dion Fortune was dead, and we find under the new regime Margaret Lumley Brown being encouraged to try to develop her psychic gifts so that she could take her place. Her magical diaries from April 1946 give an account of this process of development. In this we find her being prepared, with some trepidation, to make her first attempt at a trance address to the whole Fraternity at its Summer Solstice meeting of June 1946, a function previously performed every quarter by Dion Fortune herself.

From this event, apparently successfully achieved, affectionately known either as 'Morgan' or as 'MLB', she continued to go from strength to strength in the development of the inner side of the Society's work. The full story of this work belongs to another book, but her large contribution to it can be adjudged from the various trance addresses that we

CHAPTER ONE

HAUNTING EXPERIENCES

Most people are more psychic than they realise, the glimmerings of psychic perception being put down to over imagination or impressionability. For some, who may have a greater gift for it than most, it may remain latent for many years, but can break out in what can be distressing and uncontrolled ways, often as a result of uninstructed dabbling in various forms of psychic experimentation with Ouija boards and the like.

Margaret Lumley Brown not only had quite remarkable latent gifts, but she began to perform elementary psychic experiments in what turned out to be a severely haunted house. The results were frightening in the extreme, threatening her sanity and even life itself. In this respect it might be said that the house was but latently haunted, its 'place memories' the rooms being activitated by having someone of unusual psychic ability living within them, and attempting to make some kind of contact, even in ignorance of the dynamics involved.

So powerful was the experience upon her that she wrote a little book describing her experiences, under the pen name

HAUNTING EXPERIENCES   19

of Irene Hay, issued by a well known publisher of the day, Arthur H. Stockwell in 1919. Her motives for so doing were well described in her preface:

> *The following true sketch endeavours to present the most consecutive rendering possible of such involved circumstances...*
>
> *The object in relating these events is less to prove some special point of view than to show where conflicting opinions seem to converge. Every human experience is of a certain amount of use to other human beings, even if it only shows them what to avoid, and therefore it is interesting to note the evidence of five people in the same house, at the same time, and with respect to the same events.*
>
> *My only personal prejudice throughout is against the indiscriminate use of the term 'psychic', which too often has come to imply either a trite spirituality or a form of insanity. The sanest thing to realise, surely, is that we all possess much the same qualities varied only in degree and grade, and that, unless we entirely fail to regulate their proportions, there is nothing necessarily either unwholesome or remarkable in them.*

There follows this fictionalised account which has been slightly abridged by me at beginning and end. In an ostensibly fictional work she felt obliged to close with a romantic ending and to begin her account two years before the events in question, with how the characters involved met.

In the fictional account Kathleen Trent represents herself, and the fictional brother Theo was in real life her elder sister. Otherwise, the characters of Ruth, their live-in general factotum, and her uncle, seem drawn from the life, although with changed names.

BOTH SIDES OF THE DOOR
A Psychological Sketch

THREE PEOPLE AND TWO CATS

It was the last night at the flat. Kathleen and her brother sat on the large table by the window above a sea of bare boards strewn with wreckage of paper, boxes, books tied together, and chairs piled in couples.

A candle, in an empty Sauterne bottle on the piano, shed a feeble light.

Kathleen looked out through an uneven parting in the Venetian blind, into the starry Michaelmas night.

"I wonder," she said thoughtfully, "whether all the unhappiness we've felt and thought, 'specially in the summer when we always talked things over leaning out of this window, will infect the next people who come here. I hope not."

"It will depend upon the people," said Theo. "Some people never take infection. I'll have Ruth in, and then we can decide about division of labour tomorrow."

He went to the door and called.

"Yes, Mr. Trent – coming!" came a voice muffled in the rustling of many papers from the other end of the flat.

Ruth came. She had a wide, pale face, whose slanting eyebrows gave it a Japanese effect. She wore a kind of overall, and her hair, of that rare dark copper which is less adequately imitated than any tint, was half covered with a hideous duster of gamboge flannel. She carried a large dusty black cat under one arm, and a large dusty tabby cat under the other.

"Look at the little men," said Ruth, displaying the animals. "I can't get on with my packing, because they both keep getting into the tub where I'm putting the saucepans."

"Never mind the little men," said Theo. "We've got to think about tomorrow. When did your uncle say the van would come?"

"At nine," said Ruth. "And everything's ready."

"You and I had both better be here till everything's out," said Theo, "Miss Trent breaks herself if she moves things about. She'd much better go on first with the cats and tell the men where to put things when they unload at the other end."

"I'll take the cats with me on the bus," said Kathleen. "They'd better go in that basket thing with straps. They are too fat to take in anything smaller, and we can't afford a cab for them. I'll shut them in one of the top rooms at the new place till the men have finished. I'd also better get in food of sorts."

"All right," said Theo, "then that's that. Now we must get to bed really."

"How on earth," said Kathleen to Ruth whom she met at the door of her room, "shall we get through tomorrow?"

"I know," said Ruth, "but I feel I can't go to bed. Isn't it funny to think of all that's happened here? It looks sad to see the place empty."

Kathleen retired to her room. She was in bed in a few seconds. Then she began to cry. "I'm glad we're leaving," she reflected. "It may be better luck in the new place. One must be philosophical I suppose. And yet everything has compensation if one can only get to the point of seeing what compensation is. We've got poverty, but we've got peace. Ruth is really an angel, for we could not have afforded a servant, and if we could it would be an awful fag in our Bohemian sort of life."

Kathleen and Theo's life in the flat had been fraught with the difficulties of romance and poverty. They had many friends whom they entertained, when fate permitted, at the restaurants in Soho. Edward and Henry were added to the household. Theo became deeply in love with a girl who returned it within the limits of her nature, which was of a totally different type from his own. She therefore said goodbye to him.

Kathleen became engaged to Cyril King, an artist, who died from the result of a street accident in Paris within the year. This dual disaster in love cast a heavy shadow over the last months in Aberdeen Mansions.

The brother and sister were close affinities. Their characters and looks dove-tailed to an unusual extent. Physically and mentally Theo was a more dominant type than Kathleen, but her mind supplied the details of what his saw *en masse*. She acted as his secretary, and they worked well together, being counterparts of the same attitude to things.

Life in the flat lasted for two years. Then, to be nearer his work, Theo took the only place within their means which was available after a fruitless house hunt for some months.

The story opens on the eve of the removal to these new quarters.

The New House

The cats were very heavy and refused to balance properly, rolling together to the same end of the case and emitting infuriated comments at intervals. She was thankful when the end of the bus journey was reached and she had achieved the still more difficult task of carrying her burden over the few still remaining yards to the house, where the animals were unpacked and enclosed in a small room at the top.

This done, Kathleen came down the stairs slowly, glancing into each of the strange looking unfurnished spaces. It was curious that in spite of newly scrubbed boards and fresh paint and paper, the rooms smelt so fusty.

She opened the drawing room window wide and leaned out. A slight wind blew in, bringing a faint odour of dahlias and dead leaves from the Park, a glimpse of which could be seen at the corner of the furthest block of buildings in the road beneath.

The house was really a self contained maisonette, formerly inhabited by the landlady, a dressmaker, who still continued her business in the adjoining shop. This woman was impulsive and had had the sudden whim of changing her abode quickly. Knowing through a house agent that the Trents wanted to move immediately, she facilitated things so amazingly for them to take her former home that everything was arranged in an incredibly short time. The neighbourhood in which the house lay – immediately behind Edgware Road – was unpleasant, but the position for Theo's work was convenient, and the rooms, though low and built on an old-fashioned plan, were large and welcome after the cramped life at the flat, while the entrances to shop and maisonette were entirely separate. Fate clearly pointed to the house, which was the only suitable one to be found at a crucial moment.

Kathleen debated how the furniture should be arranged in the various rooms. Her mind went back to the arrival in their previous flat. 'At least we can start with carpets here,' she thought, for a better and larger stock of household necessities had been accumulated during the two years.

She went out to buy a few groceries and to have such lunch as Messrs. Lyons` haughty beauties saw fit to bring her.

When she returned, an errand boy was waiting on the doorstep with some flowers. She took them in and found beneath the wrappers some pointed shell-pink roses on long stems. Attached to them was a card inscribed in Eric's baffling writing, 'the first lot of furniture.' Eric was a Danish friend who had known Kathleen and her brother for several years. He was in reality over fifty, but with a curiously youthful air. He had never had the least inclination for matrimony, but displayed an affectionate and entirely respectable friendship to women, who often mistook his intentions. That Kathleen did not, constituted a real bond between them.

'How nice of him,' she said beneath her breath, 'and how delightfully apt!'

She found a jar which she washed with care, placing the roses in it. As she carried them upstairs a sheet of darkness, undispelled by the sunlight streaming through the window immediately above it, seemed to move to another position. She wondered about it momentarily, and then forgot the incident. The van soon came, and the next few hours were filled in giving directions till the arrival of Ruth and Theo. It was nearly eight o'clock before the furniture had been completely unloaded and the men dismissed.

'Good Lord,' said Theo, noting the time in horror. 'Those fellows will have been waiting in Pagani's nearly half an hour.'

They hailed a passing taxi which conveyed them – Theo fuming all the way – to the insulted guests who awaited them in the restaurant; Eric, and Gerald Lockwood, a friend who held an official position in Egypt and was over in London on business and had met them fairly often during the past few months.

Preliminary apologies and explanations ended, dinner was ordered and the four fell to amicably. Conversation always flowed easily when Theo was host, for he had the art of making other people talk.

It turned to the subject of dreams, which reminded Kathleen of one she had had a long time ago about Mary Queen of Scots.

'I suppose you'd been reading or talking about her,' said Lockwood.

'No, I hadn't. I've really read nothing much about her since she came in one's history lessons. Funnily enough too, I was never enormously interested in her as I was in the other Stuarts. I was reminded of the dream again because it's just struck me that our new house is surely near where Tyburn used to be, isn't it?'

"Just near the Marble Arch end of Edgware Road?" said Lockwood, "Yes, I believe it is. What was the dream?"

"I dreamed I was in a garden at our old home. Theo and I often have it as a background for dreams. Suddenly I saw Mary Queen of Scots…"

"But how did you know who it was?" said Lockwood.

"Because I've often seen pictures of her, and apart from that I knew instinctively that it was. She had that round lace cap on one sees in some of the pictures, but her dress was quite different from any I had so far seen in a portrait. She had a very transparent skin. It was luminous in some strange way, as if there was a light within it or behind it. She beckoned me to follow her to another part of the garden and I did so. As she walked she seemed to grow by turns visible and invisible with each step she took. She stopped on the lawn at the back of the house and said something which I could not make out. But the word 'Tyburn' came into my mind, and she pointed to a tiny cart with a prisoner in it and a driver. It was like a miniature procession of a criminal going to Tyburn, and she was coming over the lawn towards me. Then she took my hand and looked into my eyes and vanished rather like the Cheshire Cat in *Alice in Wonderland.* First her hands, then her arms, then various parts of her figure, and lastly her face. By the way, she had golden hair in the dream, and I thought she had auburn hair. But why she should point out anything to do with Tyburn to me I can't think. It was a long time before we left the flat, and so there was nothing in my mind to suggest the neighbourhood of Tyburn. In fact the dream seems a silly one, except that it was very clear and rather odd. A little later I looked through, in a shop, the illustrations in a new life of Mary Queen of Scots. In this book there was a portrait of her as Dauphiness that I had never seen before, and she was wearing the very dress I had seen in the dream."

"That was curious, but I imagine you must have read of her or seen some picture which you probably have totally forgotten about, which built it up in your mind."

Kathleen laughed. "You may be right, and I'm not the least sensitive about my dreams, but some unreasonable part of me feels certain it was more than that."

PRELUDE

The first days in the new house passed quickly. The evenings were becoming chilly. After the routine of typing and writing was finished and the last letters posted, the Trents basked in front of the fire in the drawing room and discussed any subject uppermost in the mind.

"Last night I dream of how the neighbourhood must have looked years ago," said Kathleen.

"How curious!" said Theo. "So did I! How did you see it?"

"There was a stream at the back of this house where some women were washing clothes. The houses round looked quite different, and there were a lot of trees in the distance almost as if it were the country. There was no pavement anywhere, but I saw cobble stones where Connaught Square is now."

"I didn't see any women washing clothes, but I saw the brook and the cobble stones. There were no yards at the back of the houses as there are now, and the Bayswater Road looked like a country one with trees and cottages rather sparsely scattered over it. How fusty this place always smells, by the way! Yet the windows are always open a lot."

"I know; I can't think how to get rid of the smell. But the house has been so thoroughly scrubbed and aired, I don't understand it. To change the subject, Mary Field came in today and stayed to lunch. She has found some wonderful new method of voice production. She is experimenting with it on me. She says I'm so unmusical that if this method makes *me* sing it will make anybody."

"You're not unmusical, but you've no pitch, and your voice, though it's soft and pleasant enough, is never produced right. How does her method work?"

"You make each sound vibrate till you feel it in every air passage in your head, as it did when we were children and blew on a comb wrapped in tissue paper."

"Humph? There's no new method in that. I shall be interested in the result."

"I've had two lessons already. It's a horrid sensation and makes me feel awfully queer all over, but she says it always does at first, and that it's merely because of the vibration."

"If it makes you feel ill, for Heaven's sake don't do it."

"It's only a momentary feeling. It's sure to go later on."

"Is Mary still mad on spiritualism? The last time I saw her she was always holding conversations with her great grandmother and carrying strange pamphlets about with amazing titles - *A Cottage in Borderland* and *Plain Talks with the Dead* I believe they were called."

"She's still keen. Of course spiritualism is really an excellent preliminary, but people will think of it as final. It happens to bore us because it brings us nothing new, and because we've always believed not in nothing but in everything and have had dreams all our lives. It's bound to be sometimes banal in expression, because unfortunately the dead are much what they were in life, and thousands of people are banal."

'I can't see the point of only meeting one's grandparents at séances' said Theo. 'Interesting spirits seldom come, and when they do they don't seem likely. Napoleon, for instance, usually speaks perfect English and says that all his misfortune came from leaving Josephine, and that he therefore hopes everybody will always live with their wives, and then they will be as happy as he is now. Damn – I've left my pipe downstairs!' He rose and went out of the room.

Kathleen, sitting according to custom on the hearth rug, watched him go idly. The autumn mist, which had crept through the crevices of the ill fitting windows, made the room dim despite the fire and electric light. How curiously that black shadow swept out of the armchair opposite her onto the floor! She looked in vain for an object which could have cast it. Henry, who had been curled in a compact circle, unrolled himself suddenly, got up and went up to the chair, sniffing it suspiciously. The shadow spread like folds of black velvet. It seemed to fill the chair now, and above it flashed for a second a pointed elusive face in a lace coif.

Kathleen sat up. "I must have imagined that!" she said to herself. There was no longer any shadow in the chair. Henry returned to the rug and coiled himself to sleep once more.

Theo came back with his pipe and a small table.

"What on earth have you got that table for?" said his sister.

"I know it's mad, but I suddenly felt an impulse to try table turning with you. Although we've never gone in for séances or spirit rapping and all that stuff, it would be rather interesting to try the experiment."

"When you had gone I seemed to see Mary Queen of Scots sitting in that chair. Henry got up and went to it. She vanished in an instant. It must be imagination, yet why did the cat wake up at that second and go and smell all round that particular chair?"

"How funny! It may have been a spirit, but hardly Mary Stuart. According to Theosophists, she'll have been reincarnated in half a dozen thoroughly unattractive women by now."

They sat down on each side of the table, laying the tips of their fingers on it. "Really," said Kathleen, "we look rather idiots."

The table duly agreed to tap twice for 'yes' and once for 'no', and to stop on its way through the alphabet at each letter included in the word it wished to denote.

After a while various defunct 'relations' came and spelt out platitudes in the approved manner.

"Look here," said Theo, "haven't any of you something more interesting to say?" There was a pause.

"Let me do it alone and see what happens," said Kathleen. He left the table and sat on the sofa.

"I can't understand it, for it's German," said Kathleen presently. "But it's someone called Margarethe who repeats a word that sounds mere nonsense over and over again."

"What is it? Spell it to me."

She did so.

"Now," said Theo, "that for once is not bad, for you don't know German and so can't fake. And I doubt if I ever fagged to tell you about a little music student called Margarethe. She lived in Dresden, and we had a slight flirtation. There was a joke between us about this particular word which I always misused, for I didn't speak German well at the time, and didn't know that the expression was vulgar Saxon dialect. She always teased me over it. She died two years ago, I heard. Is she still there?"

"No. It says it's Cyril now, but it doesn't seem like him."

"Meet – me – Marble – Arch – five tomorrow," spelt the table.

"But who am I to meet and why?" asked Kathleen.

"Cyril. Promise – so – that – I – can – tell – if – you – heard – right. We – want – tests – too."

Theo returned to the table and laid his hands on it again.

"That sounds fairly probable somehow," he said.

"Very well, I promise," said Kathleen. "But I am sure that you are not Cyril."

"I – am – Cyril," spelt the table.

"Tell me whereabouts you are standing," said Theo.

"By – the – fire. I – feel – so – distressingly – visible."

"Well, its very queer," said Kathleen. "I can't see that I am saying all this out of my subconscious mind, yet that is obviously the sensible way to look at it. Get me a clean sheet of paper and a pencil and we'll try automatic writing."

Theo brought them to her.

"I hold the pencil and empty my mind of everything, don't I?" she said.

"I believe so."

She shut her eyes, and the pencil wrote vigorously for a few minutes.

"It's a verse," she said in surprise.

They unravelled some of the lines with care.

TO LAIS

Don your heavy golden dress
In the phantom hours of dawn
When the Attic sleepers press
Round the jocund fawn.

Toss the heads of dancing flow'rs,
Turn the roses to your face,
Lead the yellow morning hours
To the highest grace...."

PERSEPHONE IN HADES

Poppies grow from your hair
Goddess of Sleep
Who put them there
In the air?
Do you care?
Do you lie in your lair
Under the earth?
Do you weep
For the deep
And the steep
Path of passion and birth,
Goddess of Sleep?

"They've both been written in eight minutes," said Theo. "I timed it. I don't see that your subconscious mind could have invented them quite so quickly. Also, you've never written poems. It seems to me an instantaneous *jeu d'esprit* of a person with a certain technical knowledge of verse."

"Let's do the table again and see," said Kathleen.

"It's – quite – easy," said the table. "One – can – do – that – sort – of – thing - in – an – instant. I – appear – to – exist – no – longer – so – your – subconscious – self – made – it – up – but – Mr. – Stead – would – probably – contradict – me. Good night."

"It's been quite an interesting evening," said Kathleen as they separated on the way to their bedrooms. Outside the drawing room door something waited in the darkness, as though a part of it, and then joined the deeper shadows on the staircase.

"Isn't it funny," said Theo, "that the darkness seems to move in this house, almost as if it were tangible? I suppose it's some effect of light and shadow."

The afternoon of the next day found Kathleen at the Marble Arch at five o'clock. "If anyone knew that I was making an assignation with a spirit at this place and in this century," she thought, "they would not unnaturally think me mad. But no-one will know, so I shall keep my reputation in all senses of the word."

After waiting under the Arch for an instant she turned and walked slowly down Oxford Street, looking at the shop windows. In the midst of her own thoughts flashed a sudden sentence which had not sprung from them. Her ears did not hear it, but it entered her brain through some other channel: "Thank you. I thought you might come, but I was not sure."

She told Theo of this experience. They did more table turning each night that week, always with entertaining results. Kathleen, for the first time in her life, had no dreams.

POST-MORTEM DIALOGUES

The most frequent visitor during table turning of automatic writing was a strongly defined personality who called himself 'Charon'. The Trents kept account of his conversations and their replies in an old exercise book from which the following extracts are taken.

Charon – Why not write down what you say as well as what I say? These post mortem dialogues are most engaging, particularly since I am full of *joie de vivre*. I know you love poetry. To your eyes, I suppose, the words are beautiful, but strange and sometimes far fetched. Poetry should ever be fetched from afar. Have you read the Song of Solomon and the Book of Job?

Kathleen – I love the chapter of the horse and the part about the stars.

Charon – I am delighted to find you so receptive. 'Canst thou bind the sweet influence of Pleiades or loose the bands of Orion?' How lovely! A Hebrew prince lying in state, swathed in scented linen and odorous with spices, laid along the Eastern sky on his golden bier in a hall of lapis lazuli, like some wonderful tapestry of God!

All poetry, whether in prose or verse, is music. Each word must be lovely in sound, perfectly touched to bring out its deepest melody, and perfectly judged in its relation to other sounds. For words, which in themselves are melodious, become discords if struck out of tune. Euphony is the harmony of language. Never let yourself get into hideous habits of speech, through using unmusical words. Your hands are like little white birds which fly about and won't be caught. You are like a water lily in a silver sheath. Is not that a charming compliment? I only want you to realise yourself. Don't laugh! Don't try to emulate others. Never laugh at what is out of the common; laugh, rather, at what is ordinary.

I am still puzzled as to what to make of you. If you dressed in some barbaric saffron robe and sat upon an ivory chair I could consider you better.

Sorrow always, whether it makes for evil or good in one's nature, deepens it, and through that depth one realises oneself more fully than ever could have been done before the floods of one's being rise and make the gateway of the soul break down before them. You know so much and yet so little. I have taught you more of life than you ever knew, and the amount you know about death is disgusting. Life and youth, my child, are better than your anaemic theosophical books. I wish you were a Catholic. Why are you not?

Kathleen - I don't like to be bound to anything, and I believe in all religions, not in one alone.

Charon – You must be tied in some way, or there would be neither harmony nor wisdom. Everything must manifest in some form, from cosmic essences to human spirits – abstract things as well as concrete. Form is the necessary completion of the Infinite, for all power must be centralised somewhere if it is to be of use. So Christ sent forth His Spirit before the world began, but when He came all the pain in the universe drew itself back toward the Figure which has become the Embodiment of all sorrow, and after that it fashioned itself an abstract form in what became the universal motive power of Christianity, i.e. the Catholic Church.

Poetry is the universal outpouring of spirit into matter some say. I call it the entrance of substance into shadow. For all loveliness must be veiled save from the adepts and priests of her mysteries.

This is why Holy Church holds the key to beauty and all sacramental things. On this fact hangs all nature according to the law and the poets. Christ walked upon the water and was one with the powers of the deep. He was made prisoner in a garden. He left His freedom among the flowers, and each tree bears a message of man's salvation, since wood first blossomed with the limbs of God.

Can you not imagine the scene? It was morning, and the one serene Figure among that rough horde of soldiers passed out of Gethsemane long the road to Jerusalem, the rabble of various races mingled with His own followers in the rear. Nothing to show that He was either a God or a King then. But for those who had eyes to see, a pale diadem of light was resting on the hills, and the olives in the far retreating garden began to shine in the sun, and overhead the dawn was weaving a royal robe of amethyst and fine gold.

So if we are made in God's image we must in some degree be symbols of Him before we come into the kingdom of our own soul. We cannot do this if we have not first passed through Gethsemane and Calvary.

* * *

Charon – We will now have a dissertation on psychic phenomena, which I am really in a position to give. I trust Mr. Stead will not contradict me. It is high time someone wrote a little common sense about what is called 'the astral plane.' The accounts seem coloured by dead sentimentalists and living ghosts, as far as I can make out. Nothing that I say about it will be amazingly original; it will be ordinary fact undiluted by sentimentality.

To begin with, one isn't dead. One is merely in another phase of existence in which every faculty is extended to its utmost limit, but we are deprived of all physical expression such as eating, sleeping, etc. The greatest marvel is that one is strong and well and quite passably fortunate in having found an impenetrable haven, and that one has physical form and a craving for sensation, though there is nothing to show for it except a super-subtlety of the soul. Of course the ultimate aim of existence is self expression, a thing which is directed by thought and act as in the world, and only here they are synonyms.

A man dies and steps out of one body into another dimension – the fourth as far as other people are concerned. He is complete in physical sensation, faculty and form as when he walked on earth. It resembles more than anything a new skin which has been formed under the old one, exactly like it, only younger and more elastic. The old one shrivels up and becomes a piece of unanimated, mortifying, substance.

One is in the world, but no longer of it. One sees and hears others who are of it only in a detached way. Their voices and their actions seem far off, even if there is only the space of a foot between what is visible and what is invisible. Thought travels with lightning rapidity and is the regulator of this phase because it is action. Also, things are relative to oneself and not to wholesale standards. I see, more than ever, how the individual wins in the long run. All things must come from oneself.

Except for the first few hours after physical dissolution, and when I have moods of despondency which always weaken one, I have not been through anything like Hell, figurative or literal. The magnetism of one's own thought builds a wall round one infinitely stronger than bricks and mortar. Thus none can come near one unless of the same condition and type of mind either on this or any plane. An individualist therefore, is absolutely alone as a rule. Again this is why people like – well, those with perceptions of the highest possibilities in art, say – never go near the limbo of the commonplace that haunts the usual séance chamber. *That* is *Hell* if you like.

I don't consider you a medium in its usual sense. If you were, I could not talk to you for long. You are someone who has been given highly developed physical faculties – that is all. So developed that they extend beyond the coarser fibres of existence into the finer. That is why you hear me speak.

My fiercest regret is that I allowed myself to hate or despise anything at any time, because I see how these things tell against one's soul. Harmonious blending of the forces that are in one, no matter whether in themselves good or evil, make for perfect development. Evil into good, sensuality into purity. So-called opposites are really one, for the ingredients in each are the same. They are merely different stages of a certain quality. The same pole – though in unadvanced natures each end seems a different line instead of the same one. What one must do is to organise all into a perfect unified expression of one's individual standpoint.

All harmony is intrinsically good, all disharmony intrinsically evil.

* * *

A little while before the following conversation Kathleen had been discussing food.

Charon – I will tell you a wonderful thing to eat – words, when they are beautiful. They are most exquisite. There are words of wine and words of honey, and some of wormwood and of gall. Which are mine?

Kathleen – 'The Milk of Paradise' surely!

Charon – You are delicately sweet! It is the first time I have been fit food for the young.

Gems are the art of Cosmos. They set forth, in part, the theory that Nature is great. They interpret her moods in their own lovelier hues. The tropical evening air with all its shadowy depths of blue and violet takes substance in lapis lazuli. Amber and ivory lie in the pale dawn and yellow topazes in the windy sunset. Turquoise is the frozen azure of the sky, and the curious tragic waves of Northern waters lash themselves into foaming jade.

It is an effort to remember past scenes and phases unless some experience has been deep enough to leave a permanent impression. That is why one hates so-called 'tests,' and that is why the only satisfactory people here – so far as the séance room is concerned – are the commonplace ones in whom every little detail of past life looms so large. Of course one loves one's friends and remembers them; for love of some sort, after all, is the salt of everything.

The mantle of earth has fallen from my shoulders. I do not wish to resume it in any way.

INTERLUDE

Special nails and corners had been allotted to each of the kitchen utensils when not in use. Their order never changed, so that, as Ruth expressed it, she 'could find them blindfold.'

One day a large saucepan, sacred to porridge, was missing. Ruth, who had a short time before hung it on the accustomed nail in the scullery, searched for it everywhere. Mrs. Carrington had not been that day, and she herself, after hanging the saucepan up, had only gone into the adjoining kitchen from which she could have seen if anybody had entered the scullery. She and Kathleen, looking in vain in every possible and impossible place where anyone in a sudden fit of absentmindedness might have set the saucepan, finally found it by an unused dustbin at the further end of the backyard, in a spot where no one had been for several days. Articles were continually missing in this way and were found in unaccustomed places.

Ruth had an uncle who came to see her every evening. His name was Ricks, and he was manager of a coal wharf. The bond between them appeared to be that he possessed a talent for imparting all kinds of knowledge, and she herself had a talent for never assimilating any. These differences had led to such altercations between them that Theo had finally forbidden him to come inside the house at all. He still, however, instructed Ruth outside, and was really of great indirect benefit to Kathleen and Theo – to whom he bore no malice – in giving Ruth valuable introductions to the trades people in the neighbourhood of their new house. Thus the task of living became a little simpler owing to a more spontaneous confidence being shown to the Trents by the heads of various firms who were among Ricks' acquaintances, the extraordinary list of which ranged from some of the leading clergy, to our rather sinister protectors, Mr. Billington and Mr. Ellis.

The uncle confided to Ruth that he had dreamed of the former site of the house. He had seen a brook in which women were washing clothes where a row of dull and respectable yards now stretched. His niece, remembering Kathleen's account, told him that the Trents had both had the same dream.

Kathleen had been obliged to give up the lessons in voice production. "I don't like to pile it on to Mary," she told Theo, "but those vibrations she wants me to do make me feel quite ill. I don't exactly get faint with them, for in a faint one's consciousness merely goes and one knows nothing; whereas in this case my consciousness seems to leave me, and yet I'm still aware of everything."

"But if it left you," said her brother, "you could not still be aware of things, surely?"

"It is difficult to express exactly what I mean," said Kathleen. "It might be more accurate to say that the vibrations seem to separate one's molecules all over, so that some other part of one, which I call consciousness because I can think of no better word, either partly escapes or else is no longer contained in its right place, but floods everywhere. That's as near as I can tell you. I try not to feel like that because it seems so hysterical. Yet I've never been hysterical, have I?"

"Never," said Theo. "On the contrary. Considering what we've gone through, it's astonishing that we seem so balanced. I'm glad you've given up the lessons. Very probably Mary herself after the manner of her kind, knew very little of what she was talking about."

"Another thing that happened," said Kathleen, "was that instead of the exercises she gave me, curious tunes came into my head. I catch myself singing them continually. And you know I can never tell one tune from another as a rule. I never had an ear. This is one." She hummed a light air.

Theo was amazed. "It's the first time I ever heard you sing in tune," he said. "But I can't understand how you got hold of that. It is quite different from modern music." He paused thoughtfully. "It could be an air for the lute."

"Then there is this one," said Kathleen, continuing.

"Extraordinary," said her brother. "Curiously enough you are singing quite right for once. It's the same type of thing as the first. It's like a sixteenth century chanson."

For several days it had seemed to Kathleen that her brain was being used for a species of table turning. The whole alphabet would in some strange way tap itself against her consciousness, stopping at each letter necessary in the spelling of a certain word. When this was spelt, the same process was repeated with the next word, and so on till a whole sentence was complete. When this experience stopped, whole sentences intercepted her conscious thoughts so clearly that she found her mind taking part in them and answering them exactly as in ordinary conversation. This would happen at any and every time. She would be discussing the relative value of sugar and flour with Ruth when the phrase, 'I don't like your dress – is it the fashion?' would come into her mind. She would be intent on typing an article of Theo's, when the words, 'Shall we come out soon?' would interpenetrate her thoughts on the criticism of some musical composition.

Theo had gone away for a week on business. During that time the experience, which had become more frequent and definite, continued throughout three whole nights, entirely preventing any sleep.

Kathleen was physically exhausted. It was characteristic of her that before deciding on any course of action she examined the situation from all sides.

"This isn't merely the result of disordered brain through three nights' sleeplessness," she thought, "because it has been going on for some time and has merely got worse this last week. The spiritualists would say that I was in some psychic state. But the doctors! Of the doctors we know, Dr. Henderson would think that it was the dynamic outburst from an entire life of suppressed longing for men, dating from my earliest infancy. Dr. Power might think, after learning that I habitually dreamed, liked poetry, and wasn't very keen on games, that such facts proved a mind predisposed to disease which had now definitely set in. Dr. Duncan would say that circumstances had worked into hysteria a temperament previously inclined that way, and that only my own will could cure me. Dr. Cross would insist that I had experienced a first bout of incipient insanity, would be honestly sorry, commiserate Theo, and recommend me to the pleasantest asylum – called by a more delicate name – he knew. They won't be able to make me better because they would all have made up their minds that I was bound to be inaccurate in what I described, so that it would be worse than useless to go to them.

"Spiritualism has never interested me, but its arguments in this case seem for once to be the most logical ones.

"There's no doubt that I can hear voices belonging to ghosts, or anyhow to people I can't see. Sometimes I think it is Cyril speaking and sometimes Father. Sometimes it sounds almost like archaic French, and sometimes the person who calls himself Charon and who came to the table the first time we did it; and sometimes others I can't place. It can't be my subconscious self, for the subconscious self would scarcely carry on a consecutive conversation with the conscious one, besides having utterly different points of view and an entirely different kind of mind. Nor, in any case, could one have half a dozen subconscious selves all of different habits of speech and various types of psychology. I won't worry

Theo, for he's so busy. Mary's out of town today. Ruth's no good, for she would be terrified if she knew. There must be a way to stop it, but I mustn't let myself get frightened or it will be far worse. The only thing I can think of is to go and see Francis. He's versed in spiritualism and will probably be able to suggest something."

Having thus made up her mind, Kathleen decided to go to Francis after tea, and that a walk first might do her good. She had real love for being out of doors and sought the open air in either trouble or illness with a curious innate necessity which was as far removed from the pseudo-poetic as from the athletic.

She felt feverish and strained, but had relinquished in despair her attempts to sleep in the daytime and thus make good the sleepless nights. Sleep was arrested in her. She ran upstairs to put her things on and went out, walking towards the Park.

Kathleen was surprised that nobody noticed her. Her eyes had looked so vague and her face so strange in the glass. Suddenly she felt much worse. She could no longer remember what she wanted, who she was, or where she was going. The sense by which she knew those things was being driven out or superseded by an indescribably awful blank. "This must be madness coming," she thought, and realized terror as never before. With all her will she fought the feeling and by a miracle crossed the street without being run over. She could not walk straight or do anything but wander aimlessly along, nor could she stop herself from doing so. She only knew that she was wandering aimlessly, that she could not prevent herself from being run over, that she had no memory, and that she must fight to get some sense again or she would probably never have it any more. A concise and definite command penetrated the blindness, settling on her mind and saved her, for her reason though active, was powerless to help. "Keep yourself on the pavement. Think of all the ordinary everyday things that you can, and then go home."

Kathleen strove to follow the advice. She enumerated every unimportant detail of daily life in their order. The blank began to lift and she turned round, walking in the direction of home. The terror was further off. "It was a ghastly ordeal. I could not get to you because you were too bad. Isn't there anyone who knows enough about these things to help you?" slid into her consciousness.

"I am going to Francis after tea," said Kathleen in her mind. "He's a keen spiritualist and would probably be of some use."

"Who is Francis?"

"He's my cousin, but we seldom meet him. Still he'll be good natured enough to help if he can."

"Good! You go to him as soon as ever you can."

Gradually sense returned to her, and by the time she reached home she felt more or less normal, except for extreme physical weariness.

She went to the kitchen. "Ruth," she said, "make me the strongest cup of coffee you can. I've not slept for nights, and my nerves are to pieces. After that I'm going to see Mr. Grant."

She decided to tell Ruth nothing of what had happened, for the girl was easily frightened, and indeed could be of little use in such a case. Kathleen had a momentary fear that the blank was coming over her again, but remembered that to direct her mind to ordinary and definite topics might help her a second time.

While drinking the coffee she insisted on hearing the minutest details of the dullest periods of Ruth's family life. It had the desired effect and seemed to ward off the terrible feeling. She went upstairs and forced herself to read the newspaper, but was obliged to go over each paragraph several times before she could grasp any meaning. She persevered, however, till tea time, after which she set off to Hampstead Heath, where Francis lived. She collected herself together enough to get her ticket and to enter the right trains, but when she arrived at the house the housekeeper told her that Francis was away and not expected back for several days.

She lost her way on the Heath, coming back. The blank was permanently lifted from her mind, but a newer terror sat there in the shape of perception abnormally distorted or magnified. Along the road ghoulish figures crouched with slight movements on the seats, and hounds with pointed tails and gaping jaws raced behind her. Finding she had come the wrong road, she retraced her steps, found the tube, and arrived again at Marble Arch. There too the ghouls and dogs appeared at intervals.

At the end of Edgware Road a mass of tangible blackness loomed and enveloped their shapes. The house looked utterly different as she entered it. She had some dinner, and during it experienced the worst sensation of any. It seemed as if a thousand voices poured into her mind and began to talk at once. She fell back in her chair.

"Don't you feel well, Miss Trent?" Ruth asked anxiously.

"I'm going up to bed," replied Kathleen, rising. This form of madness was even worse than the awful blank of the morning. "Try and not be frightened," floated dominantly above the deadly chatter into her mind as she went upstairs. "You see, you've become open to every current. Concentrate on talking to me only, then I can keep the others out."

"But who are you?"

"Does that really matter? Dead men tell no tales, you know. Charon is really the most appropriate thing to call me. I suppose you can't sleep?"

"I wish to Heaven I could!" said Kathleen.

The thousand voices were gradually withdrawing, and finally only the one was distinguishable.

FINALE

At the top of the stairs Kathleen felt a disinclination to go to her bedroom. She went instead into the little room next the drawing room, which Theo used as a study. She walked to the window and looked out. Grotesque figures of animals and persons crowded among the shadowy debris of the houses she was usually accustomed to see there. Some ravens croaked and flapped their wings upon the leafless trees of the high road, and far below a brook flowed between the cobblestones into the distance.

Another personality had interpenetrated her nature. It lent her unhabitual attitudes and gestures. It used her organs of speech, but the voice which came from her lips was a man's, slow in utterance and deep in timbre. Her consciousness, still in partial habitation of her brain and body, knew this, but was not averse, for in some peculiar fashion the experience gave the sense if not the act of sleep; it rested her. Alternately her tongue was used by the other personality and her own. They had a long conversation. It seemed a little later that Ruth, with a white face, burst into the room.

"Miss Trent –" she said, and stopped. "It's five in the morning, and you've never been to bed yet. I woke up and saw the light and heard a man talking to you. I thought Mr. Trent must have come back."

"Good Heavens!" said Kathleen. "I had no idea it was morning. I feel so weak." She put her hand to her head, feeling incapable of the effort of giving any explanation to Ruth. She went into her bedroom, undressed and got into bed. She felt Ruth's uncle could help her. It seemed to her that she went to him and told him so, and asked him to come to the house. Something had happened. What was it? Large discs of light were swiftly entering the room; some merged into each other against the ceiling; others settled over her form. Thin points of curious flame flickered for a moment in various parts of the room, and then were extinguished.

Through the doorway some tide flowed upon the air, and in an instant the room was thronged with dense black shapes. One had a huge body with the head of a bird. Another had some equivalent of a face sunk within the upper part, spindle legs and a pot like body, round the middle of which circled a band of fire. Kathleen was terrified. She could neither move, speak nor scream, but only watch.

"Don't be frightened," came the other voice out of her own mouth. "It makes them worse, and they can't obsess you, because I am doing so. The lights, I believe are protective. They hate light. It's an awful house, you know – that's why they come. You, of all people, ought never to be in such a place."

"But it must be my own imagination," said poor Kathleen. "There aren't such things."

"Naturally, everybody will think it's your imagination, if you tell them. I suppose they are devils – distressing to think so much is true," continued the voice from Kathleen's mouth airily. "I can tell you I had a fight to reach you through the current. It's one of the worst nights I've seen."

Swiftly and suddenly as it had flowed the evil tide ebbed again and the room cleared. In another instant it flowed again. This time a troop of animals came into the room through the doorway. These were leopards, giraffes, curious cats, and the same kind of black pointed tailed dog which Kathleen had seen in the afternoon. Some of them sprang on the bed. The other personality sat up in Kathleen's form and with her hand lifted them up one by one and flung them back on the floor. As this tide ebbed the animals which composed its waves appeared to turn pure white.

"I will show you something," said the voice. "Look on the blind." She did so. Two faces made of colourless molecules of air stood out clearly against the blind.

"One's like Napoleon," she said.

"That's right. And the other?"

Where had she seen that brow and beard? "Swinburne," she said after consideration. "Surely they aren't here?"

"No, but I pictured their faces strongly in thought, and the conditions are so peculiar that the thought is suggested to your eyes. It interested me to see if I could do it."

The morning lightened slowly. The room was insufferably hot. It was as though a current of electricity swept it, ballooning the bed clothes and the garments that hung on the wall. Something definitely separated or broke in the figure on the bed. Kathleen felt very far away – close to the ceiling.

"I'm evidently dying," she thought.

The bed clothes, which were moving apparently of themselves and assuming enormous proportions and strange shapes, recalled her back to terror.

"Leave this room! Quick!" said the voice.

She jumped on to the floor and was horrified to find that she was unconscious of touching it. She ran downstairs and fell into the arms of Mary, who was waiting at the foot of them with Ruth.

"Oh, Mary," she cried. "I've nearly died, and I'm trying to make myself think that all this awfulness is imagination. But whatever I do I can't stop it. Do you think I'm really mad? I must tell you about it. How did you get here so early?"

"Ruth phoned me and I came at once. Come in here and tell me all about it."

Mary felt on firm ground. She had read all about obsession and clairvoyance. But some of Kathleen's tale puzzled her.

"Some of course is hysteria," said Kathleen. "It must be. Remember I've literally not slept for four whole nights and days. The obsession is true enough, and thank God for it, otherwise I know those awful creatures would have taken me instead. Yet you see I've still sense enough to know I'm not normal, and my ordinary mind is conscious all the time, though it's of no practical use to me. I don't really know what to do. Oh, the awful feeling is coming again."

She recited poetry for some hours.

Mary said afterwards that different metres made her worse or better, and that the meaning she read into them was amazing. An extraordinary voice spoke through her all the time. After this was ended she laid Kathleen on the sofa.

It seemed to Kathleen that various articles in the room took terrifying shapes. A hat with long upright bows became a rabbit with long ears. The folds of a garment became the features of a face, and so on with most things. For an instant she believed that it was a fact.

"Don't notice anything," said the voice. "Those things aren't really there at all, though the other things were. This is your own imagination distorted – merely hysteria. Shut your eyes and look at nothing, or if you do, don't let any idea or its shape enter your mind, for it will be distorted there."

Kathleen insisted on going up to the bedroom again. As she did so Ruth and Mary saw a flash of light illuminate the atmosphere above the staircase.

Theo arrived that night. "Good heavens," were his first words, "the house is like a furnace!"

Ruth explained that there was only a fire in the kitchen and the drawing room. He heard versions of the case from Ruth, who was too terrified to enter Kathleen's presence at all, and from Mary, who repeated what Kathleen had told her, but was plainly at a loss to know what to do.

He went up with Mary to Kathleen's bedroom. In the doorway a fantastic sight made them pause. A tangible force of electricity was in the atmosphere. The heat was intense, and everything vibrated. The bed clothes were swelling in balloons.

Kathleen was motionless on the bed. Theo went up to her and kissed her. She opened her eyes.

"Can you tell me what has happened?" he said. She repeated exactly what she had told Mary. "Have you had any food?"

"I couldn't eat," she said.

"But you must have something. I'll go and see about it at once. And you must sleep in another room. Ruth will make you up a bed in the dressing room."

He left the room with Mary. There was a ring at the door. Ruth met him on the stairs. "Uncle's just come," she said. "He says he must see you, but won't say why."

"Have you told him about Miss Trent?"

"No; I've not seen him since she was bad."

"Well, bring him to the study, and then make up a bed in the dressing room; and here's some money. Get Miss Trent some champagne and oysters. Some of you might have thought of food I must say!"

He went into the study where Ricks and Mary joined him.

"I came," said the former, "because early this morning I saw your sister in her night dress come into my room and ask me to help her. A lot of evil spirits seemed trying to hurt her."

Theo told him, after a moment's astonishment, what had happened. "The strange thing is," he added, "my sister told both Miss Field and myself that she was conscious of going to you early this morning and asking you to come here and help her. By all means do, if you are able."

"I shall be very glad to do so," said the man. "They said in the country that I had the healing touch. How hot this place is, isn't it, Mr. Trent?" he continued. "Look at that rug!"

As he spoke, it appeared to raise itself and stood completely on end before their eyes!

"It's no good pretending we are all hysterical," said Theo. "I wish we were; it would be much easier. These are obviously things that no one understands about, and when one doesn't see them it's very natural and probably very healthy to entirely disbelieve in them." They paused as the mat sank slowly back. "Let us come up to Kathleen," he said to Mary.

As they entered a surprising sight greeted them. Shapes of light like large plates were swiftly passing through the doorway. They merged into wider circles on the ceiling. If one substituted the word 'light' for 'water', it was reminiscent of a larger scale of the circles made by flinging a stone into a pond. The bed was studded with the same discs, but they were stationary there, whereas the others were in continual motion.

"What can they be?" said Mary.

"Electricity in some form, I suppose," said Theo. They stood in silence, watching the phenomenon.

"They've been coming in for a long time," said Kathleen. "I've got used to them now. They were the least terrifying of all. Is Ruth's uncle come?"

"Yes. Now put this dressing gown on and come and see him, and then you are to have some food at once. I want you out of this room," said her brother.

Mary took the dressing gown from behind the door. It was a white flannel one with voluminous frills of lace. She dropped it with a cry. For it stood by itself, as the mat had done. Its sleeves swelled as though arms were in them.

Theo knocked it down. It did not fall in a heap of soft folds, but stiffly and full of substance, as though a form were in it. There was a soft whirr. "It's like touching an electric battery!" said Theo.

"That's how everything's been," said Kathleen. "I made sure it was hysteria, but you both see it as well."

They found another wrapper and took her down to the study. She could not talk much. Ricks held her hand, and his presence and touch seemed to soothe her.

After the oysters she seemed considerably better, and was put to bed by Mary in the dressing room.

"I'll come every day," said Mary to Theo, "and see how she is."

BOTH SIDES OF THE DOOR
Outside

Kathleen had been ill for some days. Mary was talking to Theo.

"I never do table turning idly," she said, "but last night I asked if something could be done for Kathleen. My great-aunt always comes to me; she said the spirit who obsessed Kathleen now was too strong a personality to be good for her, and that a very quiet, gentle old woman was to be sent instead."

"At first I wondered if she ought to have a doctor," said Theo irrelevantly. "But now I feel very strongly that in this case it would be the worst thing to do. What she has wrong with her is not explained by the ordinary medical theories. One can see that some of her illness, though not all, may have come from fright and sleeplessness which could have produced hysteria. But it is not the ordinary sort of hysteria, even so. There is obvious obsession by another personality, and the house itself is in a frightful condition, which four other people, who are, so far at least, not hysterical, have witnessed. We have all of us seen the lights and the devils – or whatever they are. We have all felt the heat and seen the rugs and other things stand up by themselves. Of course, if I heard such a tale and hadn't been present, I should have absolutely disbelieved it. I dreamed clearly of my father last night, He said we were to trust in God and above all to beware of having any doctor, unless it were one who properly understood these things, and that Kathleen would get through it. Personally I don't think Kathleen can get better till the house is better and these creatures can be got out of it. That brute with the band of fire that Ricks calls `Tubby` was seen by Ruth going up the kitchen stairs yesterday. Ricks met it halfway up these stairs as he went to Kathleen's room. I drove it out of her old room by sheer force of will and saw it go down as far as the first landing, and then it disappeared somewhere. You also say you've seen the same thing outside the study. Shall we go and see how she is now?"

Inside

Kathleen lay upon the bed, motionless. The November day was cold and there was no fire in the grate, but the air was burning.

"Look!" said Theo to Mary. "Your great-aunt must have been right!"

His sister had a look of extreme but peaceful old age. Her fingers mechanically performed the movements of knitting. Mary and Theo went out.

After a time a change came over the figure on the bed. Kathleen turned round. There were voices all round the room. They seemed to batter against her, not merely against the ears and brain, but against the whole body. The dreaded blankness seemed once more imminent.

"Oh," she cried, "isn't there any way of getting rid of this ghastly feeling?"

"Draw it down from the mental centre to the heart," said a voice. "That will stop the feeling of going mad, but it will probably give you great pain."

"But how can I draw it there?"

"Make the movement of breathing in the region of the heart. The pain which comes will not be physical, but will feel as if it were, and it will be the heart's counterpart, not the physical heart, which suffers."

Kathleen made a movement as of breathing near the heart. As she did so a wave of agony swept down and settled round it. The cloud entirely lifted from the mind.

"Always do that," said the voice. "It's the better of two evils. You are completely sensitive, you see."

"But shan't I get better and `ordinary` again?"

"Oh yes, you'll heal. The conditions of the house have helped to make you ill, and you've a unique psychic talent."

"I wish I had some flowers here," she said. "I should like to see and smell something fresh in this awful heat."
"You shall. What would you like?"
"Carnations and violets – and lilac."
"Very well."

Outside

Theo and Mary were bending over Ricks. He had a strange attack of acute pain, first in the head and then in the heart. His agony was horrible to witness, and he became half unconscious. When he was better he went out into the air, returning after an hour or two.
"Are you better?" said Theo.
"It's passed off, thank God!" said the man. "I passed that florist's near here. I know the manager, and I bought Miss Trent some flowers. I thought she was fond of them, and it might help to cheer her up. I wanted to get some lilac, but they had none, so I got these."
He held up a small bunch composed of a few red carnations a bunch of violets and some mimosa.

Inside

Kathleen stared at the window. How vile the house was growing. Something indescribably filthy filled the air. The atmosphere grew heavy and drugged with loathsome and stupefying odour. It seemed that drunken sailors and loafers were in the room. Their costumes were strange. There was a crowd of half undressed, coarse looking women who danced, shrieked and ogled. She tried not to hear or see them, but they were insistent, scoffing and determined. Their language was foul. She caught some of it. They said the house was theirs.

Outside

"Good Heavens!" said Theo, who was talking to Ricks in the kitchen. "What a smell!" The two men looked at each other.

"Opium!" they said almost simultaneously. "It's coming all down the stairs!"

They rushed up to Kathleen's room.

Inside

"Isn't the smell awful?" she said. "Is it opium? I've seen the lowest sorts of people. They were in a kind of tavern drinking and swearing; some of them were undressed. They said the house was theirs."

Theo sat by Kathleen's bed. "Lockwood called," he said. "I did not feel equal to seeing anyone, but Ruth told him you were very ill and sent him off. He's sent you some grapes."

"How nice of him! Thank him. How shall you describe my illness?"

"God knows! I shall say pneumonia, I think. That is comprehensible."

"Listen," she said, "I can sing in tune now." And she sang a delicate air perfectly.

"It's in quarter tones," thought her brother. Aloud he said, "Yes, that's quite right."

"I say, I'm being given oysters and champagne and the fat of the land. I suppose that means that no one else has any food at all. It's sweet of you, but I shall be perfectly all right with ordinary food. I'm not off it so much now. I'm sure I'm better. The pain is nasty, but it seems not physical though it certainly feels so. Do tell me the truth about food."

"My dear child, everybody has got everything. The main point is that you get better." He went out.

Kathleen had a bout of pain round her heart. There were green fields in mist and rain. A small house was hidden in the midst of them. She smelt gunpowder and heard a terrific crash, Ah! She was in the room again and a woman in sweeping robes of black velvet stooped over her. Where had she seen that pointed face and transparent skin?

The strains of a lute floated to her, and she could almost see the written rhymes of a song. 'Moy,' 'Foy,' 'Loy,' – that was old French surely. It was full summer in a wonderful garden. Insects hummed in the shadows, and the trees had dark cool foliage. A thousand paths intersected the terraces. Some of the paths were thorny, some were deep in flowers, some were incomprehensible, and some veiled in light and distance. Yet each had a mystic meaning, and certain people had to walk upon them all. Men were there who wore ruffs and ear rings and short velvet cloaks and swords. One man had a modern dress. She must have seen his face in some picture, for the brow and beard were reminiscent of someone she did not know. The woman in black velvet was the Queen of the garden. She leaned out through dim branches in the corner of the room. Her voice was sweet and remote as the sounds of the garden, but what she said was indistinguishable except the words: 'Messire de Boduel.' She passed into a further glade which merged into the wall.

"I suppose that was fantasy," said Kathleen, "It seemed real enough."

She felt better. There were some grapes near her. Should she take one? No; the effort was so great, and the pain might start again if she moved. It was good of Lockwood to have sent the grapes. He would disbelieve all this strenuously, but still he had understanding about other things. He was really very nice. How strange! Everything that she had ever done was rising in her mind. It was a retrospect in which all rose in a flash, and yet every detail was complete. She saw the events of her illness and before it. The life in the flat. Her engagement to Cyril. His death. She could see him now, fair haired, impetuous and uncertain in temper. They had understood each other in most ways, and each was a good lover. How ridiculous people and books were on the subject of love! Most of the modern psycho-sensuous novels seemed in this case on a par with such works as the inestimable Miss Carrey's – tiresomely vicious instead of tiresomely respectable; that was all. Perhaps it wasn't love they set out to describe at all, but that was the nearest word that could be found. Possibly the 'real thing' could only be adequately analysed in poetry or legend; and besides, few people, perhaps fortunately, wanted 'the real thing.'

They wanted tables and chairs and sentimentality – so long as it was comfortable – and the continuation of the species – ideals to live for, no doubt, but hardly worth dying for! Yet it was dangerous to lose all interest in tables and chairs and it was possible to have nice or even exquisite ones.

She remembered all the phases of grief after Cyril's death. She remembered other things. Her mother's death and their life on the Continent. The places she visited and the people she met abroad. Some amusing incidents at school. She saw her father and the incredible pile of books for the rather dreaded Latin lessons. She saw his almost physical anguish over a false quantity, and remembered with a smile that the pain she had given him had evidently been unbearable.

Then there was the garden at home – one's first garden. The paint on the garden door was blistered and had a pleasant smell in the sun. In the avenue was a tree trunk where she had found some white violets. There was a fairy ring at the corner of the lawn with the copper beeches, where on Midsummer Night's Eve one put such scraps as could be collected from the kitchen.

When she was nine she had stayed with her mother at Ostend in the summer, and there had experienced the first irony of life. It amused her to remember that. The Shah of Persia was staying at one of the hotels. Kathleen, imbued with the 'Arabian Nights' had long looked forward to seeing him. She had pictured a mysterious Eastern Prince who would pass along the sea front with a gorgeous bodyguard, and he would have a silver sabre and a turban of pearls. This was not fulfilled. One day, when she was on the sands, the bonne pointed him out to her. Kathleen saw a wearied and morose looking individual crowned with a fez, walking with one attendant on the promenade immediately above.

A wave of the child's disappointment must have reached him, for on the spot where most men smile there flickered for an instant some other aspect of spleen. He detached from the august but dingy buttonhole a purple flower, threw it to her and passed on.

She had kept the flower for some time. A royal guerdon is always interesting, even when it marks a disappointment.

She felt very weak. Was there anything else to remember? She wasn't going to think any more …

Outside

For the first time since she had known them, Kathleen was averse to the presence of Henry and Edward. They had not been inside her room since her illness. They waited, however, side by side in front of her door in that alert and upright attitude which the Trents described as 'sitting teapot'. Their object of entering the room was invariably defeated, but hour by hour they sat outside, waiting.

Ricks was beginning to fall into semiconscious states habitually. He suffered great pain in the heart and head. It was impossible to relieve this in any ordinary way, for, as he himself continually repeated, the pain was not physical, although he felt as if it were. Theo, in despair, made the sign of the Cross over him. It seemed to have a good effect. In one of these bouts Ricks had declared that a murder had taken place in the house.

The heat continued in the rooms. Black hybrid creatures were seen by all the inmates at intervals. The house was never free from the discs of light; sometimes a sudden flash or a point of flame would gleam suddenly in a corner.

Downstairs, in the kitchen, strange letters began to appear on the blind and curtains. They were formed of colourless molecules of air, and one of them bore the name of a friend of the Trents' who had lately gone to America.

One afternoon, Mary said that her great-aunt told her that Kathleen was dying. She and Ricks began to be frightened of the possibility of such an event and declared that Theo must have a doctor lest the consequences for everybody should be unpleasant. Ricks, who had just come out of the room, said that her heart had actually stopped.

"I'm willing to take the risk," said Theo. "And the risk in any case is mine. But if either of you insists on dragging the ordinary practitioner in there is no doubt that she will die or worse. I know that it sounds ridiculous in the present century to say such a thing, but something in me knows much better than reason that she will get all right. I've tried to get Francis Grant here, for he knows the psychical research people, and there is at least the chance that he might help. These events are only too obviously in that sphere. However, he has been away and is only just back. He came in this morning, and I showed him the letters on the blind downstairs. He promised to bring in one of his psychical research friends. I'm going to ring up to him now about it."

Theo went out, returning in a few minutes. "Francis is back, and is bringing tonight someone he knows, who can help – Merton, I think the name is," he said.

A strange party of four, including Ricks and Theo, sat round the drawing room lamp. Mary had gone. Francis Grant, looking rather perplexed, arrived and introduced a very matter of fact and genial looking friend – the last person one would have imagined as being connected with psychical research.

Mr. Merton got to business at once. "I would rather not see your sister," he said. "Don't tell me any of the conditions till I've found out what I can alone. Have you any article she wears, such as a comb, that I could have?"

Theo went upstairs and returned with the side combs his sister always used.

Mr. Merton took them, pressed them to his forehead, and seemed to be working out a mathematical problem. He described Kathleen's appearance and the room she was in accurately.

"She has an exceptional mediumistic gift," he said. "Circumstances which have lately happened seem to have developed it suddenly and dangerously. The medium's personality always tinges the manifestation to some extent, and therefore it is seldom that exceptional spirits can use, with any success, the average medium. Your sister is not what we call the usual mediumistic type. She is well balanced and artistic, with a strong individuality. If her gift could be used she would be one of the most valuable mediums on record, but she must never come in touch with any psychic affairs again so long as she lives, for she has not the physique necessary to stand the strain.

"The house is in an awful psychic condition. I have had much experience in these cases, but I have never been in such a place before; there are evil entities in it, and it is on the site of a much older house of bad reputation and to have been used for gambling, opium drinking and murder a long time ago. The neighbourhood is also a bad one, astrally, because it is close to Tyburn. All these conditions have been set in motion in this house, and unless they can be stopped your sister will die. They will stop, however, and she will get better shortly, but she must be got away immediately. I get that there is a man here who is also mediumistic but in another way. He has saved her from certain conditions, which would have fastened on her, by absorbing them himself. You yourself do not 'take on' these conditions, though you see and realise them, but you have remarkable force of will which has been invaluable in helping to drive the current back. On the top of all this, some powerful and unusual spirits appear to have been trying to communicate with your sister. I feel, too, some historic association in some way, but not clearly. Once she is out of the house this psychic stream will be diverted gradually. She must not return till it has completely disappeared."

Theo told him the whole story. After that they all went down to the kitchen and examined the letters on the blind and curtains. The former had been growing fainter throughout the day, and were now barely distinguishable.

Inside

Theo stood at the foot of Kathleen's bed.

"I've got some good news," he said. "Mrs. Ford rang me up this morning; she accidentally met Francis and heard from him the whole business. She and Ford want you to go and stay there till you and this house are all right."

"It's really awfully decent of them," said Kathleen. "After all, I can't be a very pleasant visitor at the moment. I might even `break out` again down there. I feel better now though. How long have I been ill?"

"Three weeks exactly," said her brother.

"Three weeks! And I had the first proper sleep, since it all began, this morning. I'll pull myself together enough to go. After what Merton said, I see I'm a thoroughly undesirable person to have in the house. You've been wonderful, Theo – you really have! Of course it hadn't been for you I should have been in an asylum. I do realise that. After all, medically speaking, I've had a bout of insanity for three weeks. Psychically speaking, I've been in an astral state, worked up by conditions of the house. Personally, I believe if I had been one degree less sane and had not tried so strenuously to think that I was being either hysterical or imaginative all the while, I should have got completely `under control` and fared better. I fought hard all the time. My normal consciousness was hardly ever absent, but it was powerless. I remember every mad thing I did, and the reason why I did it, with an awful accuracy. If I could only have got unconscious! You see I'm one of those unlucky people who, even in physical conditions, can't faint."

"Try and not think of any of it," said Theo. "Mrs. Ford says her sister had the same type of thing in a haunted house, but not nearly as badly as you or in the same ways. Ricks will take you. He and Mary have been absolutely ripping through all this. Which reminds me that Lockwood sent you a basket of various kinds of out-of-the-way fruit."

"Really! "That's good of him. I think I would like some of it now. And can I have Edward and Henry?"

Theo went down. "Thank God, she's better!" he said to Ricks. "She's slept, and she wants the cats. She was all right about going tomorrow – quite plucky – said she'd pull herself together enough to go."

The next morning Kathleen got up. She looked around the room where so much had happened. The sun gleamed upon the corner where the Queen had looked out from the branches.

"I must simply forget everything that I can," said Kathleen to herself.

Theo came into the room a little later. "The cab's here," he said, "and Ruth has packed your things."

"I'm quite ready," said Kathleen. "But it's difficult to walk."

He half carried her downstairs into the hall where Ruth was waiting. She entered the cab followed by Ricks, and Theo went back to the house. The sun came out for an instant and illuminated the cold air as the vehicle turned.

The door shut.

The Clearing

After Kathleen had gone, a double stream of evil seemed to engulf the unfortunate Ricks. He would pass through paroxysms of pain and fear which were terrible to witness.

Theo, utterly worn out, intuitively used a remedy which he himself in other days would have been the first to laugh at. "For illness as mad as that," he said later, "one could only have a mad remedy. Of course, when one looks back, it is very funny, but at the time it got beyond humour."

The basic principles of good seemed the natural antidote to evil. But 'good' was an abstract term. It had to be demonstrated by some sort of shape. The most obvious shapes were the symbols connected with religion, such as the Circle, the Triangle, and the Cross. He found himself defining a symbol, and came to the conclusion that it was really a focussing point to connect the idea more easily with the mind. It did this by presenting a shape – tangible or intangible – which the mind could readily seize as corresponding with the general outlines of the idea, the whole detail of which would be too intricate to grasp at once. A symbol was therefore not, as is so often thought, the semblance of an idea, but the first step towards bringing the semblance nearer.

The word 'chair', he argued, was a symbol which quickly presented to the mind the idea of four legs, a seat, a back, bars, and a hundred details. If all these parts were enumerated each time in speaking of a chair instead of using the word, an accurate description of the article might be given, but the mind would be unable to connect itself with what was meant for some time, if at all.

With more intricate ideas, particularly with those for which there was no adequate description, the value of a symbol was even more obvious.

In childhood, like many others, Theo had been aware of colour as a sensation as well as a vision. Their analogy was simple. Warm orange, like the sun's rays, was healing, and blue was calming as a clear sky. Theo combined colour and symbol in his imagination strongly, till the mental picture of Ricks bound in them became almost tangible. It was no good saying, in this case, "Now, now, my good fellow, pull yourself together! You've got D.T. *[delirium tremens – hallucinations associated with alcoholic addiction. Ed.]* you know," or one of the thousand things sanity would dictate. Whether it was merely a healing hypnotism working on hysteria, or whether actual devils were actually dispersed by the Sign of the Cross as in mediaeval superstition, mattered very little. The main point was that in some way the symbol cured the paroxysms of Ricks, who became slowly but surely normal again. After a while he completely recovered.

One night Theo knew that a terrible shape was encroaching upon his identity with an insidious subtlety. As he fought with the creature, a formula spontaneously rose to his lips as though from some remote consciousness: "I command you to go in the name of God Almighty, the Father, the Son, and the Holy Ghost!" It seemed that a deadly force strove to prevent the words being formed in the mind as well as from being spoken. When Theo finally prevailed, each Name was like the loosening of a cord and he flung the ghastly visitor off. The suggestion had been only too vivid, and he turned on the light. At his side on the bed was the impression of another form!

By degrees the hateful current changed its course. It turned aside from the house. As it did so the creatures it brought with it became weaker and were less frequently met. One by one Theo, with all the force he had, literally willed them out. They seem to the two men to pass through the roof.

The house regained its normal temperature, and the fustiness, so apparent in the rooms before the outbreak, had vanished.

In a corner of Kathleen's room some carnations were found. During her illness the vase holding them was upset, and the flowers had fallen on the floor and had remained there unnoticed for a week. They were still absolutely fresh.

"There must have been some chemical in the atmosphere which preserved them," said Theo to Ricks as they discussed the phenomena in calmer moments. "I wish people would use some of the energy they expend in futile wrath about these affairs, in trying to understand them and regulate them! Of course it's only fair to say that at one time I should have thought any tale of such things as have happened in this house charlatanry or madness. I've had the misfortune to go through the mill myself, though, and therefore my opinions are different.

"To put it in ordinary language, my sister, Miss Field your niece, you and myself – five people, that is to say – have had the effects of D.T. without the disease; or one could put it that five people – whether or not hysterical subjects is another point – have gone through three weeks of hysteria, and have tallied with each other in imagining the same fantasies. As the cap doesn't fit, I've no objection to being thought entirely hysterical if it makes argument easier, but apparently nobody has satisfactorily understood hysteria yet. The lights still remain, by the way, although fainter and only on the ceiling. Everyone notices them and asks what they are, and I dress up a sane lie about the reflection from some street lamp. However, I hear from Mr. Grant's friends that they are inoffensive – in fact, protective."

* * *

Here we may leave the narrative which from psychic fact becomes popular fiction in its closing pages with Kathleen deciding to marry Lockwood and go off to Egypt with him.

Margaret Lumley Brown later wrote up something of this in an article called 'A Psychic Upheaval' which although more "factual" (insofar that it does not have the fictional trimmings of *Both Sides of the Door*) is inadequate an account because of limitations of space. It does provide a less fictional description of the actual characters involved and goes into more detail about her experience with chanting verse while she was being obsessed. This had a powerful effect upon her, and twenty years later she wrote an article for the October 1939 issue of *The Occult Review*, entitled *The Occult Side of Poetry* using the pen name of H. O. Hamilton, which we reproduce in Part Four.

A Psychic Upheaval

Psychic eruptions, like volcanic ones, cannot be stopped before they have run their course. No two are exactly alike, and once they have begun to act, it is well to make up one's mind to a period of devastation such as is described below. The details are the most salient ones taken from some old notes of a psychic upheaval which took place in January 1913 and lasted for three weeks.

The household consisted of my sister and myself, an ex-dressmaker acting as general factotum, a friend who lived with us at the time, and two super cats.

My sister and I were passing through a time of great personal trouble, and all four inmates, though more or less clairvoyant in dreams, were not psychically developed in any other way at the time. The factotum was the vague, typically mediumistic type, but the other three of us were principally interested in literary, artistic and philosophical subjects. We each had an underlying individual interest in what is summed up as Theosophy, New Thought and Spiritualism, but unbased on experience or study. None of us belonged to any group of thought on these matters, and in my own family the terror of labels is a complex. This explains why we were so utterly at a loss to know what steps to take or two whom to apply for advice until the worst stages were well over.

We had just moved to the neighbourhood of Marble Arch, into a maisonette now pulled down and replaced by Connaught Mansions. There was nothing peculiar about this mid-Victorian building except the obstinate fustiness which persisted in spite of scrubbing, fires and open windows. The household began to dream repeatedly of the district as it presumably looked a hundred years and more ago. These dreams corroborated each other in depicting a brook, fields, cobble stones, and an ill-kept turnpike in place of the familiar modern surroundings. The district is, of course, the ancient Tyburn.

The next milestone in the upheaval was a sudden desire felt by my sister, our friend and myself to try table turning. *[Handwritten note by MLB: "The immediate precursor of the table turning was a noticeable sensation produced by blowing on a comb through a piece of tissue paper! This is mentioned in the book but many things in this article have been cut because of space."]* This was followed by my doing automatic writing, and under the name 'Charon', which he at first preferred, came a great deal of script purporting to be from Oscar Wilde.

As far as I know, I am the first person who received automatic writing from him. As to whether or not it was really he, I can only say it appeared to all of us to be so at the time, and I am not concerned here with arguing any of these matters but with narrating them as simply as possible.

[There follow extracts from notes already given in Both Sides of the Door *in the section 'Post-Mortem Dialogues.' Ed.]*

During this time another element was beginning to make itself felt. This was an influx of the poltergeist tribe. They were constantly materialising in front of us, all in medievally demonic shapes. The one most seen had a particularly vile appearance, intensified by a band of fire round its middle.

Kitchen utensils and other articles disappeared for days and then were found in unaccountable places. The remarkable fustiness of the house was increased a hundredfold.

At this period, the factotum's uncle, a strange, sullen, but pronouncedly mediumistic type of man, had apparently a strong subconscious 'call' from me. Feeling certain he could be of use, he arrived at the house. His niece and he had previously had an estrangement which was now amicably settled.

I am very grateful for his presence, which helped to absorb part of the terrible unloosened stream that otherwise would have completely swamped me. I became in practically an habitual condition of obsession for two weeks, during which there was nothing for it but to remain in bed. Although my normal consciousness was almost always present, so that to this day I remember most details, it was forced backwards by the encroachment of other entities, and I was powerless to act.

There was a continuous outpouring into my mind of words and streams of thought not my own. I have never known such agony (and no smaller word will do) as it suggested the tangible oncoming of madness to a person still otherwise sane. I know now my fear and my effort to fight made things far worse, but I was, of course, totally inexperienced in the ordinary medium's technique. I had no sleep for days, and whereas I have normally an unusually good sense of time, I would conceive of the passage of many hours as of a few moments. Everything in my memory, from the earliest days, was stirred into a feverish activity.

The value of the mantra was now shown by means of poetic forms. Poetry is the art I care for most and of which I have the most knowledge, and I have also an exceptional memory for it. I hope I shall be forgiven for this continuous egoism, but it is only right to admit what may also have a subconscious interpretation. The faculties in me which bore on poetry were now awakened to an astounding degree. Verses I knew were uttered by an obsessing masculine voice, and the various metrical forms, combined with sound and stress, had different effects on me in this hysterical state, which I have never forgotten. Each verse appeared in a shape before the words grew into it. Thus, a sonnet seemed a square block like a corner-stone, till it undulated gently at the sestet. A villanelle was a delicate elongated box with one end turned back, as it were, to form a much smaller box of the same kind. A ballad was something like the Greek key-pattern. A line said wrongly broke this shape and became an agony. I should like to say, however, that, judging by these occult values of verse, I have never heard in after years anyone not break its shape when speaking it, except Edmund Gosse. He had an unpleasing voice, but I would have walked many miles for the joy of hearing him say one simple line of poetry. So lasting has been the impression these poetic mantra made on me that I am convinced there must be a therapeutic use of verse, as there is of colour and music.

As I have said, all the verse I ever knew poured through me, uttered by another voice. Words, as such, lost their meaning, but metrical sound acquired an uncanny potency. Ideas did count to a certain extent, for a nursery rhyme, say, had not the same effect as real poetry in the same metre; they had a sketchy outline, and I needed something well defined.

The vowels, stressed, had marked results on the psyche: **I** bound and **E** drove it out; **O** steadied it; **A** unsteadied it; **U** was calming.

Trochaic and iambic feet had a quite gait, but prancing anapaests and dancing dactyls I dared not try more than once!

It would take too long to quote all the verses used, as their recital lasted from 10 a.m. till 3.30 p.m.; but here are some examples in which, as will be seen, certain vowel sounds predominate strongly.

I   O tell me were you standing by
           When Isis to Osiris knelt,
           And did you watch the Egyptian melt
           Her union for Anthony?

U   And drink the jewel-drunken wine
          And bend her head in mimic awe
          To see the huge Proconsul draw
          The salted tunny from the brine?

E   Yestreen the Queen had four Maries,
          The nicht she'll hae but three;
          There was Mary Seton and Mary Beatoun,
          And Mary Carmichael and me.

A   The hills and flowers are nane of ours,
          And ours are oversea;
          It watsna what were we
          Or ever we came with scathe and shame
          To try what end might be.

But the best mantram of any for steadying was in the quick sustained beat and crescendo of O sounds in:

O   I am Daniel's mystic mountain
          Whence the mighty stone was rolled;
          I am the four rivers' fountain
          Watering Paradise of old;
          Danae of the shower of gold;
          I the hostel of the Sun am;
          He the Lamb and I the fold.

At this time the whole house streamed with some kind of electricity. It was a cold January, but the heat, even of fireless rooms, was insupportable. Everything any of us touched seemed electrified. A skin rug rose on end, apparently of itself, before my sister and friend. A dressing gown stood up as though inflated by a form within it, and when touched, sank with a faint whirr to the floor. There must have been some vitalising element also in the air, for flowers fallen behind a chest of drawers in my room were found, more than a week later, still perfectly fresh. Discs of light as large as soup plates spun across the ceiling every night, some of them remaining there, while others spread themselves over us as we lay in bed. I passed from obsessor to obsessor, growing weaker physically each day. One of these encroaching was an old woman who appeared to knit. It was said via the factotum's uncle that she was sent to rest me and keep the stronger spirits out.

Once a strong smell of opium pervaded my room, and a crowd of evil looking people invaded it, saying the house was theirs. My sister and the uncle, smelling the drug, rushed upstairs to see what new terror had arisen. Meanwhile the two cats that lived with us showed the strong attraction of their kind to psychism. They would walk up, purring, to invisible presences, and would sit alert, with gleaming eyes, side by side outside my door for hours, hoping for a chance to slip into the room.

The rest of the house was infected by the poltergeists who specially attacked the uncle, causing him real agony of mind and body.

Through all this my sister miraculously kept her head, being clairvoyant but not mediumistic. She was inwardly induced to make geometrical symbols in certain colours round him, which seemed to ease his pain. One night she was herself attacked by a very strong entity. After fighting it with all her strength, she succeeded in throwing it off and commanding it to go in the Name of the Trinity. It fell with a thud to the floor and she contrived to turn on the light. Nothing was to be seen but a deep impression, as of another form, on the opposite side of the bed.

Letters in colourless molecules were now traced on the blind. In despair my sister confided in a cousin who brought up a well known occultist and clairvoyant to visit the house. He was in time to see some of the letters on the blind as they were in process of disappearing. He refused to see me but psychometrised a comb of mind and interviewed the other inmates of the house. He declared that in his considerable experience he had never before known such an awful house, psychically. It was, he said, full of evil entities and on the site of a much older building whose conditions permeated it, and which had sheltered every kind of crime, including murder and opium taking. On the top of this, powerful and unusual spirits had been trying to communicate with me, but that though I had certain rare psychic qualities I had not the physique to stand such a strain and live. He said, however, that the uncle had saved me from much that would otherwise have fastened onto me alone, and that my sister had given invaluable help by her strength of will in driving the current back and by her ability not to 'take on' conditions. The verdict was that I should be got away as soon as possible until the state of the house became normal.

The tide during the next week was perceptibly on the ebb, and I grew better and was able to go away. The elementals, dispersed by the help of a Theosophical lady who kindly offered to come to our assistance, appeared to leave, one by one, through the roof.

One thing only persisted during the five years we inhabited the house. The discs of light, mentioned before, still came each night onto the ceiling, but no longer spread over our beds. We were told they were protective. The house remained cleansed of poltergeists and fustiness all the rest of the time we were in it.

Looking back on the events from a distance of some years, they even seem funny sometimes, so much does time alter perspective. Only persons who have been through the same mill will quite understand the awful reality of those three weeks of terror. To most others I quite realise that the whole thing will appear a delusion.

There were others, however, to whom it was by no means regarded as a delusion. *Both Sides of the Door* was favourably reviewed in *Light* and in *The International Psychic Gazette*. In *Light*, a leading Spiritualist newspaper at the time, the reviewer Ellis T. Powell LL.B., D.Sc., stated:

> "It is not absolutely clear to me whether this little book is fiction or whether it is the record of actual experience....If the story is a record of real experience it certainly is a most vivid and valuable contribution to the literature of the `cosmic memory` and incidentally it demonstrates how a given locality may come to be saturated with personalities and associations surviving from a revolting past in such a manner as to be `sensed` by a psychic."

Nor was it a six day wonder for *Light* quoted extracts from it in March 1922 and October 1923.

It also aroused the interest of Sir Arthur Conan Doyle who wrote to her on 31st October 1919:

> "Dear Miss Hay, I was deeply interested both in your book and in your letter. It is a unique experience so far as I know. I have been at this subject 30 years and I have struck nothing of the kind."

He invited her and her sister to tea and also passed on his enthusiasm to the editor of *Light*, David Gow, who also wrote to say that he regarded it "as one of the most valuable and striking documents of its kind which I have ever read."

Also of evidential interest is a letter from Robert King, a leading Theosophist, clairvoyant, and Bishop in the Liberal

Catholic Church (and, inter alia, early mentor of the well known occult author W.E.Butler,) who, it would appear, was the psychic consultant who psychometrised Margaret Lumley Brown's combs. In a letter of 9th February 1920 he writes:

> *"Dear Miss Hay, Many thanks for the book which I have read with great interest. I much like the manner in which you have related `the story` and feel sure that it will do good service to the cause of true psychical research. I well recall the events you narrate, they come very vividly before me as I read the book. I shall try and be present when Miss Scatcherd gives her lecture on it."* (It was presented at the Delphic Club on 28th March 1920.)

Fortunately his advice that she never involve herself with psychic work again was not taken to heart, otherwise the rest of this book would never have been written!

Chapter Two

Psychic Encounters

Articles

The first of the articles that follow appeared in The Occult Review *for November 1919, a prestigious magazine that ran for most of the interwar years. The ones that follow were commissioned for* New Dimensions *magazine which ran between 1963 and 1965.*

Through the Ivory Gate

"Dreams out of the Ivory Gate and Visions before Midnight." - Sir Thomas Browne

The ordinary human experience of dreaming cannot be satisfactorily explained without a definite understanding as to what part of us it is that dreams. This appears to be the portion of our consciousness which is temporarily driven out or made torpid under anaesthetics and totally driven out at death. When the body is completely inactive in sleep this part can no longer use its ordinary channels, and acts in various ways.

With many people it weaves symbolic or realistic fantasies largely derived from the fleeting impressions collected in the brain during the day, dormant from past years, or temporarily developed from some state of health or mind at the time of dreaming, These it re-impresses on the brain, which, on waking, remembers a crowd of disorderly fantastic incidents of little value or interest. If the body is extremely exhausted, the brain is too weary either to take or receive impressions, and memory is a blank on waking. Often, too, when the body is not exhausted, the consciousness focuses nowhere in sleep, and the person does not dream at all.

All this is logically explained by the more progressive psychological theories of today. These, however, do not appear to account for what may be called 'clear dreams' The only explanation of the latter is that an ordered activity of consciousness can exist during sleep.

With people who have clear dreams the consciousness would seem occasionally to be loosened from the body - although the latter may be in perfect health - so much that the person feels aware of the loosening; in these cases the consciousness is not only active, but capable of consecutive thought and action. It may go on an actual journey and see actual places. It can meet people whom it knows to be dead, or others whose consciousness, like itself, is presumably loosened from the body. It may be aware of extended vision or hearing, thus leaving a species of 'second sight,' which in some way sees the shadow of the future.

This is not meant to suggest that the clear dreamer never has any dreams that arise from ordinarily explainable causes, such as indigestion, the thoughts uppermost in the brain, etc. He certainly has these too, but has no difficulty in discriminating between them and the others. To him, therefore, the idea of dreaming assumes its normal proportions as a natural faculty, which is as obvious and habitual as sight or hearing, but which is better 'kept quiet about.'

Even in 'clear dreams' there is much symbolism. The continual recurrence of a certain symbol or symbols before a certain type of event - when this is unexpected - leads, naturally enough, to a definite connection of event and symbol.

The latter appear to vary with each dreamer and to filter through the channels of class, custom and individual psychology. Race and tradition also influence dream symbolism, for instance, all over the Continent vermin is looked upon as a sign of money, but in Great Britain of sickness. It is also considered unlucky in the folk-superstition of all races to dream of a baby or of anything scarlet.

As to the reason why the future should be seen in symbols, or seen at all in dreams, one can, of course, only speculate.

It is probable that many other primitive instincts, besides the much reiterated one of sex, can wake into activity during sleep.

Symbolism was deeply rooted in the earliest races, and its ancient use was to connect the mind more easily with an idea which was too diffuse to grasp otherwise. Besides this, the lost animal sense, called 'scent' has often shown curious phenomena among primitive peoples of today, and may have, like other things, some metaphysical counterpart.

The following are some examples of 'clear dreams' collected from private sources. They are divided into three groups, which might be classed as symbolic, realistic and transcendental. It is not claimed for this collection that it proves any point, but to the unbiased examiner it seems to suggest a more definite focusing of consciousness during sleep than is officially admitted.

SYMBOLIC DREAMS

DEATH AND TROUBLE

1

The dreamer twice dreamed that a friend, who was at the time in excellent health, had a leg amputated. A year later this friend was operated upon for appendicitis and died within the same week.

II

The same dreamer dreamed that an acquaintance, who was then suffering from nervous breakdown, had a leg which was rotting and which finally became completely severed from the body. This acquaintance, for whom there was no reason to expect a near death, had a relapse and died within four days.

In neither case had either the dreamer or those dreamed of anything the matter with the member in question.

III

The dreamer dreamed that a certain looking-glass, habitually used by his mother, cracked. The mother unexpectedly died within the year.

IV

The same dreamer dreamed that a large mirror, which hung in a friend's house, cracked. The friend's wife, who was then quite well, died within a week from an operation which was suddenly found necessary.

V

The same dreamer dreamed that a mirror, belonging to some cousins, was cracked. Their aunt died unexpectedly.
The same dream happened to this dreamer on two other occasions before the death of friends.

VI

The dreamer saw an acquaintance in a perfectly empty room. Though in good health at the time, the acquaintance shortly died.

VII

The dreamer, a Protestant by courtesy but far from interested in any religious questions, dreamed that she was in a small room, which was bare of any furniture except one chair in which was a cardinal's hat. Suddenly some dignitary of the Roman Catholic Church appeared. The dreamer told herself in the dream that he must be an archbishop, as he wore the same robes in which she had once seen the Archbishop of Westminster. She wondered why a cardinal's hat should be on the chair, for the vision wore no garment suggestive of a cardinal. Knowing that it was the custom with Catholics to kneel and kiss an archbishop's ring, she was conscious of making herself kneel preparatory to doing this as the figure passed her. He paused for an instant, did not give her his ring to kiss, but raised one hand over her in blessing. and swept with extraordinary swiftness to the opposite corner of the room, where he vanished.

Two days later the daily paper announced that Monsignor S---, Archbishop of T---, had died suddenly in Rome on the morning preceding the night of the dream. The paper stated that it had been expected he would have been made a cardinal shortly. The dreamer had not heard of Monsignor S--- before.

VIII

The dreamer invariably dreamed of rats before hearing of certain attacks of slander from unexpected quarters.

IX

Two sisters - of Scotch descent, but born and habitually living in England - found that they dreamed of tartan when trouble of any sort was impending, and particularly before the death of relatives and friends, who always appeared as dressed in tartan.

Apart from these occasions, one of the sisters dreamed that she saw the King wearing a strip of the Duff tartan - she recognised it as that in the dream - round his arm, like a mourning band. Two months later the Duke of Fife died.

The other sister dreamed before a time of great family poverty and disaster, of a field or plain near a large house. It was night, and hundreds of highlanders were camped on the plain. There were bonfires and much drinking, jesting and cursing. Something, it was not clear what, appeared about to happen.

Some time later these dreams were confided to an elderly relative whom the dreamers barely knew. This lady said that she herself had dreamed of tartan before her father's death. She also related the following account:-

As a small child she had apparently been much interested by the tales of an aged great-aunt who remembered the Jacobite rising of 1745. This great-aunt lived near Prestonpans and had seen the highland camp on the eve of battle. Her husband had been a 'neutral,' and had helped to carry Colonel Gardiner off the field. Some of her relations had been Jacobites. Three had been hanged from the gables of their own house, and they had all been deprived of their property. The general horror of the time was still strong in her mind when years later she communicated the tale to the child.

It is easily understood that the elder dreamer could have been lastingly impressed with such details, but how could the impression have reached a younger member of the family before she had heard the story?

GOOD FORTUNE

X

The dreamer – English - dreamed of some sacred Indian white bulls with silver chains round their necks. He was unexpectedly offered the secretaryship to a certain philosophical society whose headquarters were in India.

XI

The dreamer dreamed of five friends, who afterwards got married, as being dressed in rose-colour and surrounded by pink roses.

The same dreamer dreamed of a certain lady as wearing artificial pink roses and a soiled pink dress. This lady married unexpectedly. The marriage proved to have been entirely for money, and turned out exceptionally badly.

XII

On two occasions before receiving a legacy, the dreamer dreamed of living Egyptian scarabs to the number of pounds inherited.

XIII

The following dream appears partly symbolic and partly realistic.

The dreamer dreamed that a friend, then abroad, produced from a brown paper parcel three pictures, which he said had been painted by Oscar Wilde. The main points of these pictures, though not all their very intricate detail, were strongly impressed upon the dreamer.

They each seemed like parts of a design rather than a picture in the ordinary sense. The first showed blue balloons rising into a blue sky with a gleam of satin somewhere and of a white butterfly and the moon. The second was rather a blur, but was carried out in different shades of yellow, for there appeared to be a thick yellow fog in it, besides a load of hay, an omnibus and a bridge. The third was of a pale, dark-haired, very slender girl. She stood under a rose-tree and pulled the petals, yet she seemed also to have a lute. She was dressed in yellow satin.

The dreamer could not think what this dream meant. The only work of Wilde's she had read at the time was *Intentions*. The man who showed her the pictures in the dream was familiar with all his writings, but had not discussed them with her. She wrote down the dream and asked several people who could throw no light on the subject. Some time later she read for the first time some of Wilde's poems, and suddenly came upon three which vividly recalled the dream.

Here are the titles and some of the verses :-

Le Panneau

Under the rose-tree's dancing shade
There stands a little ivory girl
Pulling the leaves of pink and pearl
With pale green nails of polished jade.

The white leaves float upon the air,
The red leaves flutter idly down.
Some fall upon her yellow gown
And some upon her raven hair.

She takes an amber lute and sings, etc.

Les Ballons

Against these turbid turquoise skies
The light and luminous balloons
Dip and drift like satin moons,
Drift like silken butterflies.

Symphony in Yellow

An omnibus across the bridge
Crawls like a yellow butterfly.
And, here and there, a passer-by
Shows like a little restless midge.

Big barges full of yellow hay
Are moored against the shadowy wharf,
And, like a yellow silken scarf,
The thick fog hangs along the quay.

REALISTIC DREAMS

Among many examples of this type of dream, the following have been chosen as being perhaps the most representative. The word 'realistic' is used approximately, as describing dreams which see a scene not symbolically, but as it might literally happen

In the afternoon before the dream the dreamer had been to see some married friends. It was May, and they were discussing where they would go for the summer, rather thinking of Dorking. That night the dreamer dreamed of seeing these friends with a lady whom the dreamer also knew, having coffee after dinner in a small bungalow. The dreamer noticed that the house had a veranda, and that the friends were having coffee in a curiously shaped space, which was near the entrance to the front door, and which might be used either as a room or as a hall.

Leaving the bungalow, the dreamer went into the garden and discovered that this was a small plot with a little square lawn. At the foot of the lawn was a wall with a door in it and a narrow flower bed edged with blue flowers. The dreamer went through the door in the wall and out into the road, which was straight and bare for some way, till a block of three red brick cottages was reached. Past them was a hill, at the top of which was a church. The dreamer felt sure by the smell of the air that the sea must be near, but could not see it. The dreamer went up the hill and from a certain angle of it discovered that the sea and sands actually stretched out below.

Some weeks later the dreamer described this dream minutely to the friends. They declared it could not be accurate, as they had no intention of going near the sea. No more was heard of the matter for some time.

In August the dreamer had a letter from these friends, who were amazed to find the dream accurate in all its details. They had gone to Whitby on business, and whilst going for a walk in the neighbourhood found a bungalow to let with which they were so charmed that it was at once decided to take it for the summer, and all arrangements were settled in a few days. The bungalow had a veranda and a curiously-shaped space - half hall and half room -

inside the front door. In this they usually had coffee. The lady seen in the dream was staying with them in the house. The garden was small, with a little square lawn, terminated by a narrow flower bed edged with lobelia and a wall with a door in it. The latter led into the road, which was bleak and bare for some distance. Farther along was a small block of red brick cottages, just before the hill, at the top of which was a church. At a certain angle of the hill the sea and sands could be seen beneath.

II

The dreamer, then in Germany, dreamed of a house in England. It was in the country. Going into one of the doors downstairs, the dreamer noticed the position of the furniture, particularly of a sofa, a book-rest and a window. The dreamer had the impression that some man, who was an invalid, lay on the sofa habitually. Through the window were some clear spaces of garden and some shrubs. The dreamer went out of this room and proceeded upstairs to a bedroom which seemed immediately above the first room. Here a man was lying, dead, on the bed. The dreamer felt that it was W. E. Henley, the poet, and was conscious that he had been the man who had habitually used the sofa in the room downstairs.

The dreamer was impressed with the dream, and on waking made a rough plan of the position of the furniture, etc., in the rooms, showing them to a friend. The English papers which arrived two days late - pre-war days, needless to say - in Leipzig, announced the death of Henley on the day preceding the date of the dream. Some time after, the *Bookman* published an account of Henley, illustrated with photographs of his study. Both the dreamer and the friend agreed that it corresponded exactly with the former's plan of the room downstairs and its furniture. The account stated that the poet had been an invalid. The dreamer did not previously know any personal details about Henley.

III

The person who had the following dream was English, but living in Italy.

The floor of his apartment happened to be covered with curious tiles, some of which had, by way of a pattern, numbers on them that were not arranged in any order.

By the door was a square of tiles of this sort composed of four rows of mixed numbers. The dreamer dreamed three times that if he used the numbers as they fell in the top row of this square, he would win in the weekly lottery - a municipal system of lotteries much used by the Italian peasants. The dreamer thought it would be amusing to try his luck in the lottery, but on impulse, instead of choosing the numbers in their consecutive order as in the dream, changed them and inserted a different number as well.

The lottery for that week proved to have in their exact succession the numbers on the square tiles by the door. Had the dreamer gone exactly by the dream he would have 'broken the bank.'

IV

The dreamer was abroad, undergoing an operation under chloroform at about eleven in the morning.

She was conscious of going to the house of some distant relatives in I.eicestershire. She saw one of them, a lady, with her eyes bandaged, lying on a bed in a certain bedroom. There were two doctors. The dreamer heard the words 'Graves' disease' in connection with the lady, and had the impression that the latter had gone blind.

Outside this lady's room another much older woman was waiting for the result of the operation, and sitting on the stairs crying. The dreamer recognised the latter as the aunt who had brought the patient up, and with whom she had always lived. The dreamer remembered this dream after 'coming to,' but could not understand it, as the relations in question, as far as the dreamer knew, were well. The dreamer was not in correspondence with that side of the family. The dreamer had not then heard of the expression 'Graves' disease,' and thought it must have been a wrong name. Some time later the dreamer returned to England and went to stay with these relations for the first time after many years.

It transpired that the lady seen with her eyes bandaged had had Graves' disease and had gone totally blind. She had had two doctors present during the operation, which had been performed in the room dreamed of, outside the door of which the patient's aunt had sat on the stairs awaiting results and crying. The operation had been performed near the date of the dreamer's own, but not, as far as can be ascertained, on the actual day.

TRANSCENDENTAL DREAMS

This term is used, for want of a better, to classify a collection of dreams dealing with more abstract aspects of consciousness. whether or not the list is symbolic or realistic cannot, of course, be argued here, but it may possibly be of speculative interest.

In anticipation of the theory which bases all dreams on conscious or sub-conscious thoughts, I ought to say that all the examples which hold religious suggestion were the dreams of people who were completely indifferent to and uninterested in all religious practices and doctrines. In all these cases of 'transcendental' dreams the shock of waking up has been great, so much so as to affect the physical health, and especially the heart, for two or three days later.

1

A vision of a colossal dark blue figure which seemed as if the night sky had taken shape into a form something like the human embryo on a gigantic scale. It clasped its arms around the house, bending its face above the roof. At the same instant the dreamer awoke at the noise of sharp firing, to discover a Zeppelin immediately overhead, which was, however, subsequently brought down without its doing any damage to the neighbourhood.

II

A rambler-rose in a pot was for some unknown reason rapidly dying, though every care had been taken of it. The dreamer dreamed that a thin green shape, rather like a living geometrical figure, had become disconnected with the rose and was running aimlessly about. The dreamer willed the shape back again into the plant. The next morning the rose was found to be very much revived, and in two days was as healthy as ever.

III

A primitive stone temple in the midst of forests and streams. It was entirely bare of altar, idols or any object. The dreamer joined the crowd of worshippers who, dressed in skins and of savage appearance, were kneeling and facing one way. The whole congregation, including the dreamer, joined in a mysterious chant which grew in volume and intensity till its rhythm became visible in ascending spirals of air which gradually formed into a pattern and filled the whole building like a design of smoke. The force of the rhythm finally became stronger, till the dreamer felt it was expanding his form and would soon split it into fragments. He awoke in a cold perspiration and felt extremely ill and 'gone to pieces' physically for the whole of the next day.

IV

A strong south wind had been blowing the whole night. The dreamer dreamed that she left her physical body upon the bed and went over to the open window. Looking out she saw the wind, which appeared like ribbed strands of colourless air streaming from some hidden central point. Some of these strands swept into the room and caught her up in them as if she had been a leaf, taking her some way above the earth and depositing her on a cloud. During the passage she did not feel frightened, but dazed and, the wind completely enveloping her, she could see nothing of how or where she went, but felt she had touched no physical thing of such indescribable softness. On the cloud she regained self-possession and found that she was not really at a great height above the earth, but the stars looked nearer and brighter. Presently a man came to her who asked her how she had got to the cloud. She replied that she 'had come in the wind,' and described what it had felt and looked like.

The man said it was an interesting experience, but that she had better go back, as if she woke up too suddenly so far away from her body she would probably feel a terrible shock. She then felt that he willed her in some way, and that she grew drowsy and inert and drifted into a mass of wind-loops which touched the cloud at the moment. She came down on the bed. This woke her suddenly just as a strong gust swirled round the room and out at the window.

V

The dreamer, suffering from scarlet fever, was in hospital. It was midday in winter, and the windows were open at the bottom. It seemed to her that three dark beings, half ape and half man, indescribably revolting in appearance, entered through the nearest window, seized her and took her with them the way they came. She was conscious of a great feeling of fear and loathing, also of seeing her own form asleep upon the bed, while some other part of her, borne by them, passed through the window high into the air.

The motion was of birds in flight, although the beings had no wings. After a considerable distance above the earth the air seemed to grow hotter each moment, and a clanging noise, not unlike that of hammer and anvil, sounded gradually nearer. The dreamer felt that she was going to Hell, and was surprised that it should be upwards instead of downwards. She approached a spot like an immense courtyard surrounded by a plain of sparse, withered grass. Here was situated a dark dome-shaped building, through the door of which the clanging sounded deafeningly, and the heat drifted in unbearable currents. At the left of the doorway an unseen being, whose presence, however, could be tangibly felt, gave the dreamer the impression that unless she could get back to her bed in the hospital she would die and be forced to enter the terrible doors of the dome. She woke with a bad shock and with the sensation of being brought through the window, jerked on to the bed, and into her body again. The dream was so vivid that, though it happened many years ago, she still remembers all its details with horror.

VI

The dreamer felt himself going upward through the ceiling for a considerable distance. He was shown an enormous picture of the Ascension, in front of which some spirits were rising into the air. Some rose for a few feet and then came down again; others could only rise a few inches, and wore, to help them, some inflated apparatus much like the bathing wings given to children. The dreamer tried to rise into the air himself, and found that after a time he could get an appreciable distance. The spirits told him that he was 'practising levitation,' a thing which all had to learn in some measure, and that the Ascension showed its accomplishment in the greatest and superhuman degree.

VI

Shortly before the Armistice the dreamer dreamed of a large space filled with a soft, clear amber light, in which what might be called a flock of angels were kneeling in prayer. Others flew to join them from the distance, alighting in such numbers that the light was thick with wings. The angels appeared all of the same type or height, with rather child-like faces, and their hair, features and garments seemed full of a tangible radiance. The wings, which were the shape of a swallow's, were either white or else showed the feathers grouped in lines of colour, like a rainbow.

VIII

The dreamer dreamed that one night he and certain of his friends were looking up at the stars, which seemed unusually bright and distinct. Suddenly six to eight cigar-shaped objects of light appeared in the sky, sailing overhead towards the party. The dreamer remarked at once: 'We shall have a raid to-night.' As the objects drew nearer, however, he perceived that they were not airships at all, but oblong emanations of light from some form hidden in their centres. One of the dreamer's friends gazed at them through field glasses, but after a moment said: 'We'd better not look.'

The dreamer noticed that an extraordinary expression of awe had come over the faces of his friends, for which neither he nor they could account. The dreamer then looked up himself, and for an instant only was aware of gigantic beings being directly overhead and entering certain of the planets. He noticed that they were nude, and that their bodies seemed of living flame. Their motion was not of flying but of swimming in the ether. The nearest of them, who was in the act of entering a star, had huge white wings which, outstretched, spread half across the sky. This being seemed like a boy, and carried in one hand the stem of some plant covered with small dark-green leaves. There was something stupendous and almost terrible in the beauty, and youth of the face.

The dreamer was conscious, in the second he looked at this being, that he was in the presence of something unutterably holy, and that he had never realised the meaning of the word before. So strong was the feeling that it seemed he could not look on the being more than an instant and live. He felt that he fell down on the ground, struck with a sort of blindness which was yet unphysical and extended not only to the eyes but the whole being. After a while he regained consciousness and found that the sky was clear, and that the stars looked as they had done in the first part of the dream.

His friends had disappeared, but a stranger helped him to his feet, saying: "Are you better now? You oughtn't to have looked. It is very seldom that THEY pass over. I myself have never seen them, but I can feel THEM, for THEY make the whole atmosphere quite different, and almost as it one were in church."

With this speech in his mind the dreamer woke up. The dream was so vivid that it made a lasting impression on him.

The Urwelt
The Elemental 'Other World'

There is a level of consciousness which our unclinically minded forefathers knew quite well. This level or plane, however, rarely rises to the surface of the modern mind and, when it does, is far more difficult to rationalise than, say, ghosts.

There are many words for the plane in question and its denizens. The English speak of the Elemental kingdoms. The Indians speak of the Deva kingdoms, which include beings of many grades from the greater angels to the woodland sprites. For the purpose of this article, however, the best word is probably Urwelt, which the Germans use to denote that primitive or primal sphere which includes the gods and warriors of pre-human races, fairies, natural spirits and the many projections of Earth's consciousness which become apparent to human beings under the right conditions.

What are the right conditions?

First, a sense of spiritual reality behind what we call 'nature' and a strong awareness of individual will on the part of natural forces. Sometimes this awareness will be so strong that the forces will be seen in humanised shapes. geometrical designs or in living blocks of Etheric substance. It is scarcely necessary to add that none of these things are either seen or heard with the ordinary sense perception, they are perceived with Etheric faculties.

The second essential is a sincere love of Earth herself and a desire to communicate with her 'other' children.

The third essential is a belief in the individual life of this planet and a certainty that it permeates the whole world even in inappropriate surroundings such as a city. It was in such a mood as this that Yeats noticed a toy fountain in a London shop which acted so strongly on his consciousness that the poem of *Innisfree* was brought to birth.

Those tending the land in former days were closely in touch with the Elementals. Even at the present day, town dwellers cut off from civilisation in remote country districts will occasionally become aware of the hidden a spheres of Nature and I have heard of Glasgow business men (who can scarcely be called dreamy types) becoming 'fey' when holidaying in the Hebrides and experiencing there states of other dimensions.

The call of the Elemental kingdoms seems to be especially strong in those races wherein both earth and human contacts are intertwined for centuries as with the Celts, Greeks, Scandinavians, Russians, native races of North America and Canada etc. The Urwelt forces are also allied with families which have inherited a certain tract of land for many generations. This tract of land can be either a great estate or a humble croft, for the link is with blood and not with social status as such.

It would seem that an old family thus connected for centuries with a certain area of land builds a group-entity on the astral plane. This entity links itself in course of time with bird, beast and vegetation oversouls as well as with Elementals of the district. I suggest that such a link could produce some of the hereditary apparitions which presage misfortune to the family in question. These symbols are usually of some bird or beast or fairy which is seen before a death. Among the best known bird apparitions of this kind are the Hapsburg ravens and the herons of Gight.

Ravens have been notoriously present before disaster to members of the House of Hapsburg, They are said to have followed the ship in which the Archduke Maximilian set out on his ill-fated journey to Mexico and one was also seen just before the assassination of his sister-in-law, the Empress Elisabeth of Austria.

Another case of this sort was that of Byron's mother, heiress of the Gordons of Gight whose family fortunes were connected with the herons which for centuries had nested in a certain tree on the estate. The poet's father having gambled away all his wife's property, Gight had to be sold. Simultaneously the herons deserted their ancient home and took refuge with a neighbouring landlord, thus fulfilling Thomas the Rhymer's prognostication:

> *When the herons leave the tree,*
> *The Laird of Gight shall landless be.*

The usual type of fairy connected with death is known as the Banshee (Celtic *Bean Sidhe* - Fairy woman). The Banshee is rarely seen but is heard to croon or wail before disaster and is said to reserve its visits for those of total or partial Celtic blood.

On four occasions in my own family it appears to have given warnings of this kind. On three of these occasions the announcement came in the form of an unaccountable crooning from a vase which, on examination, always proved to be quite empty. On the fourth occasion there was an apparition of a figure as well as of the sound.

The crooning started as before from a vase on the chimney piece. I was lying down and the sound left the vase and was brought over to me by a small being, embryonic in shape and of a reddish brown colour. Despite the small size of this fairy, it gave an impression of terrific force and fate. I felt myself unable to move and as if obliged to listen till the deadly little 'song' was ended. On each of these four occasions the crooning was heard by several people although I myself appear to have been the only one to see the crooner.

The belief in fairies can be found all over Europe but in Britain has been mostly derived from Celtic sources and a few from the Norse.

There are of course many tribes of Elementals of which the 'Little People' is only one. There are several instances of such beings appearing even in the present century but in this article I have as far as possible only recorded accounts of apparitions personally seen by me or else by friends.

Certain tribes of fairies are common to different localities. Thus there are Knockers in Wales and Cornwall which inhabit mines and are benevolent friends to the miners. Piskies are Cornish and have the reputation for mischievously leading travellers astray on the moors. I must, however, place on record a kindly Pisky who put a friend and myself back on the right road again; he was a tiny brownish grey being who skipped about in front of us plainly expecting to be followed. Brownies are met in Scotland and other parts where there are boulders and bracken. The elves which used to dance in fields and green clearings all over England are seldom seen nowadays for they dislike the spread of mechanical techniques and the appalling noise of modernity.

Ireland, as is well known, has a host of fairy tribes, many of them including leprechauns and others of the 'Little People'. The most renowned, however, of the fairy race in Ireland is the great Tuatha Da Danaan (The People of the Goddess Dana), that half divine, pre-human race of marvellous beauty, power and high stature who are sometimes seen to emerge in a shining host with glittering steeds and banners out of the secret places in the hills.

I had two friends who at different times and in different places encountered these beings. Both friends bear witness to an overwhelming sense of joy and vitality which affected the personality for some time after this contact, which did, however, for a time appear to cut the interests in ordinary life despite having still to carry on with this and to hide the cause of dissatisfaction for the sake of convention!

Nature spirits on which I have not yet specifically touched in this paper, are legion and detailed accounts of their hierarchies could fill a volume. Briefly, these beings are the graded denizens of the four Elements including oversouls and lesser units of natural forces such as rivers, lakes, forests, hills, caves etc. To meet these beings is an interesting and sometimes a frightening experience.

It must not be thought that Elementals are always 'seen', they are equally often 'heard' and 'felt' according to the level of consciousness active in the human being at the time. Anyone, however, who has experienced such sensations will agree with me that such things are indubitable to the person concerned. A blind man knows perfectly well when another person enters his room and is equally aware of the latter's movements thereafter

Friends of mine camping in the Welsh mountains were disturbed in the very early morning by 'something' which entered from the hills. If was plainly not an animal. It made a complete tour of the tent with a curious oblique type of movement which produced much alarm and tension to the humans visited. A torch revealed nothing to be seen. After a short time the visitor left and the feeling of fear immediately died down. There was, however, a strange vitality permeating the atmosphere.

The same Elemental can be apparent to several people at once yet produce different reactions in each. I was visiting a cave in Devonshire with two friends when the oversoul of that cave made itself obvious to all three of us. Friend A greatly liked caves and the presence brought him vitality and delight. Friend B was more neutral but had a feeling of repugnance though was not conscious of any other manifestation. I myself dislike and fear caves and I also saw the Elemental itself looming up in a green-black, slimy mass with huge tentacles which endeavoured to fasten upon my Etheric vehicle, producing physical faintness and depletion.

It is easy to understand that people with a genuine love of certain natural forces will be in harmony with the oversoul of those forces.

Elementals have not sex as the world understands the word but it is clear that they show such differentiations of force that one can only define them as masculine and feminine. The two contacts mentioned below were certainly feminine, showing a maternal gentleness and protection which yet had a profound strength within it.

I went for the first time to visit Dozmary Pool - that small lake in which Cornish legend claims Excalibur was flung at King Arthur's death. Suddenly there rose in front of me the brooding spirit of the lake in the shape of a vast white mist rising over the water. The mist took on a vaguely feminine outline of a deep sweetness and dignity.

The second occasion was one which took place in a room in which I was sleeping, exactly opposite St. Michael's Mount. At that time I had much devotion to St. Michael and a desire to get in touch with him. I was awakened very early by a feminine presence of great beauty and graciousness, like a column of deep blue lit by silver lights and accompanied by the smell of millions of flowers. So strong was this perfume that I can still recall it over a distance of many years. 'She' told me that I was not nearly developed enough to have a real contact with one of such supreme strength and spirituality as St. Michael, but that 'she had come instead'. I do not know who 'she' was but Theosophists would have called her a Deva.

One day my room was full of cut flowers and amongst them I suddenly noticed a small fairy with little wings flitting from vase to vase. He seemed to like the room, examined everything, and used to follow me about. It was noticeable that the flowers lasted much longer than usual and he seemed to emanate a delicate vitality. He remained with me about ten days and for some reason was called 'Pecksniff'. One day a whole party of small earth-spirits arrived and drew Pecksniff in with them. At first he tried to rejoin me but evidently tribal feeling was too strong and he departed with his own people.

Although the major fairy colour is green, this is often accompanied, according to folklore, with a red cloak, cap or other accessories. There are also fairies which are always clothed in red and are called the 'red fairies'. There is a well known superstition that it is unlucky for human beings to wear green because it is the fairy colour. The Ogilvies gave great offence to Fairyland by having a preponderance of green in their tartan. The latter was therefore rewoven without the fatal colour, even since which time 'On an Ogilvie green Must never be seen.' Nevertheless, people who are Favourites with the Fairies are allowed to wear green as was Thomas the Rhymer, who was given 'a pair of shoes of the velvet green'.

There is an esoteric tradition that while the ordinary man initiates the animal kingdom, Elementals must be initiated by an Adept. A duly initiated Elemental can in this way achieve a human soul. Otherwise the Elementals must fade out at the end of the evolution. I cannot argue such a point but tradition has legends of the truth of this theory. In any case it is a good principle to help an Elemental if he has helped you.

The Elemental is neither good nor evil because he is a blind force with a single pointed will. There is something akin to an animal in him for he does seem to take likes and dislikes to certain people and he is able to respond to a wish to help him and to those who show no fear of him.

NATURE SPIRITS

The living power generated by a natural force such as a river, lake, mountain, wood etc., is composed of many graded units which are comprised within one collective whole. This collective unit is the Oversoul which rules all the lesser lives of its own type in that area.

To clairvoyant vision the Oversoul appears as a personalised form and the lesser nature units owing It allegiance appear as minor shapes of the same type. A famous picture by the Swiss artist Bocklin imaginatively depicts the Oversoul of a forest. The scene shows a non-human woman crouched above the trees which evidently draw from her the dark and silent life of the woods.

These collective and individual spirits of nature have been known in all countries under the guise of folklore and myth. One might well consider them as manifestations of the earth's subconscious memories which man, on occasion, taps.

It is recognised by occultists that past events register photographically on a subtle stratum of the earth and that these impressions are known as the Akashic Records. Thus the scene of a murder or of an ancient battle will suddenly appear to the consciousness of a man of the present day who is in the haunted space and who is himself quite probably without antiquarian knowledge or interest. He may equally contact in the same manner events yet further back. He may for instance become aware of primary forms of man and beast - forms which may be indeterminate or intermingled.

To the psychic and the occultist natural objects are not 'inanimate' but show a strong individualised life and it is this fact which lies at the root of both fairy-tales and myths.

Two fairy-tales which are cases in point are Grimm's *Nixie of the Millpond* and Andersen's *Elder-Tree Mother.* A nixie is the oversoul of a pool or pond and the feminine spirit of an elder-tree might well appear like an old wise woman. Not for nothing is a giant oak described as a king of the forest, for the major spirits of the woods are deep-rooted in their own special plot of ground and resent any encroachment from lesser members of the forest.

Many people notice that trees become antagonistic at night, draining the vitality of human beings. In the daytime, however, the woods can be friendly and when one is depleted or unhappy it is curiously comforting to grasp a tree-trunk with one's hands. In this case the tree absorbs the harmful atmosphere in the human aura and replaces it with the strong and stable magnetism of earth. If one makes friends with a certain tree a sympathetic link is formed with its species.

In this connection I was once attracted to some birches which were beginning to come into leaf. Psychically, each stem was stepping out of its outer covering, in the form of a lovely naked girl pied with brown and silver like the birch-tree's bark. These spirits literally danced in the wind like some charming vivacious schoolgirls. When the rain came, they at once disappeared within the sheltering trunks. There was a definite interchange of greetings between us and since then I have always felt that I was welcomed amongst birches, as though I had been received into the home circle.

The elm-tree has a very different spirit with a reputation for antagonism and treachery. Country people used to avoid sheltering under elms in a storm and even in calm weather one may not be safe. The rhyme goes:

Ellum she hateth
Mankind and waiteth
Till every gust be laid
To drop a limb
On the head of him
Who sleeps beneath her shade.

Every unit of vegetation has its higher principle or soul. This principle, even if not psychically seen, will show likes and dislikes towards members of the human family. Those people who have 'green fingers' are types which are able to be intuitively in touch with the soul of a plant.

Flowers in a vase will sometimes tangibly move and reach out towards a person as though wishing for communication while at the same time perfume is deliberately exuded and wafted across to the favoured human being.

Occasionally however, hostility is expressed by plants. A friend of mind had a strange antipathy towards geraniums. She declared that they poisoned her when she was near them. One day while suffering from an unaccountable and singularly severe headache she chanced to go near the window. On looking out she saw that a great block of tenuous dark substance was emanating from a distant bed of geraniums and approaching the window with menacing speed. She ran into another room and the headache passed off immediately.

I once had a strange experience with a potted rose-tree, one of a couple which stood in the drawing-room during summer. These plants had both been quite healthy till one of them for no known reason began to die and, after examination by the gardener, was condemned to be thrown away. I had no especial conscious interest in the matter but that night I went out of my physical body and found myself going to the drawing-room where I took a good look at the dying plant. I noticed that a thin green shape (somewhat suggestive of a mathematical diagram) was running aimlessly up and down beside the withered rose-tree as though seeking to enter it and not knowing how to do so. I strongly willed it to re-enter and in some way helped it to perform this action.

The next morning, to my own and everyone's surprise, the previously dying rose was in full vitality once more. It went on blooming for the rest of the season and kept its good condition to the end. I think that this little episode really proves the fact of an inner vital principle behind the physical appearance of plants.

I have heard that the late Mr. Brodie Innes, a famous occultist, was obviously and indeed alarmingly in contact with a plant in his garden after his own death. There are two examples in legend to add to this list. Both refer to the renewal of life in seemingly dead wood. One episode is the story of St. Joseph of Arimathea's staff budding when struck into the ground at Glastonbury; the other is the tale of Tannhauser's staff bursting into leaf at the end of his penitential pilgrimage.

The Greeks and Romans possessed a very large kingdom of nature spirits. I would divide this kingdom, however, into two halves. 1. The spirits of Nature herself. 2. The entities of instinctive nature in man.

1. A great number of these were feminine personalisations and included oversouls and lesser units of woods, grottoes, rivers, plants etc. These female spirits bore the generic name of "nymph". Thus the Nereids were sea nymphs and the Naiads were the principles of rivers, streams and fountains. Dryads were tree nymphs and Oreads were nymphs of the mountains. Names can carry deep subconscious forces of association and there is a superstition that the name of the famous sea nymph Thetis is an unlucky omen for ships and submarines.

2. The best known of this section are the fauns, satyrs and centaurs. The fauns and satyrs were found in the trains of the great gods Pan, Silenus and Dionysus. To some extent they were also woodland spirits, for woods are associated with fear and secrecy. Their figures represent the terror, orgy and ecstasy in some of the ancient mystery rites and men wearing the masks of satyrs took part in many rituals of antiquity. Fauns and satyrs are variants of the Pan form, either as part man and part goat or else as complete man except for the ears and

horns of goats. It would seem that such forms are still built on the astral plane by the stresses of drunkenness and passion. I have heard of a very amorous gentleman who was also a fine classical scholar making an astral visit in the form of a satyr. So strong was this apparition that the white dust of the Greek road and the shadow of the olive groves built up also with corresponding reality to the person visited.

The centaurs are figures of primal speed, fierceness and energy associated with primeval man and primeval horse, partaking of those qualities in each half of their dual figure and, like the horse in the Book of Job, they are 'clothed with thunder'. I only once saw a centaur and he was a lonely and pathetic figure as though he were the last in the modern world. He was very heavily built, the equine part being that of a carthorse.

A Greek friend once assured me that centaurs were still seen clairvoyantly in Greece. In support of this he quoted a story current at the time. The tale went that some English children and their nurses were strolling in the country outside Athens. They were suddenly alarmed by the noise of galloping horses and the nurses were only just in time to withdraw themselves and their charges to the shelter of a wayside wood in order to leave room for a cavalcade of strange beings - half man and half horse - to rush past and vanish in clouds of dust.

In British folklore the fighting energy and speed of the horse is represented by the Kelpie, the terrible water-horse which rises from the Highland rivers, sometimes leaping onto the roadway near, to seize human prey and drag it down into the depths of the stream.

There is an old tradition that some rivers are male and some female. Thus the Thames is male and so is the Tiber.

Boyne and Severn are female. In Britain, certain rivers are said to require sacrifices and to claim their victims each year. Severn, Avon and Till are the most renowned for this and are thus recorded in ballad lore.

In connection with rivers I recall a dream experience in which I was in a ship sailing up a large river which was unknown to me. Suddenly the god of this river (the St. Lawrence) rose up from the hatches and confronted me. He was friendly and wished me to know that when I came to his country, he would be propitious to me. His figure seemed very real though he was not in human shape but like a vast mass of watery substance with a vaporous light emanating from it as well as some suggestion of native Canadian power. The sequel was eight years later when I most unexpectedly sailed to Montreal. I would add that I had a remarkably good time in Canada.

Wells, pools and springs are sacred to some healing spirit in many parts of the world. The Bible instances the Pool of Bethesda where at certain times 'an angel troubled the waters'. At this time the sick visited the Pool for cures. I would suggest that this 'angel' was the Pool's oversoul.

All over ancient Europe and also in Britain the Celts recognised wells and Springs as sources of healing and help and they propitiated the oversoul with offerings. Many of these ancient shrines are known to the tourist today under the guise of wishing wells. Many also have been 'taken over' by Christianity and are under the patronage of a Saint. Thus it is said that the famous St. Winifred's Well in Wales was a Celtic healing centre in pagan times.

There is also a Celtic tradition that a healing centre was known in pre-Christian days near Lourdes and was probably connected with the same spring of water. There is a story of a Catholic pilgrim to Lourdes, who had no knowledge of this pagan tradition, being startled to hear an inner voice say to him 'This all used to be mine and now the Woman (i.e. Our Lady) has it'.

There seems no doubt that during great upheavals of weather a certain type of nature spirit is active. Such beings would be related to conditions of the air. During very hot weather I have seen in central France strange living globes run along the burning earth, spreading heat in their path. When there is a violent storm, one can also be aware of great air Elementals charged with electricity hurtling over and upon the earth.

I woke one morning last winter to find a tremendous pressure in the room and a penetrating greyish light. A great grey being had evidently entered from the garden into the room. Outside, his brothers were crashing through the air. These beings were, I think, like the Gremlin tribe which some of our airmen encountered in the war. In any case they were helping to produce the worst blizzard that this country had suffered for years!

The Gods

The last of this series about non-human psychic apparitions is an endeavour to describe contacts with the gods. Such contacts are much rarer than are the impressions of encountering Nature Spirits and Elementals. The reason for this scarcity of data is probably because our minds have been for so long conditioned to monotheism on the one hand and science on the other that it is especially hard for a modern person to accept the idea of many deities unless he happens to be individually interested in myths and magic. For those who have read so far I think it may be assumed without argument that the forces of at least some of the ancient gods can be occasionally contacted and that their forms can be visualised through ritual building and certain types of psychism.

I would say that the old gods of the West come under four categories:

1. Rulers of greater natural forces such as sun, moon, stars, sea, space, etc.

2. Personalised principles once regarded as influencing man from without and now realised as being a part of human psychology such as courage, strength, love, beauty, wisdom, justice, etc. This is perhaps why Greek drama can still move us so profoundly, for the actors are of secondary importance to the principles they represent and the latter come to life and walk the stage with impersonal profundity.

3. Mighty cosmic beings recognised by Christians under the names of Angels, Archangels. Thrones, Dominions, Powers, Principalities, etc., who act as the higher servers of the One God.

4. Very early teachers of mankind who came from other evolutions than ours and who, according to esoteric tradition, once walked with men upon this earth in pre-historic days. The memory of these beings has been woven into folklore and legend all over the world.

This fourth category includes some of the primeval instructors of mankind who are now vaguely tabulated under the guise of mythological figures. The earliest religions were matriarchal and behind the stories of Demeter, Persephone, Dana, Cybele, and others, probably looms the forgotten figure of a great female teacher who helped the children of earth.

Amongst such beings who traditionally lived on earth long ago were those joint guides of primal Egypt - Isis and Osiris, Asclepios, the prototype of all doctors, Heracles, who is associated with the twelve symbolic tasks.

Besides these is the 'messenger of the gods' who brought Wisdom to the West and who came (or sent his disciples) to various races which enshrined his memory under many names. Thus he was called Thoth in Egypt, Hermes in Greece, Mercury in Rome, Merlin in Britain and Odin, Wotan or Woden among the Teutonic tribes. Odin is still remembered in folklore under the title of Herne the Hunter and as the mythical Founder of the Saxon Royal House, whose members claimed the appellation of 'Woden-born'.

Another legendary hero whose origins had traditional actuality was Orpheus, the Manu of the Celtic Race. When we remember that a Manu is the builder of some especial race and its Archetypal Man who sets the seal on its characteristics we see how the Celtic Group-soul was moulded on the Orphic pattern. This pattern was shown forth in artistic and mystical achievement, in the sacrificial death and in the tragedy of looking back, all of which has involved the Celts for generations under the name of patriotism.

A picture of Orpheus which made a great impression on me years ago was by the Theosophical painter Jean Delville and represented the dead face of Orpheus laid upon the mighty Lyre which drifted through the waves and eddies of transcendent blue amongst the stars.

There are several ways of contacting the old gods known to the present day. First, there is the ritual meeting of a certain number of people at a certain time and place - as at a Witches Coven. Second, there can be contact with an ancient power formerly worshipped in a particular shrine or locality and which 'sensitive' visitors encounter again.

Neither of the above examples has come my way and I therefore pass on to what is within my own experience. This includes:

- i) clairvoyant perception (without ritual),
- ii) psychological devices,
- iii) and one unexpected but amusing result of rather inefficient ceremonial magic.

psychic encounters

1. Clairvoyance

One day while sitting alone in a library occupied with some books, I was amazed to see an enormous figure of Thoth, ibis-headed and orange-colour, build up beside me. My thoughts jumped to a friend who had been accused of a most unlikely as well as unevidential misdemeanour. The figure of Thoth seemed determined to impress me with a warning that no judgment should be given without complete impartiality and the calm weighing of every detail.

I regret that I did not then know enough to apply the message correctly but I did refer the vision to the authorities concerned with the accusation of my friend, who were much interested but declared that the message was clearly a confirmation of the course which had already been pursued.

On the face of it I agreed, but with a feeling of intuitional discomfort. Thoth is the Lord of Truth and the Weigher of Hearts and, a long time later, it was found that great injustice had been done and the friend in question was completely re-instated. Much later still, it was disclosed to me that the image of Thoth had been deliberately built by a very strong discarnate influence in the hope that a vision seen by someone not greatly involved in the affair might convey a warning to all to be certain of strict impartiality.

The next occasion was certainly influenced by a talk with someone of highly enlightened mind on the physical plane and who had been at pains to argue that the real Pan was not to be found either in the monster conjured up by Crowley or in the 'pretty-pretty' symbolism of the pipes heard upon green slopes. The principal point raised was that Pan belonged to the type of the Living Fire of the earth when the Foundations of this sphere were laid. Like all the Elemental forces, Pan is a pure but mindless power and therefore neither good nor evil in the human sense.

That night, when out of the body in sleep, I really experienced the imminence of a meeting with this concept of Pan, which I believe to be the true one. I was in a vast primeval forest and the fires of the earth were roaring audibly and sending shafts of flame over each tree, the branches of which were laden with living sparks. The forest, however, was not set alight, but given a tremendous vitality. A sense of terror pervaded my human mind but accompanied by awe and joy.

From the distance the approach of Pan could he heard shaking the whole planet as it drew nearer. The shock awoke me, but not before I was aware that great hands parted the trees and that above their tops appeared a countenance which was scarcely a face but which was alight with vitality and power.

The following has always remained in my memory as a real appearance of one of those beings which could in fact be described as a 'god'. I was out of the body during sleep and was aware of looking up at the unusual brilliance of the stars. Suddenly a sense of great awe fell upon the whole earth while overhead about six large lozenge-like shapes approached across the sky. As the shapes came closer one saw that they were in fact auras of light emanating from beings floating within them and who were about to visit certain of the stars and planets.

I had an inner warning not to look upward again until the beings had disappeared into these spheres, but raised my eyes a minute too soon and was just in time to observe one of them entering a star immediately overhead. The beauty, youth and size of this figure, whose body was of living light, had an element of terror for me as it was far removed from humanity. 'His' appearance was somewhat reminiscent to Greek forms of Eros or Hermes and 'he' carried the branch of some green plant. I should, however, hesitate to affirm 'his' name. At the same instant my inner sight was literally struck with blindness and I passed into unconsciousness.

There are, of course, various instances of clairvoyant contacts with god-forms. William Blake must have had them and, in later days, Yeats, William Sharp and George Russell were said to have seen Angus Og, the Celtic Apollo. George Russell, (AE), the great Irish poet and mystic, painted some of his visions in pictures. I remember a painting of his depicting one of the great devas sailing above the roofs.

There is a tale of a young Indian student at one of our universities who, falling asleep in a wood on a summer afternoon, dreamed that Pan appeared, attacked him viciously and kicked him with his hooves. The young man awoke, feeling much battered, but the incident faded from his mind till, on changing his shirt that evening, he and a friend were amazed to find that his whole body was black and blue with hoof-shaped bruises. Usually stigmatisation like this comes from intensive brooding over a certain subject until the Etheric vehicle receives an impact which it impresses upon the physical body. In this case, however, the Indian had no especial interest in Western myths.

2. Psychological Devices

There is a way in which the forces of the gods can be usefully employed in the field of psychology. This method is, I think, much overlooked. It requires neither ritual nor scholarship but merely an ability and desire to use picture-consciousness as a help in ordinary life and as a corrective to ordinary failings, provided, of course, one has no prejudice against god-forms and has not achieved a more 'modern' way of psycho-therapy. The subconscious mind has nothing to do with the intellect and it is therefore useless to argue with it or try to 'talk' it out of something.

The figure of a saint can, if preferred, be used instead of a god-form, for the will does not work without desire. Many years ago Coué pointed out this fact by adapting his famous mantric phrase to individual preference. Thus, 'Day by day and in every way, I grow better and better,' could be altered, if conflicting with religious conviction, into 'Day by day, by the will of God, I grow better and better.' In both cases the method worked!

Sometimes it seems that the god-form carries more power if of the same sex as the invoker. This probably happens because the invoker 'puts on', as it were, the form of the desired force and thus attracts the latter more strongly.

During the blitz on London a very nervous woman took refuge in a shelter during a bad raid. While cowering in a corner she was surprised to find that a figure of a valkyrie built over her and immediately all fear vanished. Evidently the force must have been apparent to others also for strangely enough all the other women began to flock to her corner of the room, saying that they felt safer there.

In outer fact there was of course no reason for this feeling. The woman was not much interested in Scandinavian myths and probably, if deliberately working on her own psychology, would have chosen Mars. I suggest that the Valkyrie, an equivalent of Mars in the feminine sex, was built in the woman's subconscious mind with admirable results.

In my younger days, I made a point of invoking Aphrodite before buying any new dress - the garment to be conformable with good taste, personal type and purse. It always worked. But the complaint I have to make is that the colour was always green - the goddess's own. Sometimes I would have liked a different shade but I chose one at my peril!

This early concentration on female vanities seems to have brought through also a definite insight into them for when the era developed into the wisdom of glossy magazines, the beauticians always repeated with unction the knowledge which I had learned the hard - (or shall we say the magical?) - way.

Once, after illness, I was looking in the glass with despair at my truly hideous image when something made me turn round. My attention was drawn to a picture of Aphrodite on the wall behind me. A tenuous copper net was spread over this and the latter was transferred to my face. (Copper is of course the metal of Venus).

I felt it must be all imagination and was much surprised when my friends remarked that evening that I must have 'been doing something to myself' to look so much younger and better. Alas, such an experience has not occurred since, but I count it as a genuine magical operation of a minor kind.

A religious friend of mine had experience of saintly dressmaking and it certainly worked out very differently. Never having made a dress before, and wishing to do so, she invoked St. Therese of Lisieux. The dress was very well made, neat and black, but bore little relationship to what was either becoming or fashionable. In effect, it was reminiscent of a Carmelite extern's garb.

In the ancient days of Greece, the clients that flocked to the shrine of Asclepios at Epidaurus were made to sleep in the temple precincts and next morning describe their dream of the god. Such dreams were held to hold the answer to diagnosis and treatment. I have, alas, not been to this shrine but I have found more than once that the figure of Asclepios built in the mind can often set one on the right road to a cure.

3. Ceremonial magic.

Ritual, worked with power and intention, can, of course, have definite results and long ago, a friend of mine and myself, both amateurs, decided to carry out a rite of Venus as set forth in magical textbooks. We could not do much more than build up the Temple with colours and perfumes, and the goddess did not consider it worth while to appear! It was, however, noteworthy that a plague of pigeons and some doves - birds sacred to Venus - assembled around the house, to the concern of ourselves and the neighbours.

TRUE THOMAS - OTHER WORLD ORACLE

True Thomas, also known as Thomas Learmont, Thomas the Rhymer and Thomas of Erceldoune, is the most famous of British prophets.

Erceldoune where he lived and which today is called Earlston is now a market town on the river Leader, about thirty-four miles from Edinburgh. The Tweed runs through or near the whole neighbourhood which still holds its inner enchantment despite the spread of industrialism. For this district is the cradle of much of the ballad lore of Scotland where Galawater, Leaderhaughs, Eildon Hills, Melrose and the braes of Yarrow still keep their singing names.

The memories of Thomas the Rhymer are shadowy but it is certain that he lived during the greater part of the thirteenth and possibly on into the first years of the fourteenth century. It was at the time when Edward I of England sought to conquer Scotland where fierce opposition was offered him by Robert Bruce and William Wallace.

Thomas was a friend and follower of Wallace and one theory of his death is that he was waylaid, killed and flung into the Leader after returning from a banquet given by the Earl of March. Centuries later a huge two-handled sword, said to have been the Rhymer's, was found in the vicinity and bought by a descendant of the Learmont family.

Thomas claimed to have received the gift of prophecy from the Fairy Queen in the deep interior of Eildon Hills. She gave him the title of 'True Thomas'.

During the seven hundred years following his life it must be admitted that almost all his predictions have come true. These were always in verse form and referred to Scottish families and places as well as to historical events. Evidently the nature and racial forces of his own country were mediated by his verbal expression. Prophecies in olden days were always presented in rhymed or rhythmic language, Apollo being the god of both prophecy and poetry. The Delphic Oracle used rhythmic speech

Though many forms of divination are practised at the present time, the ancient gift of prophetic utterance scarcely exists in civilised lands nowadays and therefore one cannot draw deductions through actual observation. Occult theories, however, provide a few suggestions. The etheric structure of man (on which his physical body is based) was formerly far more in touch with what was then normal consciousness. There is a level of the earth which contains records of events and certain people were able to contact that level and gain information through it. Probably, because of this, prophets and sibyls chose to live in caves where the psychic conditions of this planet might be more readily sensed. For centuries, the vapours rising from subterranean channels were considered to assist the Delphic Oracle.

Besides prophetic verses, two other compositions are attributed to the Rhymer. The first of these is the tale of his meeting with the Queen of Elfland and the second is the earliest extant account of Tristram and Iseult. Although the authorship of the latter is sometimes disputed there is at least much likelihood that it emanated from Thomas.

The Scottish Lowlands teem with Arthurian legends which have their variations in many parts of Britain. One of the versions is that Arthur and his knights sleep beneath Eildon Hills awaiting the day when the bugle shall rouse them in the hour of need.

There are several Scottish tales of Merlin. One of these is reminiscent of the myth of Osiris for it records that Merlin was hacked to death in Dryburgh and his body flung into the river Tweed. Another local story of Merlin is that he wandered for many years half-crazed among the Lowland hills till he was stoned to death by the peasants and buried where he fell, beside the Pawsayle burn. Thomas had prophesied:

> *When Tweed and Pawsayle meet at Merlin's grave,*
> *Scotland and England shall one monarch have.*

About three hundred years after this prediction the Tweed, overflowing its banks, mingled with the waters of Pawsayle burn (for the first time on record), close to the spot reputed to be Merlin's burial place. The event coincided with the inheritance of the English crown by James VI of Scotland.

The Rhymer also foretold the Battle of Bannockburn which happened some years after his death. It was said that the slaughter was so great that the corpses were piled up so thick in the water that they made a bridge across the stream:

> *The burn o' bread*
> *Shall run fu' reid.*

Thomas' predictions are widespread over the whole country for he made extensive journeys between south and north Scotland. He foretold that:

> *Fedderate Castle will ne'er be ta'en*
> *Till Fyvie wood to the siege has gaen.*

Fyvie wood was in the vicinity of this redoubtable stronghold and, during the Revolution, William of Orange's soldiers cut down the trees for battering rams. Shakespeare described the same method when he wrote, 'Macbeth shall never vanquished be until great Birnam wood to high Dunsinane hill shall come against him.'

Especially interesting prophesies are attached to Thomas' own district. Crests and armorial mottoes seem to have guided his psychic perception. Thus, the family motto of the Haigs of Bemerside is 'Tyde What May' and so:

> *Betide, betide, whate'er betide,*
> *Haig shall be Haig of Bemerside.*

The Haigs have been in this Place for about eight hundred years and after the First World War a grateful nation, with the co-operation of the main line of the family who owned the estate, transferred Bemerside to the Field Marshal, who belonged to a younger branch of the name.

Two predictions point to Thomas' individual landmarks. The ruins of his own domain is still called Rhymer's Tower:

> *The hare shall kittle (litter) on my hearth stane,*
> *There will never be a Laird L.earmont again.*

It is recorded that a nineteenth century visitors to the Tower discovered two young hares playing among the nettles in what had been the fireplace.

The destruction of the Eildon tree so profoundly associated with the prophet's own history was also foretold by him:

> *As long as the thorn-tree stands*
> *Erceldoune shall keep its lands.*

This hawthorn, noted also for its magnificent white blossom, was already nine hundred years old when a great gale blew it down in 1814. It is said that the inhabitants of Earlston were so dismayed that they poured wine and whisky over the dislocated roots in the vain hope of reviving the Fairy Tree! In the same year all the townsmen became bankrupt and every piece of the commonland of Earlston had to be transferred. A stone marks the spot where the tree stood. Nearby is the green glen shown in Turner's picture and Huntly burn still courses through the trees where tradition records that True Thomas met the Fairy Queen.

The famous ballad in which Thomas describes this meeting is usually accepted as an anthropological document in evidence of the Witch Cult in Scotland. That cult has wide connotations ranging from the ill-wisher with a broomstick to racial memories of the ancient mysteries.

The ballad was my favourite fairy-tale as a child and for me today the old enchantment still remains in the words which read like a magical formula for establishing contact with an aspect of Persephone.

There is historical evidence to suggest that Thomas was a highly developed astral traveller and it is from that point of view that I am considering his story.

The Queen of Elfland is, of course, no diminutive fairy but a beautiful and majestic figure, one of 'the Lordly Ones of the hollow hills.'

As Thomas lay on Huntly bank above the burn he looked up towards Eildon tree and saw the vision approach. I suggest that he sunk into a reverie which took him definitely out of the body on to the astral plane, a plane being 'real' upon its own level.

The lady wore a tunic of grass green beneath a velvet mantel and the bridle of her white horse rang with fifty silver bells and nine. I do not know why this number is used unless that, added together, the figures make fourteen which is a double heptad. Seven indicates a change of phase even on the physical plane where eyesight, for instance, alters every seven years, and Thomas was about to enter on another form of life by his contact with the Fairy Queen. Bells are always magical instruments and silver is the metal of the Great Goddess of which Persephone and the Fairy Queen are aspects.

Thomas falls on his knees thinking his vision is the Virgin herself but the Queen assures him that she is 'but the Queen of fair Elfland'. Thomas kisses her and she tells him that she now has control over him and that he must come with her and serve her for seven years. She also addresses him by the title of 'True Thomas' and offers to bestow on him the gift of either instrumental or vocal music.

Thomas chooses song, finding the human voice more important. It was the day when song was impromptu and used to express heroic deeds or prophetic utterances and the choice implied that he chose predictive verse. To enhance this gift the Queen added the 'tongue that can never lie'. Taking Thomas up behind her, they ride into the interior of Eildon Hills.

After some time the Queen points out three roads - one which leads to Righteousness, one to Wickedness and the Third, lying across the ferny brae, is the road to Elfland for which they are bound. The fern is a fairy plant.

There is still a long journey before the travellers and they now pass through a grim subterranean land which harbours all the blood that is shed on earth within its springs.

Few magical ceremonies have defined anything more impressive than:

> *It was murk, murk night,*
> *There was no starlight,*
> *They waded through red blood to the knee,*
> *And they saw neither sun nor moon,*
> *But they heard the roaring of the sea.*

(For convenience the spelling and words of this verse have been Anglicised and modernised.)

The ballad of Thomas and the Queen of Elfland bears out the old tradition that Fairyland is a 'middle' kingdom, neither good nor evil, neither angelic nor demonic, neither light nor dark but a luminous and sometimes colourful twilight. Finally, the Queen and Thomas, having left 'living land' far behind, come to a green garden where he insists on eating an apple. This action confirms that he must remain in Fairyland, for to eat Other-world fruit obliges the eater to stay where he is. The myth of Persephone tells us that she was obliged to remain for as many months in Hades as were the number of pips in the pomegranate she had eaten in Hades.

Actually, Thomas only stayed three years in Fairyland as the Queen found that only thus could she avoid handing him over to her superiors who were about to claim their tithes. The Rhymer would have been liable to seizure for this by the Overlords of 'Hell'.

In this case Hell does not necessarily mean the abode of the damned. It refers to an intermediate state better translated by the word 'Hades'. In orthodox teaching Christ descended into this Hell or Hades in order to set free the souls of the just who had lived before the Christian era and were thus unable to advance further. Esoteric teaching states that the Elemental Kingdoms are a level of Hades and that Christ before his Resurrection entered also into these to give help to the non-humans.

After Thomas' return to earth his constant disappearances were ascribed to further visits to Fairyland. He certainly visited many parts of Scotland in the flesh as his widespread predictions prove. His death was, of course, presumed to be due to a final return to Elfland.

It is quite probable that he was killed and his body thrown into the river after returning from a feast with his enemy the Earl of March. The tradition is that a white hind and hart were seen pacing through the village and news of this was taken to the Rhymer. As soon as the message was given he went out into the night, uttering the mysterious words:

> *My sand is run, my thread is spun,*
> *this sign regardeth me.*

Such a man would certainly have had a premonition of his end which would have been further confirmed by the appearance of the white deer, one of the Celtic other-world symbols. He was never seen again.

There is, however, an account of a psychic apparition at a much later date, in which he led a terrified vagabond into the interior of Eildon Hill.

Despite the absence of much historical data Thomas' story will always remain of strong interest to all who care for our cultural, literary and esoteric traditions. Not only Thomas himself but his family were anciently linked with Earlston and the famous stone in the church wall records that:

> *Auld Rhymer's race*
> *lies in this place.*

After seven hundred years the Rhymer's personality still makes an impact and I find it impossible to think of him merely as one of the many magicians and warlocks living in a superstitious age.

His gift of prophecy is by no means the ordinary soothsaying but belongs to the level of racial consciousness as did the prognostications of the Hebrew prophets and also those of Nostradamus. As a man, he gives the impression of courage, power and vitality.

That adventurous courage which led him to travel up and down a war-rent country may well have belonged not only to a seer but to a messenger and observer for the Scottish National Party. There has always been the supposition that he lost his life through political treachery.

RISEN WITH HEALING IN HIS WINGS
Some Reflections on the Curative Forces

I am not usually hymn-minded but I take my title from those exultant solar lines of Charles Wesley's because they make a practically perfect healing mantram:

> *Hail the Heaven-born Prince of Peace!*
> *Hail the Sun of righteousness!*
> *Light and Life to all He brings,*
> *Risen with healing in His wings.*

Here is concentrated in a few rhythmic words the idea of Christ both as Healer and as Solar Force and, though it may seem confusing to associate wings with Christ, the last line may well be considered as a reference to Raphael the

Archangel of healing 'that standeth in the sun'. The Tree of Life, that great Qabalistic sorting-house, shows the sun as the symbolic zone of all the Healers, Redeemers and sacrificed gods of every age. Moreover the sun is the great healing power of Nature, in its own right. It is a real help for anybody who is sick in mind or body to build up the sun power in the subconscious mind by visualising the solar colour and atmosphere and imagining themselves as actually standing within the orb itself. It adds considerably to the power if one can also imagine the figures of Christ or of Raphael standing beside one there and sending out healing vibrations. The repetition in an undertone of the verse quoted above, at the same time, will increase the force for many people until the whole room seems to vibrate with warmth and golden orange light. All imagination if you will! But, I think, harmless as well as effective.

The deep golden orange tints of sunlight also constitute the colour of the Life force manifesting in matter which the yogis call 'Prana'. It has been said that they have been known to concentrate this force at tremendous speed upon a plant, thereby causing it to grow to maturity in a very short space of time. If the same force is visualised as interpenetrating a sick area in men or animals, I have also known it restore or cure in small ways, though if used by advanced occult students it would obviously be able to do much more. However, I do not claim to be a healer and the suggestions set down in this article are all on the Do-It-Yourself principle.

There are occasions when 'Prana' will not work and in its place a dim bluish light will appear in the aura of the person or animal. This, I have found to indicate that the soul of an animal or the spirit of a human being desires to withdraw from the physical plane. Thus to increase the forces of that plane, with however much goodwill, retards the subtler conditions which must now have precedence. It is not always realised that the time of death is determined by the spirit which wishes to withdraw or, in an animal, by the secret 'call' of the Group Soul. Probably we do not know the reasons behind the decision any more than the normal consciousness of the dying body knows, but it will be found useless to kick against the pricks.

Occasionally, a human being becomes, despite any medical opinion, aware that the illness will end in death. I remember a very unusual woman who belonged to no religious or occult group but who possessed a strange innate wisdom about most things saying, as she was dying, 'I have loved my body but now I want to leave it.' The transcendent sanity of this remark has always impressed me.

Sometimes I have been asked to help those troubled by 'evil spirits' and it seems callous to have to reply that, alas, I could not undertake to do so. Such cases must each be judged on the spot and cannot successfully be treated from a distance, especially when it involves people whom one has never even met. There are, however, spiritualist experts (which I am not) who are probably competent to help. Sometimes also, psychological therapy could be a better treatment. This must not be taken to mean that 'madness' is involved, for these frightening episodes are real enough on their own plane but trouble comes through lack of understanding of the conditions and the subtle underlying fear that 'unusual' things are all matters of mental disease. They are not so necessarily but the unbalance of the mind that is caused by fear is the thing that causes the trouble and not the psychic awareness of another plane.

My own experience has been that often one has to learn by going through violent psychic disturbances alone, and that after the painful lesson has been learnt, explanations and helpful people will appear almost miraculously.

We must also be really sure that we are dealing with 'evil spirits'. Often, lack of knowledge makes people think that Elementals fit this category, but Elementals are not evil any more than they are good. 'They are just entities of pure force upon their own level. However, if real evil appears to be operating and assaulting the mind, here is a very efficacious charm.

Take a lighted match and, having blown out the flame, trace with the blackened end a triangle upon the forehead. Start with the left side up to the point, go down on the right and make the basic bar between the brows. Each line is drawn in the Name of an Aspect of the Trinity.

It was once my misfortune to live in a badly haunted house near the site of Tyburn Tree - a house which was full not only of poltergeists but of the worst scum of the lower astral plane which always hangs about prisons, execution places and slaughter-houses. The skilful help of one of the leading Theosophists finally evicted these vile entities. They made their exit through the roof, being chased by a bevy of strong Egyptian forces which were set to work upon each room till it was cleared. The' Egyptians used large plate-like disks of light which spread over the ceilings and disinfected the atmosphere. I was never told the exact procedure of this magical operation but I believe that the right kind of Egyptian force can still be potent if wielded with real knowledge and desire for good. Failing those precautions, they are better left alone as they can also be used by the Left Hand Path.

I have never actually been present at what is known as 'spiritual healing', though I readily accept the evidence of its many undeniable cures. I have, however, seen a healing session conducted on esoteric lines. At this time I was aware of the figure of Imhotep (the Egyptian Asklepios) surrounded by the orange gold rays of healing. The figure seemed to point out to me certain small black marks on the bodies of the patients and, on checking up afterwards with the doctor, I found that these marks indicated the seat of the physical trouble which was diagnosed.

I once had an experience of healing which I shall never forget. I had been asked to accompany an invalid Catholic cousin and her nurse to Lourdes, mainly to help them with travelling difficulties. It was a year when an outbreak of smallpox here caused the French authorities to require certificates of recent vaccination from all English visitors. Some supplies of the vaccine used were much criticised, for many people were very ill after inoculation and some died. I was amongst the former and it was all I could do to sustain the long journey to Lourdes with two more or less helpless companions. On arrival, I went straight to bed with a high temperature and an alarming vaccination wound. Some Lourdes water was kindly placed in my room but I felt a strong disinclination to avail myself of it. I was obliged to confide in the nurse, who, on seeing the wound, insisted that I should get a doctor the first thing in the morning as it was then too late to make any arrangements.

After falling into an uneasy sleep, I was aware that the door had opened and that a man had entered the room. He brought an atmosphere of goodness, peace and compassion. In appearance he was dark and bearded, wearing robes suggestive of the East and of the pictures of adepts and disciples in Theosophical literature. He stooped over me, slid his hand under the bedclothes and laid it on the wound. After a few moments, without uttering a single word, he stepped back and slowly left the room.

I now was very wide awake and felt that I was much better. The wound also gave no further pain. I put on the light and found that the bandage which had been carefully adjusted by the nurse the night before, was folded up beside me and the whole inoculated area was completely healed, closed up and dry. I could scarcely believe my eyes, nor could the nurse when I showed her!

I did not think it wise to disclose a non-Catholic source of healing in the 'milieu' I was in and it was, of course, put down to the Lourdes water in my room (which I had never touched).

It must not be thought from the above that I am criticising the many remarkable cures at Lourdes, some of them too in the case of patients who have no religious belief at all. This brings me to what in my mind is the crux of true healing conditions. There are those who, while not Catholic, have a strong drawing towards the figure of the Great Mother, even though that attraction is unrecognised by the conscious mind. The spirit is thus open to that type of healing influence. My spirit at that time was not so aligned but was conditioned to certain Theosophical tenets.

Undoubtedly the main source of healing is the communication of the spirit of the healed with that of the healer. By 'spirit' I mean the Nucleus of being or the Essential Self of each person, no matter what his religion, lack of religion, race or status may be. The instrument of spirit is the *will* which also implies intuitional belief or 'Faith'. Thus even Christ could work no cures in a certain town 'because of their unbelief'.

Most great teachers have at least some healing influence for, after all, healing - to use the Saxon word - is to 'make whole', and for this, some measure of co-ordination between spirit, mind and body is essential. Unfortunately also, that co-ordination is often much disrupted during the human passage through evolution.

Here are some instances of the effect of spiritual contact between healer and healed.

A woman I once met described how she, as a girl, had been much helped by Mrs. Besant. She had retired to bed at the Theosophical H.Q. with apparently severe fever. Mrs. Besant opened the door and, without entering the room, looked at the patient saying 'so you've got the fever, M.?' In that instant the fever disappeared.

Another case was of a woman who had been in low health and much mental anxiety for some time. She felt that she met astrally the late Rudolf Steiner and was strongly aware of what she described as 'his healing magnetism'. The next day she was in a definitely bettered condition of both body and mind. (I should mention that she was not a member of the Anthroposophical Society, although not at all averse to its teachings.)

Deeply involved in the mechanism of esoteric healing is the so-called 'Etheric body'. This occult term is used for convenience and most people know of it under the name of the 'Etheric Double'. This is a magnetic structure which is the subtle part of the ordinary dense physical body. It upholds and frames the latter and has much influence over it by means of the Etheric sense-organs or 'chakras' which are intimately connected with all the physical processes. The Etheric structure has nothing to do with ether, neither must it be confused with the astral body. It usually dissolves after the third day of death and partially withdraws during faints, sleep or when the physical body is under anaesthetics. In psychics it is very sensitive and does not take kindly to drugs. It is attached with a magnetic cord to the physical body and should the former be ruptured, there is instant death.

Taking a wide survey of healing today we can see how the different phases of evolution have produced different types of disease. At one time sickness was looked upon as the act of God or the curse of the gods. Later on, we had processions of various kinds of epidemics which are now gradually being overcome by modern scientific discoveries. Even in orthodox medicine the trend is to realise more and more that sickness is very largely brought about by psychological reactions and far less from outside causes than used to be thought. We are also faced with the present 'de-naturing' of man, animal and plant as civilisation proceeds.

The best chances of physical health will, I think, only be realised according to the amount we are able to understand of the inter-relationship of inner and outer levels of man, animal and earth.

SCENT OF ATLANTIS

Esoteric teaching shows the connection of perfume with psychology and memory and the Qabalah links it with the etheric levels. However, in my own case, I cannot truthfully associate much sense of smell with psychic conditions apart from one outstanding example.

My experience of Atlantean contacts was noticeably ushered in with an awareness of some unusual kind of incense, quite distinct from church incense which up till then was all that I had encountered.

The first occasion was when I was passing Richmond Green and, far from being psychically inclined, my thoughts were fixed upon a possible job abroad. Suddenly the centre of the Green seemed wiped out and from the extreme depth of the earth arose an aromatic cloud which surrounded me with a smell like some remarkable incense of which the only component parts that I could recognise appeared to be burning charcoal, seaweed and pine cones. As the incense smoke cleared, the figure of what looked like a goddess emerged with the incense from the depths of the earth in the centre of the Green.

The figure was majestic, maternal and beautiful as well as being vaguely familiar in a way which I could not define. Her hair was uncovered and flowing while on her head was a curious type of crown of a spiral pattern. Her arms were outstretched and her robes were of a luminous white. Flashes of azure rose and gold shone near her head.

I felt that she represented not the usual stone image of a deity but that she was a 'real' being who had at one time been in touch with primordial man and the phrase which flashed into my subconscious mind was that she was enshrined in 'the citadel of the Temple of the Land-Under-Waves' and therefore a memory of Atlantis.

The figure cannot be compared with that of any pagan goddess though the crown was faintly reminiscent of very ancient Chinese and Cretan forms. There was nothing savage or fierce in her atmosphere but a deep serenity, wisdom and power. The effect of this experience was profound during the two or three days that its influence lasted. Then I gradually forgot it.

Five years passed before the sequel of this experience took place. At that time my sister and I were giving up our house and preparing to go abroad for some time. The intervening period was to be spent with some friends in Berkshire. In the meanwhile two series of dreams filled my nights.

The first series showed me elaborately drawn maps of what one might call the esoteric geography of England in which were marked various centres which had held the Atlantean descent of power first introduced by colonisers from Atlantis and from them, handed down through the Druids.

The second dream series consisted of constant visits to a temple on an island in a lake to which the priestesses (of which I was one) were rowed across at night by a servant. This man seemed to me to belong to a very ancient American race and my impression was that he was a Toltec. The Toltecs are said to have been of Atlantean descent and they inhabited Mexico long before the Aztecs.

My dreams never took me inside the temple though I always tried to enter it and again and again walked up through the tropical bushes, after landing from the boat. The dreams of the maps completely disappeared but the dreams of the temple (which I felt belonged to a goddess) continued for some years until I began to take up esoteric studies seriously. After that the temple dreams also stopped.

In due course we set out on the visit I mentioned above. Our friend met us at the station and, as we drove home, the car suddenly filled with clouds of the same strange incense which I had experienced years before in Richmond. This time, however, two other people besides myself were aware of the smell which could not be traced to any bonfire, house, church or conifer that we passed. The incense was never visible as a cloud but the scent built up in the middle of the car. From that time on this pleasant but strange phenomenon occurred at odd moments when we were talking in the house, walking in the garden or driving in the car.

Our friend was greatly interested in psychism and made up her mind that it would be interesting to have Ouija board sessions between the three of us and to take notes if anything unusual happened.

Almost at once a strong power took over the working of the board. At first we were told of past incarnations and previous meetings with each other. The most vivid of these records were during the Italian Renaissance. As the controlling power deepened during the weeks which followed, historical times were left behind and a mass of script relating to Atlantis was received. Notes enough to fill a large volume were taken but, alas, destroyed during the uncertainties and troubles preceding the last war. My two companions at the sessions are dead and thus I have only my own memory to draw upon.

The communicators evidently belonged to one of those teaching Fraternities on the astral plane which sometimes get in touch with people in the world. These brothers had nothing to do with the Theosophical Society though the general lines of teaching were similar. They were, however, Christian rather than Eastern.

This astral brotherhood divided into twelve sections radiating round a major centre. Each section had its own astral chapel dedicated to one of the Apostles, also its own esoteric colour, which latter would build up above the board. The centre, which was dedicated to the Virgin Mary, was the one responsible for the teachings we received. I recall, however, that the section dedicated to St. Jude had much helpful instruction on the psychology behind everyday actions. The teachings received on Atlantis included details of customs, magical ritual and the type of life lived by the three of us during those prehistoric days.

The concrete mind, as we understand that term, was undeveloped then but a cosmic knowledge took its place and the raw material of what we now call nuclear physics as well as the science of genetics were both understood. There was a system of instantaneous lighting which we have not as yet rediscovered. The science of genetics used by the priests was at first employed for good but afterwards became a means of some of the blackest magic ever known. Through this science parents were chosen deliberately in order that high and unusual spirits might be born into Earth. The legend of King Arthur's birth brought about by Merlin's magic is an example of this science which has descended into legend.

The priesthood and the chiefs represented the two divisions of the ruling caste but, as we were taught, there was constant friction between them and for a priest or priestess to marry outside the Temple was punishable by death. Because I, myself, had done this, my Atlantean life was passed in two parts of the Lost Continent – one in the Temple and the other through escape to a distant place.

This very strict taboo was in order to guard forever in the priesthood the power of clairvoyance. It would seem, however, that the true Atlantean clairvoyance was nothing like the psychism of today. It involved secret knowledge brought from far off planes which was to be used for the guidance of the race and also involved remote contacts with superhuman entities. Thus the sacredness of the blood with its inherited clairvoyance and its descent from the ruling caste of Atlantis became a fetish for long after the Floods had swamped the Continent and new lands had arisen in the world. In this blood fetish lay also the doctrine of the Divine Right of Kings – for the early rulers of Atlantis were high Adepts given special rights by supernal powers and tracing their descent from that divine primal Sovereign sometimes called the White Emperor.

The Atlantean Priesthood had intimate knowledge of the Deva Kingdom but the latter were not quite of the same calibre as the Elementals known to us now; for summoning some of these there were colours and symbols.

Through a strange experience in a dream, I came to the conclusion that the riddle of the misfortunes of the House of Stuart was due to a strong and terrible Atlantean deva being attached to each sovereign of the House by different types of contact. This contact was something in the nature of an Atlantean *bean sidhe* but far more potent and its action on the astral planes was in the nature of partnering in a dance. This was, in fact, the 'Evil Genius of the Stuarts' that we often hear about.

The family originally came from Brittany and some non-human being from the submerged horrors of Ys may have been allured to it. I cannot prove this belief, but it does I think give some reason for the remarkable charm and misfortune as well as for the extraordinary loyalty which no other Royal House shared to the same degree.

At the Ouija board we picked up the trail of several Atlantean epochs and became psychically aware of a people of tremendous stature, wearing mitre like golden crowns, slightly reminiscent of but not identical with the spiral crown of the 'goddess' seen at Richmond. A memory of these in the racial mind probably gave rise to the giants of legend.

The Peak of Teneriffe and the Kerry Mountains are said to be unsubmerged parts of Atlantis. The City of the Golden Gates sank beneath the Gulf of Mexico, and nearer to our own shores are the Atlantean outposts of Ys, which sank off Quiberon, and Lyonesse, which sank off Cornwall.

Today, if one goes to the Scilly Isles by sea, there is a spot halfway between Land's End and Scilly where Lyonesse lies beneath the waves. Several people have noticed, if they are sensitive, a curious change in the psychic atmosphere as the ship passes over this point. The Ouija board adventure lasted three months; after that the communicators withdrew.

The sitters sessions separated for a long time. The sessions were never resumed. It was an interesting episode but one which had obviously completed itself.

Chapter Three

COMMUNICATIONS

The vast range and depth of Margaret Lumley Brown's mediumship needs no further comment beyond the evidence provided in this series of addresses which were given in varying circumstances to members of the Society of the Inner Light within the years 1946 to 1950, working upon several contacts that are usually referred to as Ascended Masters or Inner Plane Adepti. No claims are made as to the identity of these contacts as the important element is the intrinsic quality of such communications rather than any alleged source. It is worth, however, comparing the style and depth of such communications of Margaret Lumley Brown working 'on contact' with the articles in other sections that stem from her own normal conscious mind.

The Pythian Power

You must take into your consciousness how civilisations and the growth of the human mind and certain alterations in the human body have changed conditions in the course of time. Nevertheless when we contact a Master or a God force with the special desire to make contact also with a special civilisation of ancient times, it is sound, though not always essential, to try whether or no the methods of that time may be again employed.

In very ancient days what was called 'the Temple Sleep' was induced in initiates who were in imagination, or in physical fact or both, taken down into a tomb. They went down and down deeply into the earth's centre within the tomb and having, if it were a case of initiation, met various terrifying obstructions and frightening beings of the other planes upon their Path, they steeled themselves to endure and to pass through the evil conditions until a place of light and safety loomed before them. Some faint remembrance of this is found in John Bunyan's *Pilgrim's Progress* - that strange vivid account of an initiatory experience, half literature and half a memory; and when there was no question of initiation but a definite trance, the Pythoness went down and down contacting the Under-Earth forces and then meeting the Being with whom it was necessary to communicate. That contact having been made, both, as it were, rose together into the light, and messages began to come through, either in the form of language or in the form of pictures and prophecies.

In Ancient Greece it was the custom for Apollo's medium to sit upon a stool above a fissure in the earth out of which, it was assumed, came great force from the depths of the earth. In both cases you will note that the first thing necessary was to contact the Under-Earth power, for that Under-Earth power, call it by what name you will, was the essential potency of Hecate, and is the special type of Isiac force reigning over the Pythoness' art.

Now as regards the Pythoness herself, there are several things to remember, for there are various aspects of the art of the Pythoness. There is the impact of mind upon mind, in which case there is not what we call a specific trance state. That impact of mind upon mind may vary from the mere sitting calmly in a chair in the right condition, receiving a message or even having a conversation, or it may entail a very far-off contact between the Higher Self of the Pythoness and remote spirits who communicate with the Higher Self, which in its turn passes down the messages to the outer consciousness, also with the mind impact. Such a condition, however, as this latter, is a very definite trance of a higher nature, for the actual bodily consciousness necessarily is completely in abeyance while the operation takes place, and it can be a very deep and indeed a dangerous state for the body if not well understood.

It is, however, technically different from what is usually understood by the trance state, whether deep or light, in which the medium leaves her physical mechanism vacant for the communicator from the inner planes.

The medium usually is guarded by those on the inner planes who are given that especial work to do, and between the medium's body and the astral self there is that delicate magnetic cord which, while life is in the physical body, must never be severed. The medium may feel aware of this magnetic cord, and as long as she be aware of it in the right way there is no harm. She must not think of it too much, or its magnetism will necessarily draw her back to the body over quickly, and the trance will not be successful. As mediums, particularly those who are beginners, are carefully watched from the inner planes, there is no need for anxiety at all as long as ordinary common sense is observed regarding health and physical conditions.

It would not be a wise thing to have as a medium some woman who had grave heart disease or some serious physical disability, indeed, it would be criminal, but ordinarily when precautions are taken, there is nothing at all to fear.

Now as you know, the human being has various centres in his or her etheric, and it is these centres that determine the type of trance. As a rule sounds and impressions of people passing and scenes are visualised by the pineal centre; but there is a very deep awareness of the inner planes, whether it be a pleasant or an unpleasant feeling, which is felt in the solar plexus, and there are, of course, when you relate the centres to the Tree of Life and its Sephiroth, various types of each sphere's consciousness which naturally come through the corresponding centre in the person.

It is the art of the magician in all his workings to employ only the centres which he chooses. It is the science of the communicator to find within his medium the best centre for expressing his message and, of course, mediums vary, but it stands to reason that a strong pineal centre and a well developed solar plexus are essential for any ordinary work to be done, for these two centres will be the most likely to be used. In all mediumistic work it is necessary to have much practice and patience - it cannot be learnt in a few hours or weeks, nor can it be given to a person who has not got some aptitude, though this may have to be especially developed and trained.

In the very early days of evolution the body was in a much softer condition, the structure itself could far more easily be permeated, the vehicles within were very near the surface. As time progressed the outer part hardened, the mind developed, and the inner vehicles were given a very much tougher shield than they had had previously. Therefore it stands to reason that a medium is one who, for some reason or another, has not got a very thickened sheath over the inner vehicles.

This may be because of physical health or it may be because of destiny, since always when you find a cosmic medium, a medium who can be used by higher Intelligences or Elementals, that medium far back probably has been used in temple service, and therefore conditions are built up in that soul which will always be there - though it is possible that it is long before any opportunity comes for them to be again exercised.

It is often remarked that mediums are so frequently women and not men and this is because with the passage of time the structure of a man's mind and his physical conditions are far tougher and harder and his inner vehicles more difficult to contact mediumistically. There are however exceptions, and when you find in a man an exceptionally good medium (which is rare) you will find, if you examine his past incarnations, that he has been in contact with certain rites of Nature Goddesses in the distant past, which induced at one time a certain effeminacy of the masculine vehicle. And though there may be nothing to show such a thing in the present life, that difference from the ordinary man will have remained, and sooner or later, if he be immersed in occult or psychic work, it will make itself felt. But as a general rule it has been so long easier for women to live in the conditions which make mediumism easier that it is usually their sex that is employed as such.

There are Masters very far away indeed and these have to be contacted in an especial manner through the Higher Self entering their conditions and bringing through the power in the form of words. Also there are certain great powers connected with this work particularly with the Order itself. These also largely use the higher planes for communication, relying on a strong visionary sense and impressing the desired picture upon that sense. The power will come through either as a picture or in words. As the contact of such beings becomes surer, stronger and more habitual and practised, the communications increase and become clearer and firmer in impact.

There is too that very remote and ancient type of communication by which the ancients said they received messages from the Gods or Nature Spirits. Those beings work somewhat differently since there is no humanity within them, which in itself could make a certain contact, however far removed. But where the corresponding force to the being in question is found within the human person, and the will is delivered up to the receiving of a message, then the power of the non-human entity can take over and overshadow the human, so that he acts with certain gestures, or may get power in the form of words which give the mental idea of what would otherwise be gestures. Such things are very interesting and of great esoteric value when well worked out.

In ancient literature we read nearly always of how the medium would become obsessed with the power of the god and have what we should nowadays call a kind of seizure or fit. That was really unneedful.

It could be that the medium was largely influenced by the idea that 'frenzy' is always divine - which is untrue, or she could be obsessed, say, with the Dionysian force, which does bring about a frenzy of a certain type; but not all beings which communicated their forces to the medium had frenzy. The Earth forces were tremendously strong but they were far more static and the Water Forces were, though not static, not quite as full of frenzy as the Dionysian ones, which reeled and fought and fell and tore. But even now you will find some mediums who, when they start to work, become over excited by the power, which has a curious effect upon the astral body, and will sometimes come through in this strange manner; but it is not essential and depends on the type of medium and the kind of power.

There were very ancient forms of all these kinds of obsessions. There were the 'Sibyls' belonging to different places: there were several of these in different parts of the ancient world. The best-known is the Delphic oracle. All these act in different ways, not all in the same way.

In a small way we in this Fraternity are, as it were, setting up the same thing, for we are making centres of different kinds in which a Pythoness of a certain type brings through a special sort of message, so that history and prehistory repeat themselves, as is often said.

We shall be approaching the Solstice now very shortly, the Summer Solstice, and it is the solstices which have a special bearing upon mediumship because the action of the sun on the earth at those times has particular influences.

At the time of the Summer Solstice, strangely enough, the Earth Force affects the medium more strongly than during the Winter Solstice, when the Sun Force has a greater effect.

All these things must be taken into consideration just as much as the lunar influences in magic. The solar influences of the Solstices and the Equinoxes are very important for magic of any kind, but they also influence mediumship, the Solstices especially. The Equinoxes in a different way bring the balance of the communicator and medium in various functions into a very much stronger focus than usual, and it is because of that that there is an especial significance in the quarterly addresses which are made to the Lesser Mystery lodge four times a year at the solar Festivals. They are especially auspicious, each in a different manner, for a Pythoness's work, and therefore it would be a very interesting procedure for each Pythoness responsible for a certain kind of work to note particularly what comes to her during these festivals, quite apart from the customary address in the Lesser Mystery Lodge. Those four great Solar Festivals are the great communicating Festivals.

In ancient days the gods had a special communication with men at such seasons both in Pagan times and in Christian times. Later they were somewhat fused together by the Church, but the essential fact, which was somewhat overlooked, was not only that a great season of Nature and some great Being were commemorated at about the same date, but that that Being, that phase of Nature, and mankind, were all in a state of inter-communication during these great Solar Festivals and quarters of the year.

We must overlook nothing in these seemingly small matters, for as we proceed upon our work we shall unearth more and more of the Ancient Mysteries.

In Aquarian days, the communications will be more frequent and more universal and the veil thinner and thinner, and the day will come, (not in this time in which all of you now live, but long years after the youngest of you has passed away) - the last phase of the evolution of this Age - when the veil may be at last rolled back entirely. For that, and to hasten that, we on the inner planes, work day and night without ceasing.

ELEMENTAL CONTACTS

The Nature-mystic, as distinct from the 'magician', relies on sympathy with the Elements; a 'feeling-with' towards the Elemental Beings in Nature from the corresponding components in the make-up of a human being. This sympathy creates a link between the human and Elemental evolutions and it is part of the work of the Adepti to forge that link, since it is only they who can give really effective help to the Elemental evolution. For the Elemental aspects of the human nature must first be equilibrated, and that is one of the requisites of an Adept.

This equilibration can be helped forward by the use of art as well as science - though eventually art and science merge. By means of the arts certain elements in man's nature can be selectively stimulated. At present such a process is very haphazard in general life and education but it could be scientifically directed, and later in the Aquarian Age the arts will be generally used as a scientific means of education. At present, in certain rituals, colours, symbols etc., are used. Their function is to help the imagination and to attune the mind but they are not essential. It is said that the higher the grade the less ritual is needed, until the Greater Adept requires only his will.

The Element of Air is connected with all the arts, but with a special aspect of each. This can be seen if one considers with what the Element of Air correlates in the human make-up – namely the 'abstract' aspect. Thus it with that aspect of the arts that it will correspond.

Let us take music as an example. There are many kinds of music: There is the primitive tribal level that stimulates the instincts and passions; the sentimental 'astral' or 'watery' music; the 'upper astral' or devotional 'fiery' music and the abstract music, mathematical in quality, which corresponds to the Element of Air.

A similar classification could be applied to the other arts. For instance, some pictures appeal to the subconscious, others stimulate aspects of the conscious mind, according to their subject and treatment.

It is likely that music is the art which would have the greatest appeal to the Elemental evolution of the Devic or Faery type because of its rhythmic nature, for the appreciation of which the concrete mind is not necessary, and to which rhythmic nature the Elementals can respond.

Dancing, too, - apart from the aspect of it that is taught and learnt for social intercourse - can be an expression of the most primitive parts of a man's nature, and the spontaneous dance that is used to express feeling springs from an Elemental level. It can therefore be an appropriate method of contacting the Elements, since it arouses the Elemental in man, and contact with the macrocosm through the corresponding aspect in the microcosm can be made. Dancing includes music because music, whether heard or imagined, is an integral part of it.

In ancient days dancers danced to the Pipes of Pan - whether actually played or heard with the inner ear. Music of this instinctual level would correspond with the Element of Earth - the 'sensory function' in terms of psychology.

The Nature-forces in general are helpful to contact because they usually contain all the Elements, but the stimulation and concentration of one Element only must be undertaken with wisdom and must be in accordance with the needs of the person. What is helpful to one might be harmful to another.

ELEMENTAL KINGDOMS AND NATURE SPIRITS

The Four Quarters make a perfect Cross and in the centre of that Cross is the 'Rose of all the World' which has written across it, from the ages to the ages, the sigils of the Nature Spirits. And as the Cross grows in the Elemental Kingdom, so does the Rose begin to unfold upon it, petal by petal, and the dew which falls from it provides the strength which helps these beings to manifest. Around are the Kings of the Elemental forces.

The Air-King is in the East standing in eddies of air, eddies which are almost like the waves of the sea standing upright on end. And the movement of air and wind sweeps down from around him, for the eddies of air stream from him with radiant light around them, and impinge upon the auras of all who are in contact.

In the South is the Fire-King, with waves of heat surging around him, and points of fire and flame searing the atmosphere and reaching up towards the ceiling.

In the West is the Water-King, and moisture and strong currents of foam swing around his feet and pour from his aura into the atmosphere.

In the North is the Earth-King, and he too has waves of the Earth-power - the Earth Element which is not like what is called 'the soil' but is a curious intermediate state of matter, slow-moving but vastly strong.

These four Kings are in the East, South, West, and North, and around each are the lesser denizens of their Element, which follow them and do their bidding. And over all is a mighty arch of elemental green, which flows and eddies and flames and roars all at once around the floor and up to the ceiling. This is, as it were, an aura which encloses the great Elemental Cross.

There are many kinds of Elemental beings, from the smallest which figure in fairy tales, to the magnificent beauty which walks within the hollow hills and around the margins of the great waters - the great powers of beauty and harmony. Or if you like better the language of the Tree of Life, the great force of Netzach, splendidly coloured and flaming Powers, beautiful and terrible as an army with banners.

These great and beautiful Beings contribute to the strength and harmony, and therefore to the happiness, of mortals - if the mortals can catch some of their atmosphere, for of course certain people are more able to contact Elementals than others, and usually such people are liked by Elementals; there is often a link between them.

You must remember that men are always tempted to give a human shape to everything but that is merely the working of their own subconscious minds. The soul of a great Elemental Being uses for a body various matter of its own type.

The great Oversouls of Water use a certain pond or lake or stream for example. There is a vast Oversoul, for instance, of a forest which is composed of hundreds, perhaps thousands, of separate lives, in one great collective slow-moving tremendous force, one 'super-dryad', if you will.

You will often hear tales of the lesser Elementals, pixies and fairies, misleading a human being, but they do not mean any harm. They have no moral sense; they want to see how foolish a human will look going the wrong way along a Cornish moor and they want to make him feel them. If they pinch or prick his etheric and if they find that he feels the prick or pinch they are very pleased - they have contacted man.

On the other hand there are those which for some reason or another are attracted to one particular human being and if, being attracted to him, they feel certain things which he might like, and if it is a thing compassed by their own element, they try to bring him that thing. They can be good friends.

You have always heard that fairies and Elementals dance - it is a curious thing that that expression is in all languages and all fairy tales in connection with Elementals. They do not dance as a human does but they have many patterned movements, and these movements represent the way in which they go about their life; they move within a pattern all the time, which is why clairvoyants having seen these movements have always described them as a dance, but it is not a dance as men mean by the word.

There are certain places where Elemental Forces, Devas of various types, are met more easily than in other places. Just as there are certain shrines to Christian Saints so there are certain spots, sometimes indeed connected with these Saints, where the Elemental Powers are strong. Sometimes the Saint has taken on the power of the previous condition. For example St. Winifred's Well was long before St. Winifred's time haunted by one of the many fountain fairies of the Celts, and these fountain fairies were almost always healing forces. There are such places on the Continent as well. Elementals like a very secret hidden place where human beings do not come very often, and where there is no noise of modern traffic, for they like complete quiet from our civilisation.

I will describe to you such a Being. It is of great beauty, surging through the green of the upper air, and its outline is a kind of stellar ray which makes a special shape as it moves. It floats in a curious way, something in it is like the flight of a bird and yet something else is more akin to the way a fish swims in the water - even so does it swim and fly in the living ether. As he passes he projects a special type of vibration, so fine, so delicately airy, it can be sensed only with the etheric body. But it affects the etheric and it gives a surge of warmth and vitality connected with that great non-human life which is all around us and in our midst and yet is not seen by us.

These Beings like to be seen when it is possible. They like to be felt, and those that can contact them can gain health and good spirits from them. Long ago people were far more attuned to these Beings because they were much nearer to Nature, but as civilisation crowds over everything men lose all connection, but they can pick it up again if they go to a lonely place, and if they have eyes to see and ears to hear.

To describe the music they like and to which they vibrate is difficult. We can only use analogies. Sometimes there is a note like a silver bell, at other times there is something like a flute in the depths of a forest. This is of their atmosphere, the vibrations which their passing makes. Sometimes musicians who have been in touch with Nature Spirits have found in composing that the music took a special life of its own, because the music itself, its notes, made, as it were, a body of vibration into which the life force of some human-loving Deva was poured for the moment.

It is music, colour, dance and rhythm that they love, flashing colour, changing rhythm, kaleidoscopic - a mass of life and yet how seldom is it seen! Our remote forefathers in Atlantis, of course, and also in our own history of very ancient times, were far more in tune with these Beings and had much to say to them and were helped by them.

Let us consider again the great symbol of the vast Rose of Life. The great sigils of golden light which go across the petals, joining up one with the other, are moving, slowly vibrating like delicate chords of music, and the petals of the Rose slowly curl and uncurl, while the dew of the great rings of space fall upon the air.

This is part of the supreme Rite of Nature. This is the Holy of Holies of the Mighty Adonai whose Name is blessed beyond all. The curves of the rose petals break like waves upon the ether light, and the dew falls from each petal and the Nature Spirits gradually withdraw. The petals become fainter and fainter, the light is dimmer and now the Rose is withdrawn upwards, but for a space it has been among us. The green tides ebb, they ebb back into the rings of space - they ebb and the air is left dry and empty.

There is a verse of W.B.Yeats (*A Faery Song*) which expresses the Elemental evolution very clearly:

> *"We who are old, old and gay, O so old:*
> *Thousands of years, thousands of years*
> *If all were told"*

Let us imagine that before us lies a green glade with high ferns on either side and tall green grass, opening into a wood of larches and beeches. There is a great stillness all around, and we enter the glade by virtue of special privilege and invitation. The ferns and grasses begin to move as though a small wind passed over, moving near the ground and not in the upper air. One by one twinkling emerald lights, almost like an eye in shape, shine amidst the blades and fronds around us.

There is a sudden patter as though a host of small animals run across the floor, but if there were animals we should see them with the outer eye; but we see with the inner eye that these are not animals but small forms of very strong and winged life, units of force which move in the wind and along the streams and within the blades of grass.

There is a strong undercurrent of rhythm, a kind of music unlike what music is normally. The fairy host passes through the glade. They are aware of us but they are not angered or determined on mischief as they might be with the uninvited. They realise that we recognise them for what they are, children of God, brethren of our own but of another Evolution. They know we realise that they have their work to do even as we have ours, that we realise that each unit of this strong yet delicate Elemental Force has an especial work to do connected with its own Element. Work which perhaps, we do not entirely understand; looking after the subtler elements of plant life, guiding the etheric power of trees and flowers, directing, under certain conditions, the mind of animals and insects and birds, helping the subtler side of the life of Nature.

There were in old England many stories of faeries, and it is noted that they often appeared to the ignorant countryman who had little mentality but who had simple, humble tasks, and who was not much better, in those days, than an animal. For the faeries were able to be near that type of human being. Even so, today, in Ireland and the far-off parts of Scotland you find still an intercourse with the peasantry that the faeries yet keep; and that when sophisticated people stay in those out-of-the-way spots it would seem that their sophisticated attitude and their ordinary mental development leave them. These become shut off and therefore such people are aware of the hidden side of things.

There are certain mortals who have always been drawn to faeryland; they have never been sent back or had the gates closed; they have been given, as it were, the freedom of the city. To those people, especially when they are conscious initiates, for some are initiates without knowing it - to those initiates who really are conscious of what initiation means, there is a special duty which is entailed by this perception of the Elemental Kingdom. They ought to realise that the initiate is the initiator, in his turn, of the Elementals even as the uninitiated man is the initiator of the animal kingdom.

In ancient days there were said to be famous wizards and magicians who used Elementals to serve them, but who did not teach them, and on such sorcerers a very grave indictment falls, for they were 'black magicians'. They had the chance of educating the Elementals but used them only to serve their own personal ends.

An Elemental creature can be trained, bit by bit, to accomplish his own evolution quicker, and to achieve in the end the right to what the mediaeval people called 'gaining a human soul.' Permission to train an Elemental must be gained from the King of his Element. It is very rarely refused if asked by a worthy person, never if asked for a worthy end, but notice must be given to the King of the Elementals first. Then you can train them according to their various needs and stages of growth, in proportion to your own ability to be sufficiently aware of them.

If the Elemental be trained sufficiently he can then, later, enter the human Evolution; otherwise he cannot continue, as the human spirit continues, after the end of the Age. It was this knowledge that gave rise to the mediaeval 'superstition' of faeries who wanted a human soul, who sought it all the ways they could, such as by marrying mortals and in other ways. There are many stories in our own and other folklore about this.

There are many groups in the Elemental Kingdoms - many sorts of Water-spirits, many sorts of Earth-spirits and so on. There are many sorts of Water-spirits which belong to the streams and brooks, the 'nixies' of the ponds or any large piece of water of that sort, the great spirits of the lakes and rivers, but these of course, are of a much higher order than the 'lower' faeries. These beings, Oversouls of a pond or a brook, for example, have lesser units which also are under them and work with them. One might call it a Group-soul with various units of the same element comprised within it.

There are certain places where these little beings are met more easily than others; there are certain days of the year when they are also met more easily than at other times, and certain seasons. They, the most beautiful and harmless type of faery, like the moonlight; they like the full moon and the new moon, especially the full moon for they are very active then. But there are other types of Elemental which work in the dark of the moon and they can be most dangerous except to the skilled initiate.

Faeries like certain days which have always been associated with them, and these days have a special current of power of the particular season of the year, and so certain days were, in olden times, associated with faeries. Such days were Candlemas, New Year's Eve, the Eve of the old May Day, All Hallows Eve. On these days there is a strong current of the Elemental Kingdom which runs through the earth and draws the denizens of those Elements very strongly. Our forefathers recognised this in what we call 'superstitious' language, but it was superstition which was drawn from an ancient, forgotten lore.

There are certain forms which have a curious humming sound, almost like a bumble bee, and people who are clairvoyant sometimes perceive this curious murmur without knowing whence it comes: certain faeries make it. Others have what amounts to a certain type of song, a curious, inner, insistent rhythm which rises and falls like the ringing of tiny silver bells. The vibrations are so fine, so tiny, that it requires a very sensitive astral and etheric composition to be aware of them.

In our green glade the fronds of the ferns wave around us and the flashing of emerald points of light are seen among the long grasses and we have been joined by other Elemental folk of the Water Element. These are floating all about in a somewhat different motion, floating up among the grasses: they have been drawn from a brook which runs through the wood close by. They are like tiny flecks of water floating in the air, almost like tongues of water just as we think of tongues of flame, but they are living, vital points of life, of great strength, capable of friendship and enmity up to a point, capable above all of education, of help beyond that point; but, alas, when taken beyond that point, they must learn the grandeur and the tragedy that the human soul must learn, the lesson of sorrow.

The faeries are all around the glade in a great circle, a faery ring indeed but not formed of grass, formed of little beings and we are in the midst of them. And those who have felt them and seen them must bear in mind what we owe to this contact, that they will help us in small ways and we must try to help them.

The help that can be given depends on the type of spirit and its actual grade and, above all on how much intercourse the spirit has already had with some human being. When an Elemental has made some kind of attachment, as they sometimes do to a human being he is very often near that human. He gets in touch with his atmosphere and therefore begins to watch him, to see what he does, even as in old days faeries liked to see a good and conscientious servant-maid being careful to clean the house and keep it spotless. They like a devotion to duty and a devotion to cleanliness very much. There are legends that they pinch the slut black and blue, but help the good servant-maid and always see that her butter is of the best, and that the clothes which she washes become as white as possible and that no mouse or insect invades her clean floor.

The best way to begin to teach them is to try - but only when they are well in touch,- to train them in some slight moral values which they have not got from our point of view. For example, it is said that faeries like something bright and pretty, a pretty ring, a sparkling necklace, something like that, and they will try to steal it and hide it, try to get it for themselves. But if the human being whom they like and to whom the ring or necklace belongs tells them that they must not take what belongs to other people but must leave it alone because they must respect property, the human in his or her turn will promise to be very careful in entering some favourite haunt or glade where the particular faery is, and not disturb the atmosphere with noise or destroy some favourite plant or injure some favourite bird or insect.

This is, briefly, how one would begin. We have been speaking of what are usually called faeries, not of the many other types of Elemental, what are called 'the Little People'.

The Element of Water

I am one who works to a very large extent with the Element of Air, that is in my own especial work here. I use that Element in a similar manner as for example my brother the Master Hilarion uses the Element of Fire and my brother the Master Rakoczi commands the Elements of Water and Earth. Therefore as I have come tonight to speak to some extent about the Elements of Water and Earth it is necessary that you realise the difference between my work and that of my brother the Master Rakoczi.

I particularly use and direct the Element of Air but I work with all the Elements. I work with and within the Elements of Water and Earth, whereas the Master Rakoczi commands those forces in his various operations. He has been described as the Master Magician, the supreme occultist, whereas in my work with the Elements I am more of the type of nature mystic than a magician. As, in the course of time, you will be coming more into contact with us, it is essential that you try to grasp, in some manner at any rate, something of our different modes of work and expression. The Masters Rakoczi, Hilarion and myself who work with the Elements have been spoken of by others as 'the Adepts of those Elements.'

Again I am one who will be working very greatly with the development of the Aquarian initiate, and it will become more and more important as time goes that you learn to recognise the Tides. How they change the actions of the Elements in any particular tide or phase, so that you shall not be carried along in any blind fashion, but learn gradually to understand and to co-operate consciously with the action and inter-action of the forces and the Elements.

You have all been taught that at the Winter solstice the sun comes nearer to the earth than at any other time during the year. This action of the spiritual aspect of Fire upon the earth stirs the earth and inner earth forces into very great activity, which means that the subconscious levels come very much nearer to the surface. Thus the subconscious mind of each of you, through this action, is very powerfully affected, and the subconscious mind is brought very much nearer to the conscious level of the understanding.

The result of this, as you know well from past experience no doubt, is that anything unequilibrated in the nature will come up, as we say, for re-adjustment. The action severely tests all that is not firmly equilibrated within the nature. Thus it means that all those things which are outworn or no longer of any value to the service of the Higher Self are destroyed. Therefore is this tide called the Tide of Destruction; but only those things which are of no value to the purpose of the Higher Self can be destroyed.

Therefore, if you can, strive to get behind the action of this present tide, the result of which works to a large extent upon the Personality and the emotional aspect of the Personality. It is because the result of the action of the Fire upon the earth works upon the emotional aspect of the Personality, that the Tide of Purgation or Destruction is known as the 'Water-tide'.

I come to speak now about the Element of Water. First of all I think I will ask you to come with me upon a journey - to come with me to the small hill opposite Glastonbury Tor, to Chalice Hill, for there we have a peculiar combination of the Elements of Water and Earth.

Let us see ourselves walking up the familiar pathway, the lane which leads to the Well. We walk up a little way together and turn off to our left and make our way around the side of the little hill. We climb up behind it now and rise to the top.

Now some of you will be able to see or be aware in some way of the faeries of water and earth who indwell this place. There is here a very strong contact with the Element of Water. You can feel it extending right down into the heart of the hill. The grass here is always very green - there is a feeling of moisture in the air. Now having made this contact with the little hill itself we will descend again to the Well itself. Let us make our way down to the Well. We will group ourselves around the Well and now I want you to imagine that we go into the well-chamber itself.

Let us now imagine that the well is all around us - we are in the well shaft - let us see its cylindrical shape, let us feel and smell the dank and the moisture of the walls, and let us see the patches of green upon those walls. Let us feel the coldness of the air within this space - we are in the well now and it is around us.

There is an oversoul in this place - the oversoul of the Well; let each of you in your several ways make contact with this Being of Water. See him, if you will, as a shaft of water. He guards this place. Contact with this oversoul of water can bring various results. It can bring you contact, if you will, with the great 'Root of Water' which is of the Sphere of Binah. If you will also, you can trace the great cosmic counterpart of water right back to your Atlantean heritage, for there the Element of Water was used by the priesthood in diverse ways of ritual and magical practices. Make contact with this oversoul and let it bring to you its own results.

The Tide of Water acts and reacts upon the emotional body of each one, and this action seeks to eliminate all those things which prevent the ever-increasing intensification of the feelings. For the action of Water should bring about a much wider, a much broader, a much more comprehensive range of feeling, so that you may learn in time to feel with a blade of grass, or with an angel, or with any of God's creatures. Anything at all that comes between the work of the initiate and the broadening and the expanding of his emotional-self will, by the action of this Tide be swept away.

I want you to feel with me now the gradual expansion of feeling, though it must at first be at the price of the sacrifice of many of the smaller personal desires. I want you to get a glimpse here within this well-chamber of the fine result in this action of Water - of this deep intensification of feeling, of this broadening of the whole range of sympathy so that the feelings expand and expand. Until, it seems, they can expand no more, and they burst their boundaries and flow over into the greater cosmic life, where the soul is made one with all things - a part of all things. As has been said: 'When the dew-drop slips into the shining sea'.

Yet because there must be an increase of feeling and a broadening and an expanding, during that process, there is bound to be pain, because of the very process of expansion and growth. Yet if you can, seek to hold on to the result of the action of Water. If you can, strive with all your hearts to get behind the action of this present Tide. If you can, seek to work with the Element of Water, allowing all the outworn forms or the blockages to be swept away. Then should you be able to rejoice and be glad at the action, knowing the joy which should come in fuller measure at the Vernal Equinox.

We who are 'the Adepts of the Elements,' and know their actions and work with them, hope and strive to bring you all to a greater realisation and awareness of the action of the forces. So that by co-operating with them you can rejoice and be glad, even in the very midst of conflict and pain. It is a very necessary part of the Aquarian plan.

It is not enough that you should accept the actions of the various phases, but you should be able to accept them with gladness and not sorrow. There is a very great deal of difference between acceptance with joy that comes of understanding, and the ability to get behind the action, and the one who accepts in ignorance and is swept along blindly by the currents of the forces.

Human temperament is composed of aspects of the Four Elemental Creatures, and when the adept is able to stand outside himself and examine the components of his temperament, he can then discern which of those Elements are in excess and which are underdeveloped. Then, by his understanding of the Elemental Creatures and by working with them, he can make good that which is deficient, and redress any Element or any aspect of an Element which may be redundant.

That, of course, is the work of the adept, and such work is not advisable until the circuit of force has been completed within the adept. But when the time comes for such work to be commenced, then I shall be at hand to help any who may call upon me - for that also is my work in the Aquarian Age - the work of the 'faery alchemy.'

It is also part of the work of the great Arthurian pattern. It is part of the work of its redemption - that you should all in time learn how to use rightfully and impersonally the four great Elemental Forces. For, as you know, in the old cycle the Lady of the Lake mis-used the Element of Water with Merlin, and Morgan le Fay used the Element of Earth wrongfully with Arthur. All these things are very closely inter-related.

Let us look around us again in this place before I bring you back. Let each of you make contact again with the oversoul of Water and seek to understand its action at this time.

Before I close I would remind you that the Master of Masters for the Western Race, the Lord Jesus, is very closely linked to this Tide and we could say that the work of this Tide belongs to the great Christian Grail. Let us see before our eyes the Silver Cup of the Christian Grail, and I would remind you that because the action of this Tide is upon the Personality, and upon the Elements that go to comprise the Personality, the Lord Jesus is Lord of the Personality and Lord of the Elemental Nature.

We are all paving the way step by step for the bringing through into fuller manifestation of the great Aquarian ideal, and so I leave you with the injunction to contemplate the interaction of the Element of Water, which leads the soul to be made one with the great cosmic life, one with all things.

The Element of Fire

Let us first consider the relationship of Fire with one particular country, namely ancient Persia.

The Persians had in their midst certain great initiates and teachers who were themselves, in the first instance, not Persians at all but who came, traditionally, from a far country of which no one in history is quite certain. These initiates are known as the Magi or the Magicians, and they correlate very well with the Druids of Britain, who also were not originally Britons but came from a far country historically unknown.

Both the Druids and the Magi came from the same country, as we know from esoteric though not from historical knowledge. And between them were many links of actual belief, symbolism and so forth, for the country whence they both derived was Atlantis, though the Magi somewhat antedated the Druids, as they came forth in a very early emigration.

The Magi brought with them a remarkable knowledge of Fire and Light. Fire, they considered, was at the root of all things created, whether of mind or of nature. Hence, very naturally, their teaching and their temples carried out this idea, and in the earliest days of Persia the first Zoroaster, the great prophet and leader, the Merlin of that race, raised a temple to the Fire, even as the great Manu Narada raised the Temple of the Sun in Ruta.

There were many prophets and teachers of tradition called Zoroaster; the first of all, whom we now consider, was one of the Great Ones who did not live upon the Earth as an ordinary man at all. He ranks with Melchisedek and Narada and such great beings, and in after ages he influenced Persian prophets and teachers who bore his name. For the power and the teaching they exercised derived from this first Great Being who was hidden behind the Veil.

The teaching had many symbols but the chief were Fire itself and the great Wheel, the great Wheel or Cycle which represented the Cycle of Creation. Therefore the ancient Persians paid great reverence, both in battle and in temple, to their wondrous symbol of the Flaming Wheel, which was borne in front of them or set up in a shrine. This also was early Atlantean teaching, with possibly very slight differences of no great importance. It was, in fact, part of the Fire teaching of early Atlantis.

Mark well the Wheel. It is a magnificent symbol, cosmic in origin. It means a Cycle of evolving life, the force of man bringing worlds or actions into being. Later it became a magical symbol also, not only in Persia but in Asia Minor and neighbouring districts, and it was called the Rhombus. It was then much degraded in its significance but its origin was immense as the worlds.

Zoroaster also taught a great deal about the heavenly beings whom you call Angels, great forces which set creation in motion, working under God Himself. And in the Qabalah known again as the great Auphanim, the Flaming Wheels.

Moreover, this cosmic teaching held much of the forgotten laws of astronomy. Indeed, it held perhaps the first astronomical knowledge since Atlantis. And the Chaldeans, who inhabited relatively the same part of the world as the

Persians, also derived a great deal of their astronomical knowledge from Atlantis. For they likewise were an emigration, and in that part of the world, which included Persia, Chaldea and Babylon, there existed a knowledge of the stars which even in India and China was not surpassed.

In those clear hot skies the stars can be seen as they cannot in a Northern climate, and in that great knowledge of astronomy, deriving from Atlantis, the well known legend of Christianity has its root. For when a particular star of exceptional brilliance suddenly appeared in the constellation of Pisces it was noticed by the Persian astronomers, who knew that it betokened the birth of an Avatar and a new Age. For the rest, all know the story of the three Persian Magicians or Magi who, following the teaching they had received from the sight of that star, set out for Palestine. It is a scientific fact that certain stars will appear in the heavens for a time to disappear suddenly after some months or weeks or days, and it is said that the Star of Bethlehem was one of such, that it was brilliant in the heavens for a short time, a star of unusual magnitude and colour, with great rays proceeding from it, and then disappeared.

There is yet another link with Persia besides the Druids and the Star of Bethlehem, for Persia is, by many, rightly considered the place through which the legend of the Grail reached Britain from Atlantis. Hence you have the strange names belonging to the East, and the curious connection with the East in mediaeval Christianity through the Crusades. But this Island was in touch with the legend long before the Crusades and long before the birth of Christ. For the Druids brought it from Atlantis, while the better and longer parts of the story itself were fitted together by filtering through the hands of the Persian Magi, who had arrived in our Fifth Root Race before the Druids.

So we have this great concept of the Primal Fire, and also a wonderful conception of astronomy, both derived from

Atlantis through the Magi - a very goodly heritage. The teaching was very pure and simple at the beginning, without a multiplicity of gods and inner plane beings, but having a remarkable intellectually planned cosmogony, never surpassed among the ancient peoples, and little debased until much later in history.

In it are presented the two great forces of 'Good' and 'Evil', so called, which are both in man, and both necessary to his development. One cannot be without the other; each is essential but they must balance. Those are the two great forces of Ahura Mazda and Ahriman - and that too was Atlantean teaching of a very early date.

It must be remembered that in the first Atlantean teaching a great deal of the earlier teaching of Lemuria was included. Much of the Lemurian teaching was singularly pure and high, though it became exceedingly debased, and to contact the earliest form of a teaching before it had become debased is a very different matter from contact with that which was current afterwards.

The Magi taught that the Eternal Fire lives not only in the forces of created Nature but in the mind of man himself. That the mind of man was a part of Fire and that the very first essence and degree of the Akasha was Fire of a particular type. They taught, too, that Fire was the highest of the Elements, containing all the others. It was indeed the 'Fire of the Wise' and never did that expression have finer significance and deeper truth than in the definitions of the early Persians.

Later, when this teaching had developed into other forms of religion, and the purer creed and the simpler form had gone, there arose Mithraism. This creed, in many ways a fine one, was spread over Rome and Greece and other parts of the world when the Roman Empire fell and was, indeed, as is well known, in some ways so like Christianity that it, not Christianity, nearly became the State religion of Rome.

Its symbols, also, had great fiery significance, for Mithras was a form of the Sun and of Solar Fire, and his initiates went through many strange mysteries of Fire and Light. He, like Christ, was born in the cave of the rock and he, too, was a Prince of the Sun.

There are very few ancient symbols so essential and sublime as the Flaming Wheel revolving like the world. Held aloft upon an iron axis, with whirling sparks and trails of Fire, bringing through the tremendous forces of creation. The forces that move the life of man and nature, the forces that are behind the stars, and that manifested before the world began. According to the early Atlantean teaching these are the forces of Fire.

The Legend of the Grail, so much belonging to the British race, may indeed be considered on many levels, and you will do no harm by considering it sometimes as an Atlantean legend which has come through Persia also. In the names of Eastern origin such as Palomides, and Perceval (and indeed, many of those with 'per' as a first syllable) you see the imprint of that first transmission of the legend.

It is a story, too, of giants and faeries, of whom the Magi taught. This, also, was knowledge brought over from the very early times of Atlantis, where there were gigantic races and races of a very 'etheric' type. There was the Fire Race, swift, beautiful and ethereal, spirits of flames that rode the air. There were dark tremendous giants, and shadows of such forms are to be found in legends of many lands, but particularly in the legends of the Grail in its earliest forms, which, as you know, are pre-Christian and Atlantean.

Think sometimes, when you consider forms of Fire, of the tremendous force of Light of Ahura Mazda, supreme in power, in holiness and in wisdom, the great Creator of the World, which was also created from Fire. Think of the fiery structure in all the bodies of man, Fire of certain type and condition. Fire, of course, is of God Himself. Think also of the great Wheels, the Flaming Wheels which are angelic forms and forces, tremendous revolving cycles of Flame that is beyond all flame, Motion that is beyond all motion as you know it. Fire is the great life-giver and energiser, the great force, the force of the stars and the sun and the earth.

Think also, when you come to Christianity, of those three gifts the Persian Wise Men brought to Our Lord, gold and myrrh and frankincense. You can think of them as symbols or as actual substances, but it is better to think of them as Atlantean ritual symbols, because they have reference to Kether, Binah, and Chokmah, and the three planes represented by those Sephiroth, and known in Atlantis in the conditions of certain substances used for incense.

The 'gold' was a type of yellow heather which had the property of blending other scents and perfumes together, and which had great potency, although it was a neutraliser. It relates to Kether, for it was one of the earliest flowers that ever existed on the pre-Atlantean earth. Its name is now unknown and there is no plant like it on the earth today. The 'frankincense' is the father of incense so to speak and relates to Chokmah. The 'myrrh' is the great astringent power of Binah, the Great Mother. And these three Supernals, in the form of incense, were offered to the Sacrificed God of Tiphareth.

And hold in your minds, sometimes, the great power and blessing of the first Zoroaster and the Magi, and build the Flaming Wheel, letting it shine above you, turning slowly North and South and East and West. Think, too, of the great Archangel of the Fiery Force of Chokmah, that all may be one in the Spirit of Living Fire.

NOTES ON THE ELEMENT OF AIR

The fragments of elemental chants given here were originally received by Dion Fortune in her earlier days at Glastonbury during the 1920's. The Arthurian

Formula, which is referred to, is also the work of Dion Fortune assisted by her former Golden Dawn mentor Maiya Tranchell-Hayes in 1940/2, and was completed and consolidated by Margaret Lumley Brown after Dion Fortune's death. Most of the material within it has been incorporated into The Secret Tradition in Arthurian Legend *by Gareth Knight.*

Having discussed the Element of Water; let us now consider the Element of Air. First let us build up a composition of place in which we can work, and this time I will choose the garden at your Glastonbury retreat, which lies at the foot of the Tor, for though I shall deal with the Element of Air, I am taking that Element in a particular sense.

It is known that the Tor symbolises the Fire Element, and Chalice Well the Water Element, whereas Wearyall Hill stands for the Element of Earth. You will observe these three hills as we stand - in this plane - the Tor behind us, Chalice Hill before us and slightly to our right, and Wearyall before us slightly to our left. The Element of Air is assigned nowhere - it is all around us, it joins and embraces the Elements assigned to those three esoteric Centres, and as I proceed I particularly wish you to keep that concept in your visualisation - the concept of the Air embracing and unifying the other Elements, for in its best sense, its most universal sense, the Element of Air is a great social and embracing factor in its practical application.

Let us invoke the mighty Element of Air - following the lines of the Chant of the Elements that was originally received in this place.

Wind and Fire work on the Hill,
Wind and Fire work on the Hill,
Wind and Fire work on the Hill,
Invoke ye the Wind and the Fire.
Oh! Winds of Space, come at my invocation,
I who am your Master.

We have now our setting, and I wish to give you something of the principles behind Elemental contacts in the human evolution. The principles behind the science that in the lower grades is referred to as the formation of the equal-armed Cross of the Elements within each initiate, and in the higher grades as the 'Faery Alchemy'.

The initiate who has contact with and knowledge of the faery kingdom is essentially one who is not dependent upon human companionship as such; he is not tied to one particular person. He is described as one contained within himself, and so contained because the doors of the faery kingdom - the subtler kingdoms - have been opened to him, and through the power from these contacts he is 'free-winged in the Aether'.

I come, at that word 'Aether', to what is perhaps the key idea of my talk for, with the initiate, it must be the 'Aether of the Wise'. This is necessary because there is very real danger in premature contact with the faery kingdoms, and it is only when such contacts are first made under supervision and control of the Higher Self, that they can be essayed with safety.

This is so because if there are premature or unwise contacts with the subtler kingdoms before the full measure of human experience has been realised and achieved, the results of the faery contacts can lead to isolation and to pathological states. It is, or it should be, realised that for the purposes of this discussion I must necessarily divide the approach to the faery kingdom into that from the adverse side and that from the side that is under the will of the Higher Self. But you will understand that there are seldom in any subject such hard and fast divisions, and of the adverse side and of the creative side there are infinite gradations of contact. This whole idea is conveyed clearly in the teachings of the Arthurian Formula.

The Element of Air particularly, because of its great possibilities when this contact is made within the individual, has perhaps a more dangerous side. This whole concept of the destructive side of premature or unwise contact with the subtler kingdoms arises from the fact that its whole science appertains to the Sphere of Netzach, and behind this Sphere is the Spatial Air aspect of the Great Goddess, which itself derives from the outer Ring of Chaos.

It is because there is that primary deviation especially, that there is the possibility of the blight of full human experience by the too early opening of the doors of the faery worlds. The great quality that rules the Element of Air is that of detachment; and detachment is a state which normally ensues at a fairly high grade of development. Therefore has adverse contact with the Element of Air been responsible for all sorts and manners of escape from the work of human development behind various forms of sex pathology, because the faery worlds are very intimately associated with the subtler uses of the sex force and its creative use - the science that is also associated with the deep understanding of the Netzachian Sphere.

So you will realise that very much wisdom is necessary before the faery worlds can be explored and essayed in safety, but when they are so essayed the powers that are then conferred upon the human are remarkable indeed. These powers will bring out in the individual any particular ability that he has. If some ability is not awakened the powers of the faery worlds will awaken that ability and give it expression in the outer world of that particular individual. Any power that he has - good or bad - will be enhanced. The powers of the Elemental world have a vast amount to offer to the Adept, especially in return for help by him in the form of development of any particular Elemental concerned.

It should be well realised that the human development of the initiate should be well in hand before such experimental work is undertaken, and that is why, although it is right for you of the Aquarian Age to realise these principles, the actual practice is usually assigned to the higher grades in the science that I referred to as the Faery Alchemy. Nevertheless, it is incumbent upon you all to realise something of the elements of your own temperament because, as you know, temperament itself is comprised of aspects of the four great Elemental Beings, who themselves derive from the Four Holy Living Creatures themselves.

It is usually understood that temperament is broadly divided into the basic temperaments of Fire and Air and of Water and Earth, but of course, that is very broadly speaking, and there are again infinite gradations of these general classifications.

When you have, each of you, understood the components of your own temperaments - understood them completely - and been brought face to face with your own particular attributes, when that time comes, it will tell you of its own accord that the moment is ripe for contact with the faery worlds. Because when you know exactly how your own temperament is composed then you will have the ground plan that will admit you in safety to the subtler worlds. For one of the aspects of such admittance from the point of view of the human is that if he realise, for example that he is deficient in the Element of Air, he can, through contact with the Element, make good that deficiency; and correspondingly he is able to redress any redundancy.

It is obvious, therefore, that such work could not be safe or wise unless that initiate was in complete control, and understood his own temperament and nature. In all these things, the right time usually reveals itself when the soul is ready to wait and ready to listen to the voice of its own guiding and directing Higher Self. As I said, it is essential that you should realise this principle, though the practice may have to wait for yet a little while.

A very important aspect of the work of this Age is, and will be increasingly more concerned with the subtler kingdoms, with the subtler uses of the polarity force, with all that goes to make up creative work and genius. I want these seed ideas to be within each of you, so let us now again contemplate this place in which we are working with the symbols of the Elements of Fire and Water and Earth around us, and the all-embracing and encompassing universal Element of Air circling around us in and through the hills, in and through our very selves as we stand here.

The gift of the Element of Air to the human is very precious indeed, and it is because its gift leads eventually to freedom that there are more dangers, perhaps, in experimentation with this Element than with the others. Where there is great opportunity, you will always get the correspondingly greater possibility of adversity.

The Winds of Space,
The Winds of Space of the Great Goddess
Are around us,
Hear ye them.

The Fire and the Air are friendly and kind,
The Wind and the Fire work on the Hill,
The Wind and the Fire work on the Hill,
The Wind and the Fire work on the Hill,
Trust ye the Wind and the Fire.

ARCHANGELS & ANGELS

There are very many types of Archangels and Angels. The ancient Jews in their mystical system knew a great deal about them and classified them into their divisions.

Angels are really types of force which act upon the various planes, units of the one great Power of that plane. They work under a particular Archangel, who directs them to a large extent. I say 'to a large extent' and not 'entirely', because angels are perfect in their own particular unit of energy. They do not go against their own laws, nor do they interfere or take part in the work of other angels. Each has his own, but sometimes some especial messenger is sent to contact some human being or to help in some especial work which, though not precisely his own, is in some way akin to it; and it is the Archangel who would direct him to go on such errands.

The word 'Angel' includes the great and beautiful Nature Beings of the higher types under whom Elementals work. Archangel, Angel, Elemental Spirit - that is the order of their hierarchy.

Certain angels work especially with the Group Souls of beasts and birds; others with the Group Souls of nations, that is to say with the National Angels of countries, who are of special types.

There are also those that ensoul the essence of beauty in the various forms of art; music especially appeals to them. They have sometimes inspired certain beautiful strains of music and the sound that is made when the musician has transcribed this music so that it can be played may be ensouled, and on occasions has been ensouled, by the type of being who first inspired it. The same applies to painting of a certain kind that has an innate sense of colour. Also to sculpture, and to poetry and drama. If these arts really touch the higher planes they bring down a great amount of Devic force which intensifies an hundredfold the appeal to the hearer or the on-looker.

There are instances, too, where angels have gone as protectors to human beings, especially to children, and there are those that look after people when they die, and animals and birds when they die, helping to adjust the outgoing life to its new conditions.

When animals die, or birds die, it is, if you are clairvoyant, a very interesting thing to see these Devic Beings especially concerned with that life guide that bird or that beast to the next plane - help it to withdraw in its various stages. For even with the so-called 'lower creatures' there are stages after physical death, and through these stages it withdraws to the great composite soul of its own species. When an animal dies and finally is resolved back to its Group Soul, there is a certain current, a certain vibration, which to some extent influences all the other animals of that species. They may not know what it is, but there is an influence which goes forth, a benevolent influence, when one of their number is definitely received back into its Group Soul.

The same thing in very ancient days happened also to man in his very undeveloped state. Peoples had a Group Soul and were very little individualised, but the Group Soul drew all units to itself in a way that has not been done since individualisation grew deeper and more intense. But in those very remote days a special type of vibration of benevolent influence went out to all the people in this tribe, or group of a race, when one of the human beings in it was received back through death into its Group Soul. And Angelic Beings helped that soul on the other side a very great deal, for in those early days these Angelic Beings were far more in touch with human beings than now, for the human beings were accustomed to think of the angels, to feel them, and to make and to seek contact with them.

It is quite useless expecting contact with something that you never think of at all. Therefore if you want angelic contacts you must think of the angels. You must imagine them as they are, great and wonderful forms of light and glory, deep protective forces in contact with you, and in contact with God, and therefore serving as a great connecting link with mankind and the far off Principles above him.

Sometimes a Deva or an Angel has become so much in contact with man, having spoken to him and protected him, that the link can become as strong as with a Master or with a great friend who has passed over after bodily death to the worlds beyond.

There are cases where angels have spoken and sent messages to man. They do not exactly send the message in 'language' but they impress the idea or the meaning very strongly on the mind of the recipient of the message and his subconscious mind supplies appropriate words.

There are, too, the Great Archangels that the Jewish mysticism described so well. Wonderful bodies of 'consuming splendour' - because they are, in a sense, consuming. The quality of the force of an Archangel is indeed a consuming flame.

If you want certain things, such as a gift of vision, and you invoke the great Archangel Gabriel, who rules over that quality in man, you will probably have your prayer granted. If you are in danger from evil spirits or black magic and you invoke that gigantic armed force that is called Michael you will get help, and so on with all. If you need healing and you invoke the great Raphael in the right way, surrounding yourself with his colours and his element, and invoking him with all your power in the name of those you know he has helped (such as, for instance, the young Tobias) you will find he will send help.

You must picture the colours of the Archangel, for they represent a great deal of colour. And if you have any appropriate music that you can play, or have played, that also is a very good means in the art of invocation.

These are the Archangels of a very great potency. They are not quite the same as what you know as 'the gods'. They are a different side of the powers of a sphere. But with some people, and for certain reasons, it is more suitable or easier to invoke the Archangel of the Sphere than the god, and the Archangel as a general rule can actually influence a man himself more, unless that man be a magician or highly evolved initiate. The uninitiated are wiser to keep to the angels in invocation.

COMMUNICATIONS

The Archangels express but one particular type of power, or one particular quality. They are more single-pointed than the god, though all extend strength. They may not be quite so difficult for the uninitiated, should he have invoked something that is too stupendous for him to handle, Also there is this to the power of an Archangel - it will, strong as it is, disappear and dissipate more quickly.

Think, too, of the very wonderful Being which is called Michael, who is the protector of all that need help from evil forces, for there are forces of the inner planes that mankind has round him, manifesting on the outer as battle and murder and sudden death. Michael is usually pictured holding a spear, armed and helmeted. All that of course is just pictorial imagination. His actual form cannot be conceived in its entirety by the ordinary mind, but that form, that conventional childish book form, built up strongly enough and often enough, will bring the force down from that tremendous flaming aura. In his beam there is a quality of battles, of fighting, of swords and spears and protective lines of war, but he is much more than a human form with wings and spear. He is beyond that kind of description as he is. And the area and radius of his force, though really close at hand, can extend for miles in your language.

That is what Jewish mystics meant when they spoke of certain angels being miles high - they put it in the nearest words they could find. The sphere of the influence was so tremendous that it covered the space of miles between the sea and earth and sky.

When you invoke the Four Mighty Archangels of the Cardinal Points you make their forms in the way that is best to build them, and you invoke all the force possible of the Archangel into these forms; but the whole of the force could not be borne by mortal man.

If you are afraid of an evil influence in your room, you can invoke Michael to send one of those he rules, lesser angels of his sphere to guard your room and keep all evil influences from crossing the threshold. If people understood how very much help can be got from speaking to the angelic powers and drawing them near, they would not neglect to do so.

In very much lesser degrees, the Faery Elementals can help people, and the lesser Elementals, as you know, come under the presidency of the Angelic Beings, or rather, the Angelic Beings rule the upper stages of the Elemental Hierarchy, for all these beings are in a hierarchy and the Elemental Kings are beneath the Angels and Archangels.

If you are in a room where a human being or an animal has died you can be in touch with certain Angelic Beings, and it will help the atmosphere around you very greatly if you are, as well as helping the human being or the animal who has died.

When a trained Adept invokes, he does so under special rules and in a special way, so that the Archangelic power comes through only to an extent that can be reasonably borne.

It would not be likely to come through to a larger extent because everything in esoteric work is balanced up and you do not invoke one great power without having something to balance it up in the opposite way, and the two control each other.

You invoke the Four Archangels, and they are 'four mighty balancing stresses'. One might say they keep each other in balance, therefore none will overflow. But it would be unlikely that anyone could, even did they desire it, bring through the whole power, because it would mean that various Cosmic forces would also have to be invoked.

Angels always act with each other and with the whole universe, and never singly and apart. It is not quite the same with a God-force. That is why I said that, tremendous as an angel is, there is less danger with him or with the Archangel.

When you invoke the Archangel of a Sphere he is, by his very nature, not inclined to overbalance, because other powers you have not invoked are always in close touch with him, and it would be unlikely that more power than could be ritually borne would be brought through. The Archangelic force works rather slowly and it comes into the vacuum prepared for it somewhat slowly, and when everything else has been properly prepared that vacuum is, so to speak, unlikely to overbalance. The force keeps itself balanced in ways that are not the Adept's concern.

As an example, we will build up the great Angel of the Moon, who gives the powers of Vision, the great Angel Gabriel, standing in the West. Imagine him first of all as the beautiful blue-green figure with silver flashes of light and a tremendous swirl of colours of various shades of peacock tints shot with silver which are his wings. And these wings, which are really a part of his great aura, stretch out to a tremendous extent; and beneath his feet and round his head are streams of liquid silver.

Now forget those wings, forget that face of silver light, forget the blue-green robes, and in their place see a tremendous pillar of silver light reaching up as far as the sky and standing on the earth; and around the pillar see clouds of peacock blue and green. This tremendous pillar is like a battery of the universe - an electric battery - and all actions of the universe are switched, as it were, on to you through this great battery, for this is the meaning of Vision, the meaning of clairaudience and clairvoyance.

Now, if you like, change from the mighty silver pillar and imagine a ninefold figure, a solid with nine sides of crystal, but reflecting silver and blue-green light, and imagine that nine-fold figure a large amount of force from the great silver and blue-green pillar, and watch it; watch this solid as you would look in a crystal globe. It will bring one of Gabriel's messengers to you - one of the angelic host he rules over, and it will bring you the help that comes from inner vision and inner hearing.

As you watch that beautiful geometric figure, this will in time change into an angel form again - the protecting beautiful angelic form which will send you the holy power of the Moon and of Water, qualities which are in tune with the visionary faculties and that are so necessary to the right understanding of the inner life, for it is Gabriel who rules the Living Water-streams, that well out from the Highest Throne.

ARCHANGELS OF THE SPHERES.

[The spheres that are here referred to are the spheres or Sephiroth of the Tree of Life rather than the planetary spheres known to astrology and astronomy, although there is a certain symbolic connection between them. The teaching of the Society of the Inner Light in this respect was based firmly upon Dion Fortune's The Mystical Qabalah *(1935) although later additions to the teaching up to 1962 were incorporated in* A Practical Guide to Qabalistic Symbolism *(1965) by Gareth Knight, as also in the latest edition (1998) of* The Mystical Qabalah.*]*

The 'Archangel of the Sphere' is broadly speaking the intelligence which is behind that Sphere's type of action. It works with the archetypal force of that Sphere and under it are the Angels of the Sphere - the lesser Devas of a certain type belonging to that Sphere, which carry out the commands of the Archangels according to their own nature.

The Sphere of Malkuth which comprises the mundane plane and the spiritual values which are immediately within dense matter - in fact the 'Spirit of the Atom' - are all under the aegis of that great Lord of the Four Elements called Sandalphon. Those who find difficulty in contacting the mundane forces successfully and sensibly should apply to Sandalphon for his help. It is through him that the soul of ordinary objects acts.

For example, could you really see with your physical eyes the exact inner plane condition of, say, a chair or a table, you would be amazed. For that chair is composed of infinitely numerous and tiny molecules which hold together its dense substance, and you would perceive psychically the legs and feet of this piece of furniture swaying and bending with a very slow vibration - for wood has a very slow vibration.

That mode of action is manipulated by the force that is in the atom, and Sandalphon is the King and Overlord of all these small molecules of life on this plane of matter. He is built up in the imagination as a great Angelic form with the Four Colours of his plane: pale yellow, olive green, russet and black. His vibrations are somewhat ponderous and slow, for they belong to the plane of dense matter, and the immediate connecting link of etheric substance just behind that plane.

When you wish to deal with the deeper and farther off etheric substance - when you deal with the *Akasha* as it is called in the East - you are under the sway of Gabriel, the Archangel who rules many subtle realms both in man and nature. He is the Lord of Dreams and the subtle vibrations of a far off kind which can reach to man's clairvoyant faculties.

He has been associated with the Annunciation to Mary partly because he is always the 'Mystic Announcer' as it were, the Lord of the special manner of message which can reach to the human mind from far off planes. He is always the Angel of Annunciation in the wide sense to many others than Mary. For this reason too he is concerned with sleep; the condition when the dense body is inactive and the subtle vehicles escape and go to other planes.

It is a large part of his work to induce what is a part of the 'Moon Consciousness'in man. He tends to draw the soul magnetically, even as a great water power draws, and therefore his influence is, as it were, a pump upon the physical body - he draws the consciousness from it. One may picture him as an immense ovoid of silvery substance with the delicate lilac and violet of Yesod in the feathers of his wings and the sound of mighty waters which are his special type of vibration.

Above that you have the great Archangel of Tiphareth - Raphael. He holds the healing and sustaining powers of sunlight in his realm; particularly has he in his control the more modern methods such as radiant heat and the ultra-violet and infra-red ray treatment of various sorts, but these are yet only in their infancy from the esoteric standpoint.

There is, too, the great Archangel of Kether, from whom the picture of the Tree of Life is said to have been given to man. He works in the great world of Cosmic Archetypes and his influence is very rare. It is of the type that comes as a blinding flash of illumination of far-off spiritual truths.

We have dealt briefly with the Middle Pillar - let us now consider the Side Pillars. The great Archangel of Chokmah brought through the creative forces in early evolution. It is difficult to formulate in the human mind such Beings as either Metatron or the Archangel of Chokmah for not only are they beyond form as we know it, but they are beyond being reduced to any adequate symbol, unless perhaps you like to think of them as great Pillars of Glory.

The Archangel of Binah has been behind the formulation of all the Mystic Cults that have emanated from the Great White Lodge. He is the Archangel of the Temple and his vast Presence shines with a certain living darkness, which has a wonderful rose-coloured glow in the centre; more than that I cannot describe him in words that you could understand.

The Archangel of Chesed has a wonderful influence of benevolence and the complete calm of eternal security and sureness. Those who are liable to become irritable or unbalanced, may well invoke his aid.

The Archangel in Geburah is the protector of the weak and the wronged; he also is the Avenging Angel, the influence that pursues the wrong-doer whether it be he who breaks his country's laws or whether it be what is really graver, he who breaks evolutionary law.

The Archangel of Netzach is not so widely known. Everybody knows about the god-form the beautiful Venus of Netzach, but it is strange how little appears to be known about the Archangelic form of that beautiful Sphere - the sphere of harmony and of beauty and above all of the whole science and value of inter-relationships, whether of planets, or plants, of Spheres or of men, the great Archetype of sympathetic vibration. He shines with a green and golden flame and a rose coloured light is over his head.

Now we come to the Archangel of Hod - the great Michael. He is the Archangel of the sphere of magic because he holds in control the demons and the evil influences which otherwise might escape into the world of men. He is a very essential protector in magical formulae - especially when the would-be practitioners are novices.

The ancient Jews had whole choirs of angels and a whole list, besides these, of mighty Angelic Beings. I cannot attempt to deal with them all in one session but it is useful to take ten of these mighty Beings which are of such importance that they are respectively in charge of the great Emanations of God.

Many initiates are not so much in touch with the Angelic forces as with the God-forces of these Spheres - although, in practice, there are certain archetypal powers of these spheres which the Archangel can bring through much better.

Let us for a few moments contemplate the great Archangel of healing - the great Archangel Raphael who stands within the Sun. He can be pictured standing in the East blazing with golden light with a touch of sky-blue within it, and a rush of fire and of air is in the movement of his wings, and the curative force of the Sun streams from him, down into the Earth and into the auras of those attuned. The light streams from him and his aura fans the air.

FORMS OF THE EGYPTIAN PANTHEON

There is a cheap concept of Egypt held by many people who play with occult notions and attempt to act up to them according to their notions. Through these foolish, albeit well meaning people, has come a very false idea of Egyptian myth and magic.

The Egyptian gods are not to be confused in their types of power with the gods of any other pantheon. There are many resemblances no doubt, but a particular Egyptian aspect is not found in other races: that of occult rigidity. As the Egyptians carved their gods and statues and raised their temples, they used very remarkable angles most of the time, and circles relatively little. Such things are by no means a chance development of primitive art. They express the esoteric trend of the soul.

The Egyptians were rigid in their teaching and their outlook; they became in the end over conventionalised and fell through it. But in the beginning that rigidity referred to a supreme knowledge of one-pointedness, of absolute and intense pursuit of the Ideal, tracking it down as a hawk tracks down its prey with unerring sight - and the hawk is the bird of Horus.

Manifestation must come through pairs of opposites, and it was Horus that issued from Isis and Osiris. Horus, that divine symbol of the bird of prey, with that wonderful gift possessed by birds of prey especially, the gift of longer sight than humans have. The sight that tracks out miles ahead, pursues, and falls with exact precision on what it has marked. Therefore is Horus a notable symbol of the highest trend of the soul according to Egyptian ideals.

Those rigid lines have another outstanding quality, namely that probably no divine images of gods or goddesses can be so clearly memorised as the Egyptian. The most foolish and least educated person, having once seen an Egyptian statue of a god, will be able to recall the statue more or less accurately to mind, far more easily than a more beautiful statue of Greece or of Rome or some aspect of deity in another nation.

The Egyptians used those straight simple, symmetrical lines which helping the eye are easily fixed in the mind. They have in the sphere of statues and pictures the same qualities that verses and rhymes have in the sphere of literature. They are invaluable to the memory and therefore those great Egyptian beings, once thought of in the mind, may be marvellously quickly and strongly built up by the magician. And may even be effectively thought of by the non-magician who practises it enough.

That is one reason why the Egyptians were so noteworthy as magicians; they built the form so very clearly. I do not say that that cannot be done with other pantheons, far from it, but I speak of the general trend of Egyptian statues and of their general value in magic. The simple and the easier the figure of a god is to build, the stronger can you make that form and the forces within it, and that can be its danger too.

Those who built so strongly the forms of the gods found meditating on those forms of especial benefit to the growth of the soul. The symbolic figure of the Hawk and the Man in those few rigid lines (you can almost make a child's drawing of them, the hawk's head and beak, the angular outline of a man standing with a wand in his hand or an ankh) repeatedly drawn within the mind and dwelt upon, was meant to produce the aspiring soul that Horus represented, the soul that tracked down its prey from a far distance.

And so it was with other gods and goddesses. The Egyptian pantheon is simple. So simple that people do not realise the intricate elaborations of which those forms are capable and in which they can be used if necessary. Egypt was the great source of power in the Mysteries. Its Gods were always extremely powerful because magic is what is done with the mind, and the form the mind held was simple and strong and rigid in outline.

When you read the Book of the Dead and the Egyptian liturgies then naturally somewhat the reverse is noticed. The language is hieroglyphic and secret, almost over burdened with hidden meanings wrapped in occult outlines or a beautiful image. Every liturgy is also something to be studied, for every sentence is a mantram, and if repeated with power and intention can be of great value or of great destructive force.

It is such things as this that excavators come across when they take upon themselves the opening of a tomb of the dead, where some departed prince has been laid away under protective magic, which can pursue any that attack the stronghold where he has been laid. Magic that can still act today, thousands and thousands of years later, because when those princes or pharaohs were laid in the tomb, Elementals were brought into touch that should for limitless periods protect his tomb, and which can still act today.

For that reason also it is not wise to have Egyptian amulets which are genuine. Usually however those who are connected with the Mysteries are protected against evil designs of that kind because it is understood they would not use the amulets amiss, and would understand why they are charged with that magnetism, but for the uninitiated it is by no means wise unless the history of an amulet be very well known.

There are of course a vast number of gods in the Egyptian pantheon, forms of Isis, forms of Osiris, all of them 'black' and 'white'. There is also that mighty Being whose force with Horus comes in to action in this Age, the mighty Thoth. He who weighs all in the balance. He who measures the days and the seasons and the heart of man. And they are both bird-headed. They are both easy to remember to build within the mind.

Should you desire truth, contemplate Thoth, and you will find, if you are sincere and one-pointed, that your mind is guided many degrees nearer to the vastness of truth than before. For those lines of which that mighty form is composed have in them a great esoteric plan which sets forth a great principle in all its lines.

So indeed with all the figures of the gods and goddesses. Their lines were hieroglyphs, though simple. And dwelling on the figure of the God held, through contemplation, a whole wealth of knowledge and teaching. That is why they were used so much in the Mysteries, because they held chapters and chapters of teaching within each figure, if they were dwelt upon, quite apart from their magical value.

There are also, equally strongly marked with the Egyptian gods, definite aspects of power, much more clearly felt than is often the case with other god forms. The power of Ra as the Sun, the power of Osiris, of Kephera, of Anubis, of Great Isis, are all very distinctive and can be very strong. There is no doubt about the type of power that descends in a strong Egyptian ritual: it is well marked out, clearly defined, even as the figures of the god.

The Path of the soul may also, in certain natures, be very well studied by the Egyptian methods, for certain natures respond to them better than to other methods. Those who are better taught by what is clearly cut and outlined and very definite in statement, such souls are better helped by Egyptian teaching and Egyptian esotericism. I do not here speak so much of magic, which is another matter and requires those that are trained a great deal more highly, but magic is at its most remarkable in some ways when well worked with Egyptian methods. Many of these methods have been forgotten but they can, to some extent, be found again in the old books and in dwelling on the old Egyptian liturgy, which is full of such things.

I would also charge you not to forget that Great One, Thrice Greatest Hermes, but on occasion to invoke him and learn what you can about him, for his power and his teaching are very great.

The Lord of this present Age of Aquarius is Horus, he who proceeds from Isis and Osiris, who contains within him Isis and Osiris, who is both of them in a sense. But the time has not yet come for that mighty power to descend on all mankind to its full extent as it will eventually. What you can do now, however, is to contemplate that power and draw it to your mind sometimes. For the more you do so, the more will you become harmonised with the present Age.

The Cult of Hathor

All the great deities of Egypt had their priesthoods and those priesthoods were versed not only in ritual and certain orders of Temple work but also in certain methods of development of the soul, the method of each priesthood differing somewhat from those of all the others. In the great colleges of Thebes, On and others, the secrets of all these cults were known and deeply studied. For in these gods, especially those of very ancient date, Egypt had an inheritance from an older world, long since swamped by the waves, but still the source of much Egyptian magic and many of the gods and goddesses.

One of these was Hathor, who can be described broadly as the great Concreter of Seven Spheres, representing approximately the Earth power of the seven planes. She was not exactly the same as the great Negative Force called the Mighty Isis, save that all the goddesses were aspects of Isis, but was a form already ancient before the Dynasties came to Egypt.

She represented fertility, not only the fertility of the Earth but also that of the Underworld, which means that in his passage of the Underworld in initiation or physical death man learnt of Hathor to grow. She fertilised his soul and he progressed through her influence, which may be compared, to some extent only, with that of the Greek Persephone, who was a less concrete and more gentle form than Hathor.

She has also been compared with Aphrodite but a more correct comparison is with the Syrian Ashtoreth in her sex aspect, although she did very strongly and strangely represent the sevenfold force associated with Aphrodite. She represented it on the seven planes of the planets we know and she also represented the seven planes of Sothis, of which she was a form, for stars and suns and planets have all their various planes and levels of existence. She therefore represented a very deep working of true spiritual development, for not only could she show the advancing soul how to gather the fruit of the planes he must travel through after death, but she could do the same for the seven secret planes of the planet of Isis, Sothis or Sept.

She had a certain amount of the power of the Moon, but she had a great deal more of a particular type of Solar power and Martial and Earthly force. The particular sphere of the Underworld that she ruled had to do far more with the sun aspects, for she was the daughter of Ra, and always accompanied him herself in the form of another and mightier sun.

Think of the sunsets of Egypt, great shafts of red and rose, and golden light lying above the hills and beyond the desert, and you will have some idea of how the people thought of the passage of the Boat of Ra, in which he and Hathor journeyed to the Underworld, a mighty passage through waves of flaming red and golden clouds until the Disk was lost to view. Though such things are but imagination do not despise them, for it is imagination that opens the gates of the other world and through imagination the soul understands much that it would not otherwise understand.

She was also a kind of figure of Fate, a sevenfold Fate which followed man and showed him his different conditions on the seven planes of manifestation which had to be worked out on this plane of the world. And she was, too, the Lady of the Sycamore, one of the few trees in Egypt, a land without many trees that gave real shade, and also the Lady of the Mountain of the West.

The Mountain of the West was one of the Theban Hills, one on which the sun seemed to rest as it set, and this particular hill showed the great Disk of the Sun in his Boat as he journeyed to the Underworld, while over and above him shone the great Hathor in her aspect of one of the powers of Sothis. Wherefore she was called the Lady of the Sunset, the Lady of the Mountain of the West, for she influenced the sunset of man which is the world of death and the road to initiation.

Her cult was not one that would seem to modern thought very intellectual but it was not meant to develop the intellect - that was the province of the cult of Thoth. It was meant to develop the soul itself on certain lines and to certain grades, for the great value of the cult was that it made things more concrete than did the others, since the goddess represented the Earth qualities in far-off planes, and through her were those qualities brought down, to some extent, to this Earth.

Her symbol was the cow and in the great festival during her month, corresponding approximately to the modern October, a snow-white cow decked with beautiful gold and silver symbols and wreathed with the leaves of the sycamore, was led to the front of the Temple to be adored by the people. In her honour at these rites great cow masks were sometimes worn by the priesthood, and there was Temple dancing and music, and great litanies were spoken, invoking the goddess by her many Names until the power in the Temple grew and she herself built up above the altar in black and white and gold and green.

She was represented as a black goddess for she was old, old as the Theban Hills and the earth of Egypt was the mud of the Nile, black and rich with fruitfulness and nurture, which the goddess represented not only in the earth but also in the soul of man.

The grades of her priesthood were described in terms of cattle; there were Cows, Bulls, Calves and Heifers; there was grazing - a term of adepthood - in certain parts; there was the great Herd of Heaven to which the initiate aspired and whose ranks he desired to join. An initiate of Hathor of a high grade had a very high degree of power.

Picture such a one with the dark skin and the slight, somewhat narrow form of body typical of Egyptians, robed in black and white robes and upon his head the great headdress from which up-rose the horns of the Cow. When such an initiate brought through much power these horns extended, as it were, into beams of light, enabling others to see that his soul was indeed beloved and guided by Hathor.

Her initiates took on largely the strange peacefulness and earth - quietness that the cow, which was considered a sacred animal, so particularly has. The fertility of the soul and the knowledge of contemplation come into mind when one thinks of cows, and it was held that the great calm and ruminative quietness which, as it were, held the Earth in its compass, descended from and united us to the Earth of that far-off sphere which belonged to Isis, the sphere of Sept, for only in quietude and ruminative contemplation and calm can the spirit grow.

It must not be forgotten, however, that this goddess had other aspects also symbolised in the cow. A cow, no less than a bull, can be very savage and Hathor had the aspects of battle and stampeding force, and could drive the soul to destruction in her harsh and terrible aspect, for harsh and terrible she could be as can all the Immortals.

When you would enter into contemplation and ruminating peace think of Hathor and her symbol, the cow, and this thought carried into the sphere of the soul will indeed bring a remarkable peace. Think, sometimes, of yourselves in terms of cattle, sacred cattle, a herd of peaceful creatures grazing in secret pastures. Picture yourselves as wearing the mask of Hathor, the cow mask, and gazing out upon the sunset on the Theban Hills. See, streaming around the tremendous horns of the mask, light which leads up the sky and is in contact with that other mighty sphere shared by Hathor and brought down to Earth by her, who concretes all.

In contemplating her remember that she represents the seven great planes from which, in a remote and secret fashion, all are built, and her great calmness and earthy wisdom will help each of you to align himself once more with those Inner Planes.

Hathor bore between the horns of her head-dress a great shining disk and you may wonder whether this disk was, as generally thought, a lunar symbol or whether it was a symbol of the sphere of Sothis. This depends upon the degree of understanding of the nature of the goddess. There was the fertilising aspect which combined the action of the lunar powers upon the Earth and upon the animal nature of man, but the full understanding of this aspect marked the threshold of the inner reality of the goddess who held indeed between the horns the symbol of the sphere of Sothis.

Hathor was a symbol of the separation of the tremendous drive of the instinctual life from the higher states of consciousness; the separation that results in the understanding of the passionless states of being and which brings that great strength that resides in contemplation. She was a great symbol of the power and drive of the animal nature which are freed by the action of the lunar tides and rhythms. She was also a symbol of the animal nature in its liberation. A symbol, that in the contemplation of these two, lies the divine mystery of union, the 'Marriage of Heaven and Earth'. There is symbolism of this separation in terms of cattle, in the making of butter from milk.

On the Tree of Life, Hathor relates much to the Daath-Yesod circuit of force, to the 13th Path and to the inner reality of Netzach.

Orpheus

I have been considering what would be most helpful to speak upon today and I have concluded that it would be a good subject to take the power of the great Being you know under the name of Orpheus, for there is much that is completely misunderstood about the Lord of the Green Ray.

All Rays work with each other, and with these great Beings, the two other Rays are always included but in a more latent sense. Therefore, with the Green Master you must consider the devotional side and the wisdom side as well.

It has been sometimes said that the Green Ray is without wisdom - that is complete nonsense. It is not the keynote of it, but there is a great wisdom aspect which develops from the Green Ray, and its wisdom in this case is the superlative knowledge of the subtleties and secrets of what is called Nature. Of the very deep inward knowledge of fish and bird and beast, and of their ways and their needs, and above all of a remarkable communication with their Group Souls. Such a thing is very rarely found in man completely but you do find among country men a knowledge of animals and birds – although I mean a much more complete and a much deeper power of wisdom, which really knows the Group Souls of these creatures.

Now that complete and remarkable knowledge was part of the mission, incredibly long ago, of the great Being and Teacher called Orpheus. In that remembrance, vague as it is, of his power, is drawn the legend of his making the trees dance and the birds sing as he played upon the heavenly lyre. And this great lyre - what was it? It was the atunement with the Seven Great Spheres of Manifestation. The knowledge of those Spheres. The ability to draw down their influence through feeling with them, as well as by knowing all about them intellectually, for the power of the Green Ray is also a power of understanding, sympathetic vibrations and being harmonised at will with those vibrations.

And that Great Lyre brought down the knowledge of the planets, of those Seven Spheres, so that lessons could be given to mankind through them, for the Great Being called Orpheus was a Teacher of men.

Of course there are many legends and myths as always of these Great Beings, and these legends are a way of expressing a truth, for where you have a great myth you may be sure you have, if you contemplate it, a key to a great truth. And when the knowledge and history and legends of this Great Being were assembled together they formed a part of worship in some of the cults of Hellas. And they also formed a very remarkable philosophy, which is a great deal forgotten.

But one thing I will say, the great teacher Pythagoras was one who studied the great Orphic philosophy and belonged to it, anyhow for some time. For in it was a very great knowledge of number, and the teaching of sound and number, which was in the teaching of Pythagoras. He did in fact to a large extent elaborate from his knowledge of the Orphic myths and from the illumination which he as a great initiate drew from those myths.

There is a very great deal of connection between the Green Ray and the laws of mathematics and proportions and rhythms and such details are all associated very strongly with the Green Ray. There was, as you no doubt know, a great cult of worship of Orpheus in Thrace, and Thrace was a country of wild and rocky scenery, of great hills and rushing streams - the powers which drew down the great mysteries of the Sevenfold Lyre.

There is also a myth which you may well apply to yourselves when you meditate on the Green Ray. It is of the nymph who after Orpheus had been drawn from the Earth and the wonderful Lyre had been lost to the world, found it by the stream in Thrace and bore it with her, yet did not think herself fitted to touch the strings which such a Master had touched. She therefore only bore upon her heart the Lyre, silent, beside the roaring stream.

That really may be seen to apply to those who get a very deep contact with the higher side of this Ray and have it in their power, by the virtue of reverence and dedication to understand it through meditation, and in that way this beautiful myth may be applied to all of you.

I do not wish today to go in very particularly to the side of the legend in which the great One was torn into pieces and killed. That is, of course, the sacrificial side, the tearing of the elemental self to pieces by the wildness of the instinctive processes so that through this terrible path of suffering and of sacrifice the great and glorious Spirit shall be freed from the torments of the wild instincts and shall reign within the sky even as the great Master did when he withdrew.

He belongs to such antiquity that it is impossible to give a date for his appearance in the world, but all the myths of him are derived from a great teacher and guide of very early days. And so you see in this great Lord of the Green Ray his wisdom side and a great devotional side which is shown by the sacrifice as well. The Orphic Path of the initiate is by no means an easy one, for it does mean the tearing asunder of the instincts that does not happen to those who have less of the Green Ray in them.

The great knowledge of the Group Souls of lesser creatures also belongs to the great Orphic teaching. Here again much of it has been lost but I think that were a real Mystery cult of it revived, not in the same way, for you have not now got the memory and knowledge, but some kind of revival with intention, with the help of ritual, built on these myths, I think you might find that interesting planetary, geometrical, and Group Souls of plant and animal contacts might be made - at least I would suggest that.

There is a whole history by itself alone of all the geometrical shapes which exist in all things, whether in planets or numbers or music, or any form of nature or art, and that too again is a part of the Orphic Mysteries - that strange geometrical knowledge of a special type bringing through the geometrical forms of non-human life - for these forms are higher symbols than the reproduction of the subconscious pictures of human forms, really.

When the volume of *The Cosmic Doctrine* was translated there were many teachings and suggestions of vast planetary and other cosmic and geometrical shapes. Such shapes and teaching, in essence, though less elaborated, was also much in the Orphic doctrines. There was this great difference between Orpheus and the great Egyptian Osiris, that Osiris had to be re-membered again, his limbs had to be pieced together again and made anew, but with Orpheus the opposite was the case, he had to be dismembered and scattered to the elements forever and not re-membered again. But the immortal power is there overhead, diffused among the elements, diffused and spiritualising and harmonising the higher sides of the elemental power to those who would seek the knowledge of that power, sending it through when they have contacted the great higher subtleties of that marvellous Ray - the Green Ray.

I would have you try to contact this great beauty, which is also the soul of measures and of mathematical exactitude. This great essence of harmony that inter-relates all, once it has become free of the tearing instincts and the cruelties of the lower elemental states. I would have you think of the great sevenfold vibrations of that tremendous lyre, with the vibrations of which the planets throb and turn and reflect their light upon the Earth. The Great Being which you call Orpheus could still be brought into touch with this Universe anew - he is in touch with other Universes now.

COMMUNICATIONS

So think upon the nymph beside the stream who found the lyre again. And the blessing of the Lord Orpheus and the shadow of the eternity of the stars be upon you through the great Ray of Orpheus.

DEMETER AND THE MYSTERIES OF ELEUSIS

I will raise a picture in your minds from which we will begin our talk. You are standing around me in the great plain which is outside the city of Athens. It is night, and dimly before us rises up the gigantic outline and height of the Acropolis. Around us in the plain there are one or two statues, one or two stunted olive trees, and the vast planets look down on this. We are going some miles away from Athens, along the road across the plain. We are going along the road to Eleusis.

There have been many tales told of the Mysteries of that place, but very little indeed is known today, because those who talked at all were not people learned or proficient in the Mysteries but were either neophytes, or would-be neophytes, and did not know very much about what they spoke of. Those who really knew what was behind those great Mysteries and had really been through the complete initiation did not feel any desire to talk at all.

There were two great sets of Mysteries there, the Mysteries of the Mother and the Mysteries of the Daughter. They were the great Earth Mysteries of Hellas, though they had drifted down there from Asia Minor.

Within the courts of the great Temple you might see animals being taken for offering or sacrifice and long processions of people, who were probably not going to be admitted but who watched certain ceremonials to which the ordinary public might go. They were the great Mysteries of the Life of the Earth, the corn ready for the food of man, which was Demeter's contribution; and the seed of the corn which sprung up in the dark earth, and finally pierced it and raised a green shoot in the spring, which was the Mysteries of the Daughter.

You all should know well the tale of Demeter and Persephone so I will not repeat it, but I will try to make clear the great power that these Mysteries had upon the hearts of men. For it was not only those who had been themselves initiated who felt the power, but the outsider who saw only certain of the public manifestations and who was so brought up in awe and reverence of the great Goddess and the forces of the Earth that even the relatively small amount of the ceremonies he was permitted to see had a great effect upon him; and he considered that it had an effect also on the cultivation of the soil and on material prosperity connected with the soil.

The priests and priestesses of that great company had been through a severe training of a very profound type, somewhat like that which took place in Egypt, though there is always a certain difference according to the country. The Mysteries of Demeter were not quite the same as the Mysteries of Osiris and Isis, although the fertility of the land and the growth of grain were implied in both cases.

There was said to be a great Power which went round the Temple at Eleusis on the occasions of the great festivals, and this Power touched certain persons who were present, and not perhaps present in the Mysteries themselves but present in the festival as onlookers. Such persons would then probably do all they could afterwards to become initiates, for the great Power of Demeter had touched their hearts in a special manner and they were no longer content with the ordinary ritual of the outsider which was attended by pious crowds merely because it was the custom.

There were, too, the great and secret festivals of the Daughter Goddess, of Kore, the Sacrificed Maiden, sacrificed to the power of the deep Earth, which you call Pluto, in order that, after she had been carried away and learnt the secrets of the hidden Earth, she should bring back those secrets in the form of the green corn springing once again.

There were those who said that they saw the apparition of the great Earth Goddess within the Temple, and it was seen in a special way, usually surrounded with gold and yellow, the golden yellow of the corn. It is quite true that those who invoked Her on such occasions did seemingly have a special blessing on the fructification of their land.

Those who were actually initiates spoke very little about any matter which had to do with the Temple, but it can be assumed that there was a ritual of initiation and there were various rituals which had to be passed through. They were not as terrifying, perhaps, as the Egyptian, but to some extent they aroused a more inward sense of awe. There was always placed within the Temple a very large stack of bound corn, and a certain Power appeared to pass over the corn at certain moments as it lay heaped in the Temple, and I need not say that that was the occasion of a very great sensation in those who witnessed it.

Like all great Mothers Demeter was not all gentle, she was severe and even could be harsh, because it was her duty not only to comfort but to teach and to bring up, and how could she do that only with gentleness? Therefore, of the immortal gods, she was one of whom men stood in very great awe. She had also a great deal of sorrowing and suffering which people remembered in some of her rituals of mourning - mourning for the daughter stolen away from her and taken underground and hidden, so that for months she wandered in great sorrow and tragedy, unable to find her daughter.

Therefore, with all these great Beings of this sort, you find that great power of tragedy, which is the basis of drama, and, therefore, of great value in various ways to man. It is the basis of drama, and drama is what he can model himself upon. It is the life of the hero or heroine of his especial race or religious teaching upon which he can model himself.

The drama of Demeter and her daughter was a very great drama in which the soul of man faced many of its factors, and we have a Mother cult rather than a Father cult, whose basic ideas and tragedies and needs went to a deeper part of the soul than would be on other occasions with other gods who were not mothers. They brought up the spirit of man, as it were, conceived him and brought him forth in the Mother Goddess cult as an initiate; and it is in that way that the Mysteries of Eleusis had such very great and wide sanctity and teaching.

They have been, of course, completely forgotten and overturned and what I can tell you is after many centuries. It is usually a matter of surmise or of what one or two people themselves initiated, let fall later. There is very little left upon which you could build anything to copy, but there are eternal verities in the Cult of Demeter and her daughter, and those eternal verities belong to man and belong to nature. And if you base yourself on nature, you will find that her seasons, her strength, her changes, will not only affect you, they will benefit you. So that when the leaves put forth their green again, your mind will begin to teem with ideas in a special way and you will burgeon, as it were, like the spring morning; and when some tragedy has happened to you, you will learn, after much searching and sadness, what exactly has happened and what you must do in order to regain what you have lost.

That is just what the Goddess did. She regained her daughter and she understood the reason of the loss and she adapted herself to it, so that there should be no conflict which should affect man again; she accepted that her daughter should go under the earth for a certain season and be on the earth for a certain season.

You may say all that is just a rather foolish poetical allegory which means nothing to man now. Yet man has lost so much. Had he the roots of his being firmly planted in the earth, as his forefathers had, with the mind that has developed during the centuries, then, indeed, there would be a straight run-through of power such as you have no conception of. The great forces of nature, whether of the Earth or whether of the starry skies, were meant to be linked with the life of man, and he has forgotten that link. Where and when he remembers it, an added power is his that nothing else can give.

If you can imagine to yourselves the long line of the Temple of Eleusis with the steps going up to it and the columns bearing up the roof, you will find that a great deal of benefit will come to you down those steps, and there will be a reviving life of the Earth which will come out of the Temple and fuse itself with you, and this will help you, for it is a steadying power.

The power of the Earth is rhythmic and steady. It gives calmness to those who have not sufficient control or poise, for the Gods do not go against their own laws. I wish you could see the long processions which we saw going to that great Temple:- man and beast laden with offerings, and the poise and reverent bearing of those setting out for the Temple; well-known men on horseback and many others of lesser condition following on foot; a long procession coming out of the city towards Eleusis.

Had we not had in Hellas those deep-rooted teachings of the gods, gods of different manners of work and gods of different types, I question very much whether we should have evolved the many different philosophers whom we did evolve. For philosophy, true philosophy, comes out of religion, and extracts from religion all the hidden things that the purely outside worshipper cannot understand. Philosophy lets us add that mental process to the great truths that man has always had. As we had so many great truths under the form of gods, so had we so many great philosophers and teachers.

The Rites of Eleusis, as we knew them, will not come to the world again, but you who perform certain Mystery work might well endeavour to constitute in some form a Rite of the Earth Mother, for it is of very great benefit on all planes, for, in the mystic Earth, which she represents, all planes are in touch with her.

She was said to be seen seated in a great cave on certain occasions - a cave of the earth - and this cave was full of the vital powers of the Earth, also to some extent of the Moon, which is in near juxtaposition to the Earth. Unless you know Demeter, you will not know the Stars. Think well on that, my friends, for the Earth herself is a planet. And the tragedy of Earth is the tragedy of sacrifice, as with other Gods, for Persephone was a sacrifice, a sacrificed goddess, a sacrificed maiden.

I dwell a great deal on this twin drama of the Mother and the Daughter, for even in their names there are untold mysteries written for you to find. In Eleusis meditation was conducted upon both of them, and there were two great initiations of Demeter and of Kore; of the Mother and of the Daughter. They were very great and perfect powers, and the correspondences with them is in man, for man has his correspondences with the gods when he works in harmony with Nature and when he understands and controls his own nature.

All those who have work to do on the earth, in so far as it is related actually to certain work of the earth, should meditate on the great Demeter. They would find happiness, counsel and help from that great power of the Mother, even as they could find a great deal to learn from the power of the Sacrificed Daughter, who goes and returns and adjusts herself to both lives - the life with her Mother upon the surface of the earth when the right time is there, and when the right time again comes, the deep unknown and mystic life, hidden from all, in the very depths of the Earth's soul. That is Persephone.

The Sea Cult

The sea much more than what we call 'inanimate nature', is a life tremendous and full of enigma: helpful if you understand how to conform with its laws, baneful if you cannot or will not do so. The sea is a great deal more "alive" than a force of inanimate nature is in the usual sense of those words.

We have lost very many secrets and among them the great secrets of the sea-power known in Atlantis. There was, upon the Island of Ruta, a great deal of knowledge of the Great Being, the outer 'body' of which we call the sea.

In different parts of Atlantis there were certain centres which were especially devoted to the Sea-cult and its study; the cult of the Sun, which was also a very great force, came later. The cult of the Sea was first, and it is on that occult knowledge that a great deal of the hidden ceremonies and knowledge of the Withdrawn Temple in Atlantis was based.

There were great ceremonies connected with the four quarters of the year, less at first in connection with the Sun than with the Sea, which was their remote origin. What was it that the Atlanteans and the early races were seeking in this worship? They were seeking the origins of Life itself; not so much the life of the Spirit which depends on the evolution of mankind - that became the Sun Worship - but the knowledge of the basis of Cosmic life and force which was, in effect, based upon Space and the Sea. The very first beginnings, even mentioned in Genesis, were from the water.

Initiates should try to return to certain things in Atlantis, to rebuild the great power from which the Mysteries sprang in the City of the Golden Gates, and they forget a great deal if they forget the Hidden Temple. They must remember not only the Sun Temple, but that other Temple, the Withdrawn Temple of that time. For just as the Sun Temple had all its individual Temples related in some way to that great spiritual and healing power behind all, so was the Withdrawn Temple related to the great Cosmic life of Space and Water in its first unfoldment which we call the Sea.

There are various aspects of the Sea, even as there are of the Sun. Different nations and races specialised in one or other aspect just as certain races specialised in the Sun worship, but if you come to examine the history of cults you will perceive that behind and originating each phase of the early Sun worship was a Sea cult - yet older, fiercer and stronger - and in some way all should again make contact with that worship and that powerful atmosphere - the Mother of Birth and, therefore, the Mother of Death: the beginning of Life and the End of Life - of Life connected with the Cosmos, linking man not only to the Solar Logos as does the Sun but to the Worlds beyond, to the other Solar systems - to the great Cosmic whole. For that belongs to the Sea, the Mother and the Genetrix of all Life.

Were the actual occult symbols and powers belonging to the Sea rightly remembered, 're-collected' from the earliest time, you would have a vast sum of experience to handle which could be applied to this Work - to the handling of powers, and above all to the esoteric development of man when he has reached a sufficiently high grade. Obviously it is not a form of development to be applied in the early phases, or even to those in the Outer Greater Mysteries, for the knowledge brought back would confer a great deal of self-sufficiency and power which could only be justified for one of whom the Masters were definitely certain.

So the knowledge of the esoteric life and magic connected with the Sea-power has been very largely withheld but you do get glimpses of that ancient worship - which is the cult which very far back in the roots of time made a special greatness, a special development among Island races. We all can think of our own Island but Ruta, too, was an Island, and here in Britain where these later Islands of ours are, there was a great deal of early Sea-worship before the worship of the Sun took on the significance among the Druids of which we all know. The Druids knew well of the other worship but it was not their work to dwell upon it overmuch for it had fallen into disrepute and had degenerated, and it is far better (as they being wise men knew), when something has so degenerated that it is sinking down into the abyss, not to recall it but to replace it with something else. For when something sinks into the abyss it means that it must rest for an Age, perhaps several Ages, before it may be recalled upon another arc.

Therefore those who gave us the great Sun-worship and knowledge did well. Now, however, the time has come not indeed to replace the Solar powers but to start recollecting and piecing together again this lost body of legends, this lost body of Osiris as it were, and to fit it together again that it may begin to reign once more in the hidden world and come again upon a new day. Those who are trained to recollect and fit together these pieces are indeed Servers of the Great Mother, and they are the teachers of those who will come after. They lead a retired life away from the world - a life that will give them the power to recollect these teachings once again, for later people to use in another way, when the Sun worship shall, in its turn, sink down and the Sea-worship shall completely return, for so it is with all great Cults on which life has been based.

Solomon, who followed the great Solar monotheistic teaching, found that his Temple lacked much of the ancient life and usage which was given Israel in the beginning via Chaldea and Mesopotamia, and he sought to replace this life. He went to the great master of the forgotten knowledge, the King of Tyre. The Tyrians were a Sea-people who had guarded much of that ancient belief, and so with the help of the king of this Sea-people he began to try to make perfect the great Temple of Israel.

In Britain itself certain parts were once especially sacred to that very ancient ritual which is now mostly forgotten, and a great deal of it was also in Ireland, and it is from that vague remembrance of the ancient Cult that many secret powers and strange and imaginative symbols in Ireland have been drawn. Within our own midst there were great Sea-cults in forgotten days off Wales and Cornwall and also, particularly, in Brittany, which was at one time an island and has ever been isolated in a curious way both from France and Britain - always a small country entirely by itself with ancient customs but half-understood, and the remains of curious symbolism and worship mixed up with the Roman Catholic faith.

Brittany has an especial message for all of us because it was there that the last great secrets of Sea-power, drawn from Atlantis, were kept. There was for long a great Atlantean Sea-Cult in Brittany, but it became so abused and defaced that it was useless to try to conserve it. Nonetheless, there was the genuine power and secret knowledge, and here in Britain there was nothing so strongly drawn from Atlantis relating to the Sea as in Brittany.

Those in Britain had imported more of the Sun magic, for it was the Sun Temple priesthood, not the Withdrawn Temple, which went out colonising. Nevertheless, on the downfall of Ruta there were certain people moved from the cataclysm who were competent to bear the most secret knowledge with them, and of those a small party at one time landed in ancient Amorica and hence you have the legend of Ys and such fables, which have much truth and history behind them, though distorted by time and the Church's adaptations.

It must be realised that the Sea is something that can never be controlled by man; but by innate knowledge from his most ancient past man may learn, as it were, the balance of humanity with that great Force and all it stands for in his evolution. But such knowledge comes only after considerable development and after spiritual stability is proved and established. People unsuited to such knowledge and such worship used its symbols wrongly and became drunk with power and applied it evilly as is shown by legends of those who were not evolved enough to be safely given that Sea knowledge which at first was only intended for the highest initiates.

We have had in human evolution very great systems which recur at different times, the Solar system, the Stellar system and the Sea system. These recur in the Mysteries at different times and, of course, in all Mysteries you find a residue of all three.

ROBIN HOOD, THE CRUSADES & THE QABALISTIC TRADITION

It is forgotten sometimes that the remains of the earlier race went back into the hills of Wales and Northern England and the caves of Somerset, Devon and Cornwall at a far slower rate than is suggested by orthodox history. There was much more intermingling of its blood therefore with the Saxon and Norseman than may be supposed; so that by the time the Normans came England contained a larger admixture of non-Saxon blood than perhaps is realised. We will now go forward beyond that time into Norman and early Plantagenet days and first I will speak about the very early cycle of the songs and stories relating to Robin Hood.

The Robin Hood cycle is a kind of interlude in English legend - an interlude between the Grail and the later Tudor days which brought in printing and the Reformation. It might well be called the English Green Ray Legend. Whether or no an Earl of Huntingdon really set up a brotherhood of outlawed men does not matter; the story under the name of 'Robin Hood' contains Green Ray lore of a certain period and type. It was a very strange order of outlaws - a small Aquarian circle long before the present Age.

We have the head of the company acting as administrator of rough laws and of a code of chivalry. With him were various companions in arms, all of different types and different social standing and different trades, yet a brotherhood in which the administrator, though the head, was also included.

Into this company composed of men of different types, trades and ages finally comes one woman - one woman alone in that company of men; and she is known by the title of 'Maid', strange as it may seem. What type of woman could live in such a way with all those men and yet be known by such a title?

Whether or no she was, as legend says, a virgin while living in the forest, because of all the various hardships that would arise otherwise, does not count much now. The fact that is of interest is her title. 'The Maid' - that title so much misused by narrow-minded people who ignore the real meaning of virginity of soul - that which is without alloy, integrity of the Self and of the level it works upon - nothing to do, necessarily, with physical virginity. Such a woman will work with all kinds of men at different levels, understanding every level. Maid Marian was the better type of Aquarian woman long before her time.

In history we find rather the same idea (but carried out quite differently) in Joan of Arc. One woman with a universal mind, the Archetypal Feminine Mind in one woman - that is the Aquarian Ideal.

Regarding the other outlaws we have the priest, Friar Tuck, who has very little friarhood about him except his name; yet he used his priesthood on behalf of the outlaws, ministering to them spiritually when needful. Such a man brought down into the forest when needful the Christian side of Pan. The other companions are perhaps more obvious in their meaning - Little John, Will Scarlet, Allan-a-dale and all the rest of the band.

There was within that forest outlawry an inner bond of union of each with all; it was almost a forest Order, a brotherhood; those who broke the code of chivalry were punished and dismissed. All had to abide by the laws agreed upon among them. The strange story has no parallel in other tales and contains many things which would be good to try to discern in meditation, This legend of Sherwood should be dwelt upon by all of you because it is an example of Aquarian discipline long before Aquarian days.

There is another well-known figure of the same time - the King under whom Robin Hood lived, Richard I, who led his people to the Crusades and lived abroad from his own country too much to be accounted a good ruler. Nevertheless he was a symbol of the Mysteries, for by his meeting with Saladin and his journey to the Holy Land he let into England an influx of foreign ideas. Above all he let in many occult matters and suggestions taken from Near-Eastern countries.

When the English king and other Europeans mingled in battle to defend the Christian Holy Places they invoked without knowing it the power that was behind those sacred spots and influences. Hence we know that when the Templars had formed themselves into an Order they met with the last remnants of ancient tradition in Syria and the Mysteries began to come into their own after having nearly disappeared from the world. They had been crushed out before that day by Early Christianity. We who are descended from those same powers invoked by the Templars again are with you now.

In the recesses of the Eastern mountains there dwelt a last remnant of brothers belonging to the Essene school. These gave secret methods and symbolic messages to their pupils and a School of Initiation was founded out there in Palestine among the armed knights who called themselves Templars, We who descend from the same Tradition also know that these knights deviated from the original pure tradition, intermingling it with matter drawn from Judaic and Islamic traditions, which were not so pure as the traditions of the Essenes - pure in the sense of 'untouched'.

In those early days in far-off Palestine the Knights met those few brethren holding this ancient knowledge. Those brethren dwelt beside the hills close to the Dead Sea and they held a Qabalistic knowledge superior to some that evolved from the Templar school; nevertheless the Templars used that knowledge first through them,

The Qabalistic Tree of Life system was committed by secret signs and inner plane messages over many hundred centuries, and though there have been many schools of thought counting it as untouched literary tradition, very much of it also has been an oral tradition and has been sent down from the inner planes.

I would be strongly averse to making a new system of teaching regarding the Qabalah, for it has come down to us from various sources, mingled and pure. But nevertheless there remain upon the innermost plane of consciousness a great many more schools of thought of Qabalistic knowledge than already exist. We who are custodians of the teaching must be careful in our choice of these to whom we give it. Even now there are people not worthy to receive it, who have used far too much of a modern standpoint upon it without sufficiently considering the ancient beliefs.

Your own tradition is a very much better type of learning than is sometimes given out by other disciples. We who have the keys to this great mine of information must be doubly sure of the character and purpose in each person receiving it from us.

The links forged by those who made the Tradition descend into Gentile and European minds; those links are yet here. They are given from beyond the plane on which I now stand; they are part of the power that is behind me; therefore I say of this Tradition - be careful of it. We are behind all the schools of knowledge that have arisen from this traditional method. No truth is too deep for those fitted to receive it but all truth must be carefully guarded at first.

Far away from this world, we who are beyond it send our solemn assurance that we are in touch with those truths and work with them. We are all the time training our own selves and those beneath us must carry on in the same manner till they reach our level. Nobody may stand still here. Those who stand still in earthly work and practice and those who feel no deep significance in the Work and will not take trouble to understand and live it, had better leave it. We do not work with idlers. This applies to all.

The Essenes and Melchizedek

I wish to speak of the very great teaching brotherhood who lived in secret in Syria and were known among men as the Essene brotherhood - these scattered brethren who managed to hold out for some centuries secretly in Syria and who guarded the Secret Tradition of Israel.

They had a very remarkable philosophy and teaching of which scarcely anything has remained to pass into ordinary history, but certain Jewish teachers claimed connection with them, and Jesus of Nazareth was trained amongst them for a time before his ministry began. He did not adopt all their teachings publicly because he had to deal with ordinary members of the world, and the Essene teaching was a secret doctrine.

The Essenes were a great power on the Inner Planes, for they had a truly noteworthy astral working power, one of the finest, in its own way, which has ever been known, And they worked a great deal with the Tree of Life, using its symbolism in very many ways, and infusing into the various Sephiroth a tremendous flood of knowledge and of symbolism.

They developed the Tree to a very remarkable extent but it was all secret and there are scarcely any traces of them as a brotherhood now. But certain of the prophets belonged to them, Elisha and Hosea, for instance, and they used mount Carmel as a centre. And although in the orthodox external Jewish tradition it was purported to be only a vast patriarchal system, the Essenes knew that behind that teaching there was the 'feminine power' of the Almighty. Indeed they used a very great deal of the power of the Sephirah Binah, and worked with it extensively, and it was from them that many centuries later the Templars took their teaching.

They too worked with that great force and within the name 'Templar' is hidden the great Grade of Binah, the Master of the Temple. Outwardly, of course, the Templars said that they were guardians of the Temple of Jerusalem and that was also true, but the Inner Temple was not spoken of outwardly to the uninitiated, although that teaching they took from the small body of the Essenes whom they contacted.

The Essenes guarded within their secret doctrines the inner knowledge of the great Manu Melchizedek and all he came to teach - for there is a vast amount of knowledge, still undiscovered, that circles around that tremendous figure lost in the mists of antiquity. The Essenes had contact with him and kept a certain contact with that knowledge for a very long time, and even when in the course of ages the deep contacts were lost, the tradition and symbolism of those contacts remained.

And remember, you who know about the Round Table, that there is something of the same mighty symbol which concerns Melchizedek. The Table of Melchizedek was a great and secret formula and the great Manu had contact with the earliest of the Essenes so that certain doctrines concerning him were handed down and kept for the initiates only. But sometimes they were, to a certain extent, given out, as when Paul of Tarsus compared Melchizedek and Jesus of Nazareth - for Paul, an initiate, knew of that mighty figure and his Order. And all this, of which I will not now speak too much, is bound up with the Round Table Order and the Grail, with the Christian Mysteries too, and with the off-shoots of mysticism which you have in the Middle Ages such as the Templars and the Alchemists.

Certain, of course, of these Essene principles passed into the teaching of the Gnostics of Alexandria, for indeed such was only to be expected seeing that the founder of Christianity was himself a trained Essene.

It has been said that this could not be so because Jesus of Nazareth did not denounce war and fighting, and as an Essene he was bound to take no part whatsoever in war and fighting, and to have nothing to do with those who fought. But he had to teach in the world among ordinary people, and above all things he used that divine quality which we call plain common sense, and he put as few rules and laws as possible, especially when they were almost impossible to fulfil for the man in the street. The very difficult laws and rules were certainly meant to be fulfilled by the initiate, but that was another form of his teaching, and one that was always kept secret, having in it a great deal of the Essene principles as well as his own especial teachings and revelations. It is a thousand pities that so much of this has perished (all has perished as far as documentary evidence goes) but like much other secret teaching it can be picked up by traditional symbolism and meditation.

Thus there is an especial link for the Essenes and the Templars with that very early great tradition of Melchizedek. There was among the Essenes also, as naturally would be with esoteric descendants of Melchizedek, a great interest in the stars, and the Essenes guarded an especial lore of the stellar forces which also has all been lost - part of the invaluable teaching which had descended from Melchizedek.

In addition to that, you have yet the other, called Rosicrucian, which also descends from many of the same sources, because the tradition which is this mighty stream also bears a great deal of teaching which came through the Essene tradition - such as the Tree of Life for example. And it also has that wonderful symbol within it, the symbol of the Great Banquet, the Supreme Table, the Table of Melchizedek, the Table of Merlin; different levels and indeed sometimes not quite the same type of symbol, but always the same principle behind.

You will find also that the Great Names that belong to these mighty potencies have a great deal of continuity also, they belong to the same stream. The name of Jerusalem and all it means and stands for, of which the outer city is merely an outer symbol - the name of Damascus also in the same way - they were both great centres of initiation and you will recall that Paul of Tarsus was initiated in Damascus - that centre later connected by tradition with Rosicrucianism - and in the same way it was he who gave the teaching of Melchizedek and of Israel to the Western world.

So you see how all these things link up in a very remarkable way - it is a vast symbol system which may all be found upon the Tree. We are going through the same things again upon another arc: we are living through these ancient traditions and teachings yet again in this Age and also in other esoteric groups forming the Western Tradition - the Tree with its many branches and its prolific fruit - the Tree that is rooted in the Universe and holds the great subconscious of the Most High.

I would not say more now because these subjects are so vast that each of them would take years to be fully discussed, but I leave to your imaginations the seeds sown, to take root and to shoot in your minds and flower there. For indeed we in the West are heirs of a mighty tradition; and Atlantis, which I have not mentioned, is by no means forgotten, for the Manu Melchizedek existed in Atlantean days and taught in those days also. What he taught, in a slightly altered form, is of the same things and is also the Atlantean Tradition.

If you read your Bible and read the prophet Hosea and read about Elisha and Mount Carmel it may be that from the few words perhaps which you find suggesting the Tradition there may be great ways opened up to you.

The Holy Grail

There are two great Centres of the Grail in its history - one is called Avalon and the other is called Montsalvat (there are various spellings of this Mountain). They represent two different racial heritages connected with spiritual truth.

The Temple of Montsalvat exists upon the astral plane complete in its building. It is the Castle which contains the Chapel that is the home of the Grail Mystery. It is, perhaps, less known in this country than the legends which pertain to Avalon but it is none the less important,

There is upon the inner planes a company which might be called the Company of Avalon, and there is also upon the inner planes a brotherhood which we call that of Montsalvat. They are not in any way rivals but they work in different ways and the contact with each is somewhat different.

Within the Great Hall of Montsalvat behind the Chair of State whereon sits the King and Master of Montsalvat there is a small doorway which leads into the Chapel of the Grail. There is very little furniture in this chapel but a central altar, on which there burns eternally, in the midst of jewelled flames, the mighty symbol of the Spirit through all the ages of man.

The stories of Arthur and his Knights which include the history of the Grail and of the Round Table are well known, and these Knights can be taken in one interpretation as spiritual presences ready to overshadow the individualities of those dedicated to the Grail service, and bearing a warning in their failures as well as inspiration in their successes.

The Grail power represents a great spiritual essence existing in different forms upon every plane and this essence is open to every soul who is going to undertake the Quest, hazardous and dangerous though it may be.

It is also of importance to remember that individual souls contacted to the Grail-power in their turn add more force to that power, and it is a power which should link together in itself not only Britain but Europe as well, for in the beginning the Grail was for the world itself and certain races have inherited certain traditions of it - chief among these races being the British and French. There have also been contacts in Spain, Italy and Germany but not so strong as in Britain and France. It is because of that, that there is, despite certain racial antagonism, a spiritual link between Britain and France, which should not be lost sight of - and also, the link with France establishes the link with the rest of Europe.

In the ancient legends the Grail appeared and disappeared very suddenly, even as the good and spiritual impulses come to man very swiftly and unexpectedly and then withdraw. Will that man act upon that impulse or will he not? Only he can decide. That 'Vision of the Grail' comes not only suddenly, but it comes to any man who is likely to respond, whether he be of high or lowly station, but his soul must have the mettle of a Knight.

There are four great symbols which ever call to mind the Grail. They are the Lance, the Cup, the Sword and the Stone. They belong to the most ancient spiritual impulse, since it is a basic one, and dates from the days of Atlantis.

There have been within the Grail ministration several very Great Ones who have led it forward in their several ways. One of the earliest of these was the Great Being called Melchizedek, and 'after his order' came another Great One who founded the spiritual side of religion at that period in the world's history - the Lord Jesus: He too is a Prince of the Grail.

There are many phases in evolution - they have to be trodden out in certain ways and one phase gives place to another - but it also prepares for the other as can be seen on close inspection. Therefore the Age which is now past prepared the way for the spiritual impulse of the Aquarian Age, which could not have entered as quickly or have been based on such a strong foundation without the Sacrifice of Jesus and without his teachings, which must be rightly understood. Before him there were great teachings relating to spiritual laws brought through from Egypt and Greece and Syria, which, too, belong to the Grail teaching.

This is the Age of the Aquarian Grail - the highest spiritual teaching of which this Age is capable. It is the Age of the coming of the Cosmic Christ, not to any special Group or Church but to the individual Spirit of Man when he shall have attained to worthiness of it.

Let no one make the mistake of setting on one side the Lord Jesus and his teachings. Search these teachings well and you will find the pre-knowledge and preparation for this Age - not a setting forth of an ideal of man belonging only to an Age that is passed. Remember that the simpler a structure, the simpler a thought, the stronger and more enduring it will be.

The Lord Jesus left fewer words inscribed in books or memory than any other Great Teacher who ever came, yet each sentence of his that has come down to us holds great significance read aright and felt aright.

The great religious teachings of the last Age kept within certain Churches have many good points but sometimes they were mistranslated and misapplied in order to bear out something which it was wished to keep in a Church's creed. You should consider these things from another standpoint, for Christianity should become a 'movement' in the individual rather than a movement within a certain Group - although it had to start like that as often movements do start.

They begin frequently with hot-blooded enthusiasts, sometimes over-stating facts, working people up emotionally, being unbalanced in their desire to set up a great truth. They will try sometimes not only to set aside but to stamp out other truths. It is the history of all religious movements, because in those ways they are men's movements, not God's. But the spiritual impulse that gives breath to the movement is God's for that only is the real influence - the great influence of the spiritual truth sent down into whatever pure vessel the heart of man can devise for it.

We in this work upon the inner planes need help from you even as you need it from us, for the whole Creation is joined together. It is not meant to work alone. Everything belongs to the great system of the stars, and the smallest cog in the wheel must be willing to do its part - for even a small cog misplaced or broken may spoil the work of the engine and spoil the work of its fellow man.

A strong contact should be established with the picture in your minds both of Montsalvat and of Avalon, for these two are greatly linked together: and there is beyond those astral points also a still greater and stronger one, the great Church or Temple of the Grail upon the Inner Planes - a very real edifice in so far as the heart and mind of man can make it so. And those who are fitted to enter this mighty Temple of the Grail are those who have achieved the Quest. But on their way to it there is the Sacred Chapel of Montsalvat, where the contemplation of the Spiritual Mystery is profound, and where much teaching may descend to the faithful and believing soul who tries to worship therein.

The contemplation of the well-known stories of the Knights and Ladies is one of the Paths to that great inner plane Temple of the Grail wherein the mightiest Masters behind the spiritual teaching await the aspirant.

ALEXANDRIA, GNOSTICISM, AND THE GRAIL

Consider the mission behind the Grail influences; not what the Grail itself implies in individual and in general application, but rather a certain aspect of it which is often somewhat forgotten or overlooked. Namely the Grail centre in the city of Alexandria in Egypt.

Alexandria was the centre of a great renaissance of learning and esoteric knowledge after the Dynastic days of Egypt. In its great University was set up a seat of study of the Mysteries where the Gnostic power was inaugurated. In that Gnostic knowledge was combined the great revival of Egyptian and Greek mythological beliefs united with the teaching of Jesus the Christ.

It may well be asked what this has to do with the previous statement about the mission of the Grail teaching. It was in that University, in the researches made there, combined with the secret esoteric practices, that were first brought through much of the revived history of the Grail, drawn from Atlantis by way of Egypt. The teachings were very secret and into them was fused the then new teaching and belief given by Jesus the Christ.

In this inmost teaching of Alexandria, the Mysteries of Osiris of Egypt and of Dionysos of Greece were unified with the teaching brought by the young Galilean; for he combined - and he knew he combined - Dionysos and Osiris in himself in yet a third aspect.

The remembrance in men's minds of this Alexandrian knowledge of the Grail mixed with the stream that formed in Britain and Europe later on, bearing with it a curious trend of Eastern history, as can be seen from close study. In those early Mysteries of Alexandria were used the most potent symbols and rites that could be traced as prototypes of the Christian Mysteries.

The power that was gained in this way was of a very important kind. It was what was lightly called by non-initiates 'Earth Mysteries' but inwardly it combined the Sun and the Earth Mysteries into one whole. Previously the Mysteries were, as it were, separated into certain lines - the Mysteries of a certain deity - but this combined them all in the new Christian dispensation.

In Alexandria there was a special Mystery language and certain symbols were especially used. Many such were incorporated into the Essene Brotherhood later on from whom the Templars learnt. Also they passed into local tradition to some extent as the brethren in Alexandria were scattered by travel and persecution.

The very great symbol of them in Alexandria, interestingly enough, was the same symbol as is used for Mark the Evangelist - the symbol of the Lion. The lion that is wild and the lion that is tamed and the Lion that is one of the Four Holy Creatures. This Lion symbol of Alexandria may yield much to meditation.

It is from this Egyptian city wherein were many exiles and Jews and men from nations all over the known world of that day - a great cosmopolitan city - that many parts of the Grail story came to Europe. But it originated in Atlantis.

Those in Alexandria knew the Egyptian Mysteries of Atlantis, but in the burning of that library of Alexandria was destroyed nearly all of the stored learning of ancient times, including books and accumulated knowledge of the Mysteries. In that esoteric work in Alexandria was built, according to esoteric plans, the great inner plane Temple of the Grail, on secret teaching laid down by the Lord Jesus himself.

This Grail Temple was, as it were, projected down to the Astral by his power and it is full, in the hidden parts of it, of the tremendous forces of the far distant plane in which he now moves, for he partakes of the nature of a very remote 'Sun-sphere', which is not what we call the Sun, nor even what is called the 'Sun behind the Sun', but the Sun which is of another Evolution for which his teaching largely prepared. Those of you who are able to be sufficiently withdrawn on to remote planes can contact this Temple, and the more it is contacted the more will be brought through - especially of the Christian contact, the forces of the new phase of Christianity.

In the Gnostic Alexandrian version of the Grail, which was also called the Round Table, the completed history of the whole Mystery was the contact of this remote Sun. It is necessary that the part played by the Christian side of the great teaching through the Gnosis of Alexandria be remembered, and on occasion used with the others, for the Grail is many-sided.

That remote Sun-sphere to which the Lord Jesus passed on was called in Egyptian phraseology the sphere of Aton. Some slight knowledge of it in very early days was expressed by the Pharaoh who worked to bring into use the knowledge and philosophy and mystery of the Solar Disc. His teaching was much more than an attempt at monotheism, it implied an early knowledge of, and contact with, a super-Sun sphere.

The Wisdom Aspect

There can be neither Power nor Love in proper function without Wisdom. And, as you all know, in the three great aspects or Rays the two others are latent. Therefore the Wisdom side of the Green Ray and of the Purple Ray will now be considered.

The wisdom of the Purple Ray, the wisdom of Devotion, is that understanding and complete realisation of the necessity of sacrifice, and of the impersonal love which does all to raise others to the highest. These cannot be brought about by mere emotional feeling, however worthy and admirable such feeling may be. They cannot exist at all without those very great attributes of wisdom; namely, *understanding* and *realisation,* otherwise that Ray is grievously incomplete.

Understanding is of the intellect – it is the intellectual approach to wisdom. Realisation is of the spiritual approach to wisdom, it is the complete assimilation of the experience of the Spirit itself.

In the same way must the Wisdom Aspect be brought to bear upon the Green Ray of Power and Beauty. There must be understanding of the intellect and realisation of the Spirit.

Therefore, even on the Green Ray, as well as the great 'blind forces' of the gods and of nature, you have the teachings of the Ancient Wisdom, which have given the knowledge of these powers to man, have explained these powers to him and have made it possible for him to understand and realise all that lies in these powers.

Philosophies have thus arisen as a means of teaching the great Power Ray in its right manner - not only by the feeling of power but by its true explanation and realisation, for therein lies the wisdom of the Green Ray.

There is a very significant and ancient symbol of Wisdom - the great magical instrument of the Master of Knowledge - the Caduceus of Hermes. It is indeed one of the greatest symbols which esoteric lore possesses, and meditation on it will bring more to the mind than pages of teaching.

In it is shown the Staff of Power with the great Pine-cone on the top and the two Serpents intertwining up the Staff, one Serpent being black, the other white. Yet these are two aspects of one Serpent, the Serpent of Wisdom. The white serpent represents the great wisdom of the eternal, which has foreknowledge from the beginning - that knows how things will happen. The black serpent represents the evolutionary knowledge of man himself, for man learns through his evolutionary experience. Yet all the while, those two serpents intertwine and touch each other, starting up the shaft from the same point, meeting the end of the staff at the same point, symbolising the great union of God and man.

This staff was borne by Hermes the great teacher, the One who in his various aspects knows all things. He bore it when he brought messages from great Zeus to the Earth or the Underworld. He bore it when he led the dead in the Underworld to their appointed places, symbolising that he always had full knowledge - that he had the eternal wisdom bound also with the wisdom of man himself. Indeed the symbol works out only too consistently, for on the lowest planes the god was depicted as cunning and as a thief - which is the using of understanding in a debased way.

Wisdom is like the serpents on the staff - developed into a spiral pattern - going and returning on another arc over the same place. And the wisdom of the ancients has returned to us again upon our level, and much of the wisdom of Atlantis we are gathering together again and using on the Aquarian level.

All should strive to develop far more the great Hermetic Ray. I have remarked how very little, relatively speaking, students know. How often relatively little even their teachers know in this work. There is admittedly a vast amount to assimilate, but nothing can be done, nothing can be made clear, unless you are prepared to devote yourselves to the Understanding and Realisation of the Ancient Wisdom. It is on this that our work itself is based.

Everyone should try, if only for a few moments, to reflect on some point in *The Cosmic Doctrine*. It would be of great value, for wisdom is not only intellectual understanding, but is also realisation. And when a thought incubates in the mind for some time - especially a thought somewhat difficult to assimilate and to understand intellectually with clearness - that thought has a very great effect upon the mind. It not only gives sound instruction but, if truly reflected upon, it does much more. It intensifies the power of that idea throughout the whole spirit and mind. It becomes a kind of inner food by which indeed the soul can grow.

This applies to all our teachings. Never shirk a book or a concept which appears to you difficult intellectually, Try always to get some kind of understanding of it. Never let it go by as being too difficult to comprehend. Every idea that concerns this work is worthy of study in this work. It is worthy of study and devotion.

It is strange but true that when something has seemed complex and confusing, if you leave it alone for some little while after studying, it will suddenly rise up in the mind, clear-pointed and full of light as a star. Of such a kind are the difficult concepts, for instance, of *The Cosmic Doctrine*. They will rise up as a star in your mind - quite suddenly - if you have sincerely tried to grasp them. And the light they will bring is a light that illumines far more than the mere intellect. It is the light of the spiritual realisation.

What is called the 'illumination of the mind' is in fact a deeper aspect of the Wisdom Ray coming into contact. For wisdom illuminates every dark place and makes lighter every light place. A full illumination is a stupendous spiritual experience. But if you dissect it, you will find that it is really a sudden realisation and tremendous power of understanding of some concept. And this understanding reaches far beyond the sphere of the mind.

Nevertheless, the initiate must be able to some extent to bring it down into the mind, for all power must be 'earthed' in some way, else it can do damage on the inner planes to the person concerned. The great concepts of 'The Cosmic Doctrine' and of our teaching must, to some extent, be brought down into the mind, and put into action also in the sphere of Earth. True wisdom lies in that.

In the Western Tradition the Power Aspect and the Devotional Aspect yield fruit which is gathered together and presented in the form of deep knowledge, great ideas and concepts that the Work brings forth in the minds of men - and must continue to bring forth in the minds of men - for its own sake as well as for theirs.

You should think of all great initiates of the past. How they lived out the Three Rays in their lives, how they suffered in their devotion to the work, how they used their great force for the work in order that teaching should be given to all, including yourselves. It is a matter for great gratitude on your part, and for a great realisation.

Think especially on this great concept of the Western Tradition, the concept of the Wisdom Tradition which has all these other qualities in it, all the great Power and Devotion and Wisdom.

You are units of the Group, and the Group lives, in a sense, in each one of the members that compose it. Each unit must bring its quota of the three great Aspects to the

Group, that your light may so shine before the world that the Western Tradition may come forth in public once again, on a far larger scale than we have been able to do before. This rests with each one of you. With the least of you and the greatest of you. With each one of you in different ways and in your different degrees.

Look round for the great god Hermes who bears the Staff of Wisdom before you and realise *within yourselves*, each one of you, that same great Staff with the two Serpents entwined. For to the Microcosm as well as to the Macrocosm applies that symbol of the Caduceus.

All of you should think on what has been said, that it may sink into the mind of each of you as a seed which grows and unfolds into a flower in time. You must understand how these vast ideas connected with this Work are very difficult to put into language. They have to incubate, so to speak, in the mind, and then come through into intellectual exposition. And it is in that period of dark growth, when you may feel you can grasp nothing and that you are learning nothing, that the seed is beginning to grow. And if you keep devotion and the power of will, the wisdom will come through that seed in due course, without fail.

MAGICAL KNOWLEDGE & THE BIBLE

The study of the Bible reveals a great deal of magical knowledge and development of occultism; even when only the Scriptures in the Authorised Version are considered.

It is very interesting that almost all the highest contacts were made on the tops of mountains. This is explained by the fact that the great spiritual power of the race of Israel worked largely in the upper air, the rarefied air of the highest mountains. Moreover the higher the mountain was climbed, the more certainty was there of great solitude and silence. And the mysticism of Israel was largely dependent on the contact with the Highest, made in complete solitude.

The Prophets lived very largely as hermits - solitary and lonely lives - and their mysticism and their prophecy mainly took the form of inspirational language. The breath, indeed, of the mountains impregnated by the Highest. Their prophecy came in a spate of inspired language when what they called 'the Spirit of God' was on them. There are many interesting instances of this.

For example, Moses was given the tremendous spiritual urge of prophecy when the enemy was attacking Israel. It was promised by God that he should not only have the full force of protective power for the people of Israel during this terrible time of battle, but that those with him should receive part of his spirit - that they should take on from him a large measure of the spiritual force which came down upon him, as much as they could bear and were able to receive.

That is a very interesting point, because it means that when a super-mystic is in a condition of especial clairvoyance, a certain amount of that spiritual faculty he exercises can pass from him, and influence in a lesser degree others who are with him, provided they are also clairvoyant.

Consider too the theory of witchcraft, which was condemned very greatly in Israel, for Israel had no belief in, or rather was not allowed to follow at all, the 'dark side' of the Goddess. It was the white side, the prophetic side, and not the other in which they believed. Therefore witchcraft and wizardry were violently condemned and punished with death.

By witchcraft was often meant, not what passed for it in later medieval days, but what we should nowadays call 'spiritualism', Such is shown in the history of the 'Witch of Endor' who was not necessarily a sorceress. Her 'familiar spirit' was probably some departed human being who helped her, and not necessarily a devil.

We find, also, various forms of magic used in the Bible. It was said that Moses was a Priest of Osiris. He had certainly been brought up in Egypt and trained in the Egyptian priesthood for a long time before he led Israel out of Egypt. And that he was able, by this added power given to him, to overcome with his magic the magic of the Egyptian priests.

And it is, if you regard it dispassionately, magic of a very definite type. He throws his staff down, and it becomes a snake. Was that a mere clever optical illusion? No. There was a very great deal of magical secret in that work. Physical particles do not change forms but etheric particles can change form when directed by a higher will. And the etheric part of the stick or staff will be strongly influenced to become a snake, and all who were there who were clairvoyant (and most people were in those days) observed the snake.

More wonderful and striking than the magical matters in the Old Testament are the amazing works of the Lord Jesus himself, and all that that great Master did. He raised the dead after they had been dead only a very short time. There is a magical feat by which those dead a very short time may be called back provided they have not gone too far, and this is what he did. He gauged the exact state that they were in, and saw that there was a possibility of calling them back, as with Lazarus and others.

There is the remarkable phenomenon of the gift of speaking in other tongues, by probably uneducated people. This was the great gift of Pentecost - the sudden rush of knowledge of another language, not hitherto mentally known. That, of course, is shown in what we now call 'spiritualism'. There are various cases in which quite uneducated people have spoken correctly in another tongue. There are, of course, cases in which it is an awakened memory of another life, but also it is a spiritualistic condition as well. And in the case of the Apostles who did this, it was what we should call a spiritualistic condition. There were those on the inner planes able to help them when they wished to address certain people in another language for the cause of the Lord, and the words poured mediumistically, through them.

But in general the great mystical and occult strength of Israel was the inspirational language which all the prophets had. A kind of ecstatic communion with God, in which very often literally speaking, prophecies of the future, which were all fulfilled, poured through them. All, as you see, of the 'white aspect' of Isis, though they would not have used that expression.

Now we may well ask is there, or was there, in the ordinary people, any kind of contact with Atlantis? There is at the beginning of Genesis evidence of the memories of Atlantean conditions, which came via Babylon. For it must not be forgotten that Abraham came out of Chaldea, and that the very early Jewish traditions were inherited from Chaldean memories, and transferred therefrom. There are references to the giants - the Atlantean people of terrific height. There are the references to the flood - to the great water, cataclysms of Atlantis. And under a single name such as Noah, Adam and the like, there is really a whole race described in the one word used.

It must be remembered with the various translations of the Bible, that there has been mishandling and 'correction' in order to bring the Bible into line with a preconceived doctrine, and in that way the sense of certain things has been lost. I refer particularly to the translation of many Hebrew words, meaning quite different things, by the one word 'Lord' for God, whereby has been obscured a great deal of teaching. When God is the Elohim, He is both male and female. When He is the Highest, the All-Father, (the Absolute as other Jews would call Him), Who is constantly referred to in the Old Testament, it is quite a different name, and it has quite a different significance. That is why biblical reading is so fall of pitfalls and difficulties and liable to cause misunderstanding in discussion.

There is no doubt that many things in the early part of the Old Testament were memories of Chaldean teaching - teachings of the stars, for instance.

In Reply to questions.

(1) Enoch was one of those very early members of the early Atlantean race, when men were scarcely developed in the way they are now physically. That is to say, when they were so largely etheric, and only just beginning to live on the Earth in the solid condition. That they were, as it were, half 'here' and half 'away' all the time. Enoch was certainly one of the earliest Atlantean-Lemurians.

(2) There were many different kinds of miracles performed by the Lord Jesus, He commanded, for example, unclean spirits to come out of people - such were cases of 'obsession' which often happened in Eastern and savage countries and which to this day are more frequent than in the West. He ordered in human language, but it was the directed Will behind which mattered. He willed the demoniac obsession to come out of the man.

He would also speak when he helped people. He spoke, as it were, to the diseased part itself. He really spoke to the etheric of the diseased part of the body. For example, if he were dealing with an ear, he would speak to the etheric part of the ear, and that etheric part 'heard' him and began to work, and naturally the physical parts of the body followed suit. Those are two examples.

(3) Elijah was really carried up etherically/astrally, and people often were so strongly aware of the astral and etheric happening (even as certain mystics are today) that they have compared them with a physical happening, which did not occur.

Conclusion. There are many other things that could be said on this subject, and many other matters which could be brought in, for the Bible contains everything within it if rightly understood and dispassionately considered and studied. But what I have said I hope may have given a certain amount of fresh interest in the study of the Bible; for when such a book is too much hammered into people, as it were, they are liable to be bored and leave it, or else become fanatical about it. If you can read it dispassionately as any other book, it is astonishing what it gives, whether you be a Christian or not.

SOUNDS AND LANGUAGE

Deep down in the subconscious mind of our race there is, far below the surface, an ancient tradition linking it up with Atlantean traditions. These traditions came direct to this land at one time - quite apart from all those which have also been adopted from other racial creeds and interwoven by later incoming races.

In Atlantean days there was a far more intricate knowledge and study of certain matters than is generally attributed to the Atlanteans, who were, of course, quite undeveloped as regards the human mind as we understand the term today. The ordinary consciousness of the 'man in the street' today was unknown to them. Nevertheless into such mind as they had, which is practically our subconscious mind, were instilled great forces which manifested as a kind of telepathic vision and knowledge.

For example, the wheel (which they knew in Atlantis) came from the visionary knowledge of such an implement impressed on the minds of the priests from beyond the Veil. Hence very great and strange feats took place in Atlantis, not exactly because the Atlanteans had remarkable intelligence, but because they had remarkable vision. This vision is now known as clairvoyance, but clairvoyance is a very poor imitation. The vision of the inner planes, the communing with the inner planes by the priesthood in Atlantis was advanced to a degree undreamed of in the greatest psychic powers known today.

Some of the things that came through in Atlantis from behind the Veil were the knowledge and vision of details connected with medicine, astrology, art, and above all, electricity. There has been no such knowledge of electricity since. Little by little the world has re-discovered certain elementary principles concerning electricity but the knowledge of electricity in Atlantis was far beyond what even the most advanced scientists know today. What amounted to electric power of a curious kind was used in moving large weights, in giving relief in sickness, and in producing sound, words, messages and many other things.

There was a notation of music which has not been approached in later ages. This notation, composed of 'electric notes' and vibrations was received by specially trained adepts and made into a system of musical tunes and mantra. Such tunes and mantra, could they be recovered, would provide material for notable achievements among musicians, but it would require a trained psychic to receive such notes or vibrations and bring them to the ordinary register of sounds.

You have now the register of sounds brought about by vibrations upon the human ear, or rather transmitted to the brain by the human ear. You would need something transmitted from beyond the ear and then translated into what the ear can accept. Certain notes are colossal wavelengths which could not be transcribed at all. All you could do would be to get their approximation. There is in the notation used in the world today nothing that could even suggest the great notes that Atlantis had.

There were certain instruments specially made to record some of these notes. They registered them, and then they were brought down a little further into the ordinary consciousness of the day, and transcribed by certain kinds of musical scoring which no longer exist. But these instruments of music were better able to reproduce the 'shadow' of these sounds than modern instruments. Some of these instruments in Atlantis were not intended for the human hand but for a certain type of electric mechanism.

Certain chants were, of course, used in ritual, and they were vibrated very strongly. The low notes and the high notes were vast sounds sometimes, and the human voice of that period was far more amenable than it now is. The vocal chords were slightly different, the larynx was hardly developed at all and the voice had a more flute-like quality.

There is impending upon the world today a new era. In it will be quite different forms of work and art and science, but a great deal more knowledge and power will be brought down from the higher planes. Some of the Atlantean music and science are gradually being rediscovered but by different means. Vibration is the foundation of all things and rhythmic sound allied to vibrations helps to beget everything that we know in the world of matter.

Far down in the depths of racial memory there lies a substratum drawn from the very same knowledge that fed Atlantis. Therefore it is very important to plumb the depths of the human being. Knowledge of music could be invaluable in this connection. When Orpheus had his wonderful Lyre which drew all the world to listen, it was not because he played some beautiful melody, but because he used some of the ancient knowledge of notes, and drew down from the atmosphere a great many overtones and quarter-notes and less, belonging to the higher planes - knowledge forgotten even then in early Greece.

Such notes sometimes stumbled upon by a musician will make a great difference in an atmosphere suddenly. They may make a great difference to some beast or reptile or bird; hence we say the creature is 'charmed'. But the truth is that the vibration on which the creature's basic nature is set has, as it were, been struck.

Harmony or discord in human life whether individual, racial or even international, can be brought about thus. When in a ritual the gavel is used, even very gently, it makes a great change in the atmosphere; the same when a gong is struck.

Naturally when psychic atmospheres are in question the sound on the physical plane must be low - not high or loud. The gong and the drum are percussion instruments of very great age. Savage tribes employ the drum when they work up into frenzy, and soldiers marching are led by it. The Chinese and other ancient races employ the gong - different arrangements of blows marking different occasions. The gong as well as the gavel is a very important astral accompaniment in ritual. Bells also were used in magic a great deal.

There are tremendous chords whose sounds have Elemental bodies. A tremendous note can be embodied in a shape. When Elemental music enters the consciousness it is really vibrations of entities moving and living their life. Those who are far beyond this world, remote from all the life around you, also live in the midst of mighty vibrations.

Far down in the subconscious many of the mighty notes of the Universe reverberate; they are Atlantean sounds reborn. Chanting more than singing often touches this subconscious depth; it has a mantric effect, hence the value of chanting in ritual and religious services.

In order to bring out the value of sound you must also remember the distinctions of language Words of the same meaning chanted in different languages have not the same effect - just as in the various pantheons, a god, equivalent perhaps to another god of another race, yet has differences; Apollo and Balder, for example, are not quite the same. Words sung in English, in Latin, in Greek, in French, may mean the same but their vibration is different. Hence when the Reformers insisted on using the common tongue instead of Latin they performed an occult act - they made religion racial. It is, of course, a moot point whether it should be so but that is not now being discussed.

Different languages make different calls upon the cosmic vibratory laws. Certain sounds in some languages will link up with certain cosmic vibrations better than other words in other languages meaning the same. We all know how when we want to be light-hearted and gay we think of French despite the many grave and solemn works that have been written in that tongue. English has an excellent effect in legal matters and common sense dictates and sport. It is forthright and yet not necessarily harsh; it is a language of those with the concrete mind. The French have not the same type of common sense and mental outlook as the English. They have far more meticulousness but no broad outlines as we have, so that they lose themselves at times in minor details; but their logic is admittedly very fine. Many magical things are better in dead languages or very ancient ones, for then vibrations touched the magical plane a great deal more. That is why any word remembered from Atlantis is so valuable in magic even if all the context is forgotten.

Chapter Four

Poetics

The Occult Side of Poetry

Published in the October 1939 issue of The Occult Review *under the pen name of H. O. Hamilton this article by Margaret Lumley Brown draws upon her experiences recounted in* Both Sides of the Door, *here characteristically describing herself in the third person. This experience of the power of chanting and repetition in poetry when recited aloud became a matter of continuing interest to her. It is referred to in her correspondence with Colonel Fawcett, which drew forth some of his own experiences of mantra (see his letter of October 12th 1924 on page 201)*

So far there has been very little study of the psychic effects of poetry though, like music, it seems to have had therapeutic results in certain cases. Just as music and colour can alleviate nervous difficulties, poetry also can have a harmonising power if the patient is sensitive to it – not, of course, otherwise. It reaches the emotions first through the mind and not through the outer senses, and therefore has naturally much less popular appeal than any other art. Music has been known to stop toothache, and I have known a poetic rhythm, insistently repeated, do the same, for when the etheric body is disorganised the repetition of certain verses will either stabilise it or – and this is important – greatly increase the trouble.

Some years ago this happened in the case of a woman 'sensitive' who had a great love of poetry and an unusual memory for it. During a psychic upheaval of the worst kind in a haunted house, she fell into a semi-trance, and for some hours steadily emitted, by recitation, probably all the poetry she had ever known. She chanted it in a curious way, and as she recited, the verses appeared to take shape in the air in front of her and in some cases before the eyes of people listening, the form coming first and the words filling in afterwards. The ballad's shape looked much like the Greek key-pattern and was quite unaffected by variety of sound or transposition of rhymes. The sonnet was held within one large and one small oblong square, interlaced, and subject to a recurring motion like a tide of ebbing and flowing geometric lines. When, by chance, the metre of the verse was broken, the effect on the medium's face and feelings was terrible. It was as though her whole personality disjointed itself with the verse.

Here I would remind people that poets themselves usually disagree entirely with the ordinary methods of verse recitation. These generally spoil the poetic form in order to give dramatic effect, or sacrifice the metre to the merely intellectual sense of the words. In the psychic case I have been speaking about, the meaning of the words undoubtedly had an influence on the medium, but the vowel sounds combined with the metre had even more. Thus, although Wilde's 'Sphinx' is written in the metre of Tennyson's 'In Memoriam', and the form itself was evidently beneficial:

> *O tell me were you standing by while Isis*
> *to Osiris knelt, And did you watch the*
> *Egyptian melt her union for Antony?*

was more strengthening, if less soothing, to the medium than:

> *The Danube to the Severn gave*
> *The darkened heart which beat no more;*
> *We laid him by the lonely shore*
> *And in the hearing of the wave.*

The medium found that Swinburne's anapaests were unsafe for her to say. They appeared in horizontal spirals with the energy of uprooting winds, and made her want to throw herself from the window, not with suicidal intention, but because the swing of sound was too great for the room to hold her.

The case of this medium helps to show the mantric power of verse, but it is interesting to find that poets themselves endorse aesthetically the semi-chant in which she recited while in trance. Tennyson is the best known example of this. He had an extraordinary method of declaiming poetry, chanting his words in such a peculiar manner that no one who had once heard could ever forget. Yeats also, who had strong views on the speaking of verses, has recorded of himself that: "Like every other poet, I spoke in a kind of chant when I was making them."

In short, one might say that the perfect speaking of poetry must include acting outside the sphere of drama and singing outside the sphere of music, and it certainly accounts for the almost universal failure of recitation, no matter how excellent the voice or choice or dramatic appeal of the reciter.

Undoubtedly, in early days, poetry was connected with prophecy and with religion. Apollo was the god of both poetry and prophecy, and the Delphic Oracle's words were delivered in an hypnotic chant. The Bards of ancient Britain were of a Druidic order. The Hebrew prophets thundered their curses and lamentations in some of the most magnificent poetic stanzas that exist. The Greek poets believed themselves to be definitely inspired by divine forces, and 'Sing, O Muse' was not a mere metaphor. Whatever name we like to give the powers behind inspiration, they certainly exist and can work today, though the present age may have no belief in them.

Rudolf Steiner said that poetry is drawn from a remembrance of the life between death and rebirth, and that it is inspired by some of the more remote spiritual beings. He spoke of each art as being pressed down into man's esoteric principles, or bodies, in descending scale from the principle immediately above. Thus poetry, which is, according to him, the highest art developed today, is pressed down into the Ego by the Higher Self; music, in its turn, is pressed down into the astral by the Ego, and so on.

Now, just as in the striking of notes of music some people are conscious of the presence of devas, so, during the reciting of poetry, beings of other planes have been known to intensify the vibrations and, as it were, 'pick up' the lines and continue them into space. I have heard of poets in the act of composition seeing waves and sheets of azure light, sometimes empty and sometimes with beings of various size and appearance moving in it. Blue, according to some occultists, is the colour of the cosmic current which surrounds the arts, though it is sometimes tinged with green or violet according to the type of production. Sappho, in a lovely line, speaks of 'the violet-weaving Muses'. On other occasions inspiration has come simultaneously with another sort of apparition.

William Sharp (Fiona Macleod) relates how when he was a child of seven years old he fainted and saw a white lady in the wood, standing in a mist of bluebells. She seemed to lift the blueness out of the flowers and thrown it at him, and she 'unlocked new doors in his mind and put him in touch with ancestral memories of his race.' Æ wrote a great deal about the subject and was as strongly conscious of the details of poetic inspiration as St. Theresa was of the details of religious vision. He said of one of his poems that it seemed like an oracle delivered to the waking self by some dweller or genie of the inner planes, and he mentions a vision of Angus Og (the Celtic Apollo) surrounded by his cloud of many-coloured birds appearing to Yeats when the latter was asleep out of doors.

Once, when I myself was in that sensitive condition between sleeping and waking, I saw a bearded man in long white robes like an adept of some kind, showing me three golden crowns. 'James II' were the only words I heard as I awoke. But during that day a short poem on James II evolved itself quite effortlessly in my mind. It mentioned the fact that James had lost three kingdoms for his Catholicism, and it was later published in the *Dublin Review*, not, I need hardly say, with any account of its unconventional origin!

The inspiration of actual words is not unusual. We all know of cases when someone has found that either in sleep or in automatic writing they have written down some verses, usually of indifferent literary value. But there are more exceptional cases, notably the writing of Coleridge's 'Kubla Khan'. The facts, according to Coleridge himself, were these. He had fallen asleep in his chair one afternoon from the effects of a drug, just as he had read the following sentence in 'Purchas's Pilgrimage': 'Here the Khan Kubla commanded a palace to be built and a stately garden thereunto, and thus ten miles of fertile ground were enclosed with a wall.' At this point Coleridge fell into a profound sleep which lasted about three hours, during which he was certain that he had composed between two and three hundred lines if, as he said, 'that indeed can be called composition in which all the images rose up before him with a parallel production of the correspondent expressions without any sensation or consciousness of effort.' On waking he had a clear recollection of the whole composition and instantly began to write it down, but being called away on business for an hour, he could remember nothing but a few scattered lines and images on his return. Hence the poem's shortness and fragmentary form.

Yeats' poem 'The Jester' was written down word for word after a dream, and its astral inspiration is unmistakable.

> *She opened the door and the window,*
> *And the heart and the soul came through;*
> *To her right hand came the red one,*
> *To her left hand came the blue.*

Æ's lovely and too little known 'Krishna' was got in sleep line by line from the inner planes, and its starry texture could surely only have come from there:

> *And yet He is the Chief among the*
> *Ever-Living Living Ones,*
> *The Ancient with eternal youth, the*
> *Cradle of the infant suns,*
> *The fiery Fountain of the stars and*
> *He the golden Urn where all*
> *The glittering spray of planets*
> *In their myriad beauty fall!*

William Sharp, while at Glastonbury one day, lay down at the east end of the abbey and, vaguely staring at the broken stones, was suddenly inspired with three unpremeditated lines:

> *From the Silence of Time, Time's Silence borrow.*
> *in the Heart of Today is the Word of Tomorrow.*
> *The Builders of Joy are the Children of Sorrow.*

If the origin of poetic images could be certain, what a new fund of knowledge one might have both esoterically and pathologically! Yeats once said, with regard to this subject, that images welled up before the poet's mind from a deeper source than conscious or subconscious memory.

Poetic images can sometimes be visible psychically. I know of someone who, shut in a room alone, murmured under her breath Gray's words on Pindar which are, according to Tennyson, the most melodious four lines in the whole of English poetry;

> *(Though he inherit)*
> *Nor the pride nor ample pinion*
> *Which the Theban eagle bear,*
> *Sailing with supreme dominion*
> *Through the azure depths of air.*

Outside the door, the two year old child of the house was discovered spreading out his arms like wings and jumping in the air. It was elicited that he was trying to copy 'a big bird which came through the door'.

Yeats related a strange story, apparently true, of a painter's image. I will insert it here, because, although it is forbidden to speak of one art in the terms of another aesthetically, occultly they overlap. A Japanese artist of remarkable genius painted some horses on a temple wall. The horses are said to have slipped down after dark and trampled the neighbours' fields of rice! Somebody coming to the temple in the early morning was startled by a shower or water drops on his head. Looking up, he saw the painted horses still wet from the dew covered fields and now 'trembling into stillness'.

Repeating poetry, for long, to oneself has an ecstatic effect on the subconscious. Some people become so hypnotised with the auto-declamation that they jump in the air and wave their arms with all the appearance of a drunkard. King David before the Ark and a Cambridge professor of recent times are good examples of this peculiar 'madness'.

There is a very interesting connection between poetry and wine. Reverence for wine as beverage, product and image seems to exist even in the most abstemious poet. Apollo and Dionysus were interchangeable deities, and art, in essence, cannot be puritanic, however regrettable this is to Puritans. Marlowe died in a tavern brawl, Swinburne wrote his best when drunk, Milton's spirit was about as far from his politics and creed as it could possibly be. Some years ago Isadora Duncan summed up this standpoint in her famous criticism of Americans: "They have taken the art out of life, the sex out of love, and the alcohol out of wine!" In any case, some spiritual quality analogous with intoxication is bound up with poetry. It shows in the eyes of every poet and is quite distinct from the glance of any other artist. Look at the eyes in the portraits of Keats, of Goethe and of Tasso – one can but say the spirit reels within another sphere.

Curiously enough, when persons have been aware of a Devic manifestation with regard to poetry, the Beings have sometimes shown a bewildering slantwise movement, so far as words can describe it. I believe that Steiner attributed the art itself to the inspiration of those remote Powers known as the Spirits of Motion.

The Litany of the Sun
The Poetry of Margaret Lumley Brown
Selected by Gareth Knight

A collection of Margaret Lumley Brown's poems was published in 1918 under the imprint of Erskine Macdonald and her pen name Irene Hay. It received encouraging reviews from *The Times Literary Supplement, The Spectator, The Scotsman, The Glasgow Herald, The Publishers' Circular, Library World* and *The Financial Chronicle.*

The title piece moved the reviewer in The Scotsman to protest that it read 'more like a triumphant hymn of sun worship than a litany', evidently feeling that its sentiments a little too strong for conventional religious sensibilities despite the quasi-religious use of the second person singular to address the (evidently Solar) deity:

The Litany to the Sun

Thou who standest at the portal
Of the Heaven's great highway,
Mortal Light of Light Immortal,
Take the prayers our hearts yet say;
Thou whose worship faileth never
From the Temple of the Day
And who wast and shalt be ever
Lord of Love and Life and Lay:
Strike again thy silent lyre
Through our dullness of desire,
Walk with us as once in Delos with
mysterious song and fire!

…and so on for another seven stanzas hymning of the Solar Logos.

However, the good reviewer seemed reassured by a 'more restrained exaltation of feeling' in the remaining pieces, and one called *Claverhouse,* written at the site of the battle of Killiecrankie, was one singled out as 'strongly as well as delicately touched and effective.'

John Graham of Claverhouse, (1649-89), Viscount Dundee, had firmly supported the Stuart cause in Scotland, and fought against King William III and won the Battle of Killiecrankie although he was mortally wounded in the fray. From the first stanza of the long poem it would seem that Margaret Lumley Brown had long felt a sympathy for this Jacobite hero. We know of her sensitivity to place memories and this occasion was possibly heightened by being written in 1914 when the whole of Europe was erupting into war.

CLAVERHOUSE
Killiecrankie Pass, 1914

Strange it is to stand above
Where you fell;
Hero of my childish love,
Take to-day this last farewell!

Age and reason look askance
On these things,
But once more the old romance
Wakens from the hills and sings.

In this soil the last hope lies
Of King James,
Where the harebells bluer rise
Out of unremembered names.

And continues to celebrate various events of his life until the last farewell of:

Still the Garry crashes down,
Running black,
And the misty mountains crown
All the battle's former track

Where the sable charger paced
Midst the whirl,
Rise your buff coat silver-laced
And your white face of a girl.

Conqueror who won in vain
Parting nears –
Take my message since this rain
Well may cleave two hundred years

With thin crystal swords in line
Unto you
Who were keen and cold and fine
As the rapier you drew!

The Scottish papers naturally welcomed poems with a Scottish element to them, and *The Glasgow Herald* in particular an *All Hallows Eve Toast* which it hailed as 'a bold variant on the old Jacobite toast – To the Kings across the water!' However, although Margaret Lumley Brown had very great sympathy for the Jacobite cause, and possibly died for it in a previous life, in fact this poem is addressed to a wider confraternity. It salutes all who have nobly served causes they have held dear, as was indicated by the rubric under the title

All Hallows Eve Toast
"Every man is born a king, and most people die in exile, like most kings."

To the kings across the water-
The Immortal River brink,
To the host self-led to slaughter,
Let us call this toast and drink!

To the shadowy flag-streamers
On the hidden shores unfurled
Over all the fools and dreamers
And the outcasts of the world!

To the soul that feared no censure,
And the life that feared no quest,
Till the last and high adventure
Lay achieved beyond the rest!

To the thief whose soul was juster
Than the law through which he died,
To the strength the weak can muster
When the mind is crucified!

To all those unseen, yet near us,
Who have led their souls in might
Down the darker paths to steer us
And the life that feared no quest,

> *To the kings across the water-*
> *The Immortal River brink,*
> *To the host self-led to slaughter,*
> *Let us call this toast and drink!*

However, more personal and more poignant I find the companion piece on *All Souls Eve*. She mentions in 'Both Sides of the Door' a lover who died. Could this be he?

ALL SOULS' EVE

> *I know that I shall meet you soon*
> *Without grief or fear,*
> *Between the dusk of night and noon*
> *When daylight is sere.*
>
> *The secret silver cord was loosed*
> *From out life's control,*
> *But now it has been freshly noosed*
> *To draw back your soul.*
>
> *The stinging scent of autumn bloom*
> *With haze-covered hue*
> *Pervades the dimness of the room*
> *In honour of you.*
>
> *Chrysanthemum perfume is rife*
> *With late-quickened mould –*
> *The resurrection and the life*
> *Of new out of old.*
>
> *I feel your voice beat with my heart,*
> *Your hand on my hair,*
> *You are around me and apart*
> *Like air within air.*
>
> *Your thoughts surge on me in a sea*
> *Of words left unsaid;*
> *I know so well you are with me*
> *And never were dead.*

And in the same tone we find *Absence,* which to my mind is the most moving poem that she wrote:

ABSENCE

To some are given many days
For love in earth's familiar ways;
To us the narrow house of dreams,
The undercurrent of the streams,
The wordless meaning of the phrase.

I may not find you in the years,
But where your absence still endears
The stronghold of the heart's defence,
The ecstasy of reticence,
The strange divinity of tears.

Oh! stretch your hands forth from afar
And draw me to you star by star;
Make all my mind articulate
With silences whose delicate
Still thoughts reach out where you are!

Mary, Queen of Scots, is a figure of considerable almost archetypal power as we have seen in one respect in the account in 'Both Sides of the Door'. Another of Margaret Lumley Brown's Scottish poems that attracted critical attention was one named *Chastelard to the Queen.* Pierre de Chastelard was a poet and highly romantic young courtier whom she had met at the French court when she had been married to the Dauphin. He followed her to Scotland and pressed himself upon her with such abandon that in the end he was brought to trial and sentenced to death on 22nd February 1563 which he awaits as the poem opens upon his last romantic thoughts

CHASTELARD TO THE QUEEN

It's a shining axe with a swift, sharp edge,
　　And the day is bright and keen,
For the penalty of a lover's pledge
　　And the pleasure of a Queen!
Will thine eyes turn unto me, Mary,
　　Or thine hand lie on the ledge?
For the mood of woman must vary
　　Lest her heart perchance be seen!

I was never one whom the Church could mesh
　　In the fears of sinners` lot,
If the grass grow over me green and fresh
　　I shall know that Hell is not.
Is the spirit whiter than flowers –
　　Is it fairer than the flesh?
Is a soul condemned by its powers?
　　I shall learn full soon, God wot!

Though the priest hath shriven all sins of mine
　　By the Lord upon the Tree,
Yet my soul is nailed to the fibres fine
　　That have raised the form of thee!
Is it not with grapes I am drunken
　　But the flower of the wine,
Through the fairer thing am I sunken
　　And may Christ forgive it me!

Now the wind, the sun, and the morning break
　　On the world as heretofore
And I go where sunrise nor mornings wake
　　And the winds will blow no more;
I shall lie afar from thy scorning
　　With the dreams no axe can shake,
But the wind, the sun and the morning
　　Shall entreat thy chamber door!

The figure of the romantic *femme fatale* seemed to attract Margaret Lumley Brown, as one might expect by one who had a particular feeling for Ishtar, Babylonian goddess of Venus. In *The Other Woman*, in the figure of Lilith she brings an almost metaphysical element to this. Heloise, incidentally, was another to whom she felt a great affiliation.

THE OTHER WOMAN

Eastward in Eden, musing, Lilith lay
And pondered on the world's eternal ban
Since Eve supplanted her beside the man;
For her nothing was changed and yet today
God's Footfall shone upon the lily spray
Within the Garden as when earth began;
Yet green and shrill the four great rivers ran
Beneath sword-flames which kept the world at bay.

Then Lilith looked upon the world and there
Marked well the hatred that could never cease
'Twixt Eve's daughters and those herself did bear,
And Lilith knew revenge and was at peace:
For lo, the names men gave her children were
Helen and Heloise and Beatrice!

And there is plainly a magical element that caused her to write a poem invoking the four quarters of the universe in *The Cap of Winds*:

THE CAP OF WINDS

[Eric, King of Sweden, who made the wind blow from any quarter to which he turned his cap.]

Behold me turning
My cap to the North,
With unleashed waves and churning
The waters rush forth
To the land where the ice-girdled peaks
Send their breath through the fir-forests swarth!

Behold me turning
My cap to the South,
And this soil which is yearning
With hardness and drouth
Is as moist as Arabian caves
With the touch of a distant sea's mouth!

Behold me turning
My cap to the East,
And with frighted discerning
Look mankind and beast
At the sun that the morn's ashen cup
Overturns at a black wizard's feast!

Behold me turning
My cap to the West,
And the light that is burning
The hill's highest crest
Coaches violet fire in the fjords
And the flowers smile on the snow's breast!

Four winds men know not
Within me are rife,
When the other winds blow not –
The cold rage of Strife,
The warm strength of all infinite Love,
Death's black blast and the fair force of Life!

The deepest magic in her poetry probably lies, however, in the Babylonian Fragments, which she elsewhere records as having come to her when she was very young, almost ready written, rather than needing composition.

A BALLAD OF BABYLONIAN FRAGMENTS

I
ISHTAR

She came as primal morning forth
And older than all sin,
The Queen of war throughout Her land
And every love therein.

In scarlet sheathed and forged within
The firmamental flame,
Her godhead was the guardian
Of that which hath no name.

For She in fullness of the earth
Did bear its full desire
From out its utmost depth of sea
Unto its inmost fire.

The red pomegranate of cool eve
Hung low behind Her ear
And in Her hand the mellow dawns
Fell burnished, gold and clear.

The morning and the evening star
Were sandals on Her feet;
The cord of life did string Her bow
To deadly things and sweet.

II
THE RIVER

From out the far Armenian caves
The green Euphrates swept
And down a thousand vales and hills
Its current poured and crept,

Until across the hot, pale plains
By Ishtar's courts it curled,
And thence into the Persian Gulf
Did sing her through the world.

III
THE KING

The King paced in his saffron robes
Where granite bulls were crouched;
Upon his head, with fangs of fire,
The dark male emeralds couched.

He vowed Her from the lion-hunt
That all his soul held dear
The comeliest sun-coloured beast
Which fell before his spear,

And veiled his face in front of Hers
Whose brightness none might dim,
For was he not the lord of all
But She the lord of him?

He was the Warrior of the World,
His galleys swept the seas,
He was the Firstborn of the Sun
And King of the Chaldees,

The Chieftain of Assyria
And all of Babylon,
Whose fame was spread from Crete to Tyre
And over Lebanon,

He brought ten thousand Hebrew slaves
Across the Syrian line;
And many mighty Arab lords
Did cede him corn and kine.

He built a blue mosaic house
Of symbols strange and old,
Where twenty thousand fighting men
Hung shields of beaten gold.

Around his ivory turret-room
Were tawny frescoes drawn,
And five fair casements fitly set
Did open on the dawn.

V
THE CITY

Amidst the hot, pale plains below
The green Euphrates wound
Through many miles of palm and vine
And arid desert ground.

Upon the banks on either side
Rose up into the sun,
With burnished tower and battlement,
The walls of Babylon.

And in and out through court and street
The river water fell
In rainbow jet and foaming fall
And ilex-girdled well.

A myriad spears did file behind
The captains of the host
And wingéd lions at the gates
Looked forth along the coast

Where curious and stately ships
Came sailing through the heat;
The painted masts of Persia and
The blazoned Indian fleet,

> The dark Arabian frigates came,
> Which bore perfumes and bales;
> And in the towered harbour moored
> By Ishtar's moon-like sails . . .

V
THE RIVER

> The dust and sand that once were bricks
> Float downward on the stream,
> And bubbles break upon its surf –
> The bubbles of a dream.
>
> Through many miles of palm and vine
> he green Euphrates falls
> Across the hot, pale plains above
> The sunken City walls.

And in a similar vein is her evocation of Atlantean traditions which, as she states in her article 'Scent of Atlantis' in Part Two, she felt a strong connection.

THE CORNISH SEA

> Beneath my room the water twists,
> Great flanks of foam and green:
> It writhes, a dragon of the mists,
> And coils the rocks between.
>
> But far away it changes hue,
> Where many fathoms press
> Upon the reef of nether blue,
> Which once was Lyonnesse.
>
> Across the night a triton horn
> Blows dream and sea-desire,
> Till in the first clear cold of morn
> The ships come in from Tyre.

Thin as moon-hazes are their sails,
Their masts are shadow-rods,
Their cargoes are forgotten tales
And fair, forsaken gods.

For here in Cornwall nature weaves
A garden strange and walled,
Where Ocean like a dragon heaves
His scales of emerald.

Her last word, however, as I am sure she would have wished, shall remain addressed to a cat, the one in question surely being Henry in the adventures of 'Both Sides of the Door.'

TO A GREY CAT

Silver cat with golden eyes,
Restive form of vital plush,
Surely some strange spirit sighs
In that body lithe and lush!

Evil lurks in your repose!
Some steel soul in velvet sheath
Hides behind your vibrant nose
And your deadly, pointed teeth.

All those wondrous, circling lines
On your breast and on your paws
Must be cabalistic signs
Traced by wicked heathen laws

That sepulchral resonance
Mellowed through your throbbing throat,
To a deep reverberance,
Is some lost archaic note.

Well I know you lay of yore
Languorous and leonine,
On the purple-paven floor
Of the temple's inmost shrine.

So perchance your padded tread,
Stealthy, stately, yet abashed,
Was some rite obscure and dread
Of the Secret House of Pasht.

Is it true your seeming play
Masks a strange and potent will –
That you go the Ancient Way
And the gods are with you still?

Acting ever, real to none,
Sacerdotal veiled in jest,
Slanting upward to the sun
Eyes where moons are manifest!

Appendix

A Letter to Margaret Lumley Brown from Arthur Conan Doyle.

WINDLESHAM
CROWBOROUGH,
SUSSEX

31 Oct. 1919.

Dear Miss Hay,

I was deeply interested both in your book & in your letter. It is a unique experience so far as I know. I have been at this subject 30 years & I have struck nothing of the kind. My publisher will send you my new book on the subject.

I have no sympathy with the diabolists because I look on Evil spirits as poor undeveloped souls

who need sympathy & help. But
you really seem to have got in contact
with something sub-human & elemental —
the D.T. section of the other world.
Prayer – intense prayer, and the invocation
of good spirits was your only sure
defence. I fancy those discs of
light were guardian spirits. Wilde
seems to have played up well. he
will get promotion for that, for even
to him it must have been pretty
awful. He would seem to be
pretty near the earth – Tyrrell the
clairvoyant described him accurately
as standing near me & gave the

message "I am happy with my wife, Constance." I had no notion of his wife's name, but I find now that it was Constance.

I should like to know if you have had any hauntings since. I should like also to meet your sister & you when the times are a little less strenuous.

Yours sincerely
Arthur Conan Doyle
ACD.

INDEX

Abraham, 218
Absolute, 219
Absence, 236-7
Adam, 218
Adepti, Inner Plane, 130
Adepts, 95, 127, 137, 168-169
Adepts of the Elements, 148, 151
Adonai, 142
Æ., see Russell, George
Aether of the Wise, 160
Ahriman, 156
Ahura Mazda, 156, 157
Air, Element of, 138, 148, 158-163
Akasha, 156, 171
Akashic records, 96
Alchemists, 203
Alexandria, 203, 209-211
Alice in Wonderland, 25
Allan-a-dale, 199
All-Father, 219
All Hallows eve, 146
All Hallows Eve Toast, 235
All Souls Eve, 236
Amazon, 10
America, ancient, 124
American Geographical Society, 15
Anapaests, 227
Ancient languages, 224
Ancient Mysteries, 137
Ancient Wisdom, 212, 213
Andersen, Hans Christian, 96
Angels, 103, 154, 163-170
  Of the Spheres, 170
Angus Og, 229
Animals, 45, 165
Annunciation, 171
Anubis, 177
Anyte of Tegea, 9

Aphrodite, 108, 109, 179
Apollo, 111, 131, 224, 227, 228, 231
Apostles, 218
Aquarian age, 137, 161
Aquarian circle, 198
Aquarian Grail, 207
Aquarian ideal, 153, 198
Aquarian initiate, 148
Aquarian level, 213
Aquarian plan, 151
Arabian Nights, The, 56
Archangels, 103, 158, 163-174
  Of healing, 173-174
  Of the Spheres, 170-174
  Of the Temple, 172
Archbishop of Westminster, 77
Archduke Maximilian, 91
Archetypal Feminine, 198
Arch Pythoness, 1
Ark of the Covenant, 231
Armistice, 87
Armorica, 196
Art, 138, 164, 231
Arthurian Formula, The, 158, 160
Arthurian legends, 111
Arthurian pattern, 152
Ascended Masters, 130
Ascension, 87
Asclepios, 109, 120
Ashtoreth, 179
Asia Minor, 154
Astral body, 135
Astral plane, 34, 114, 125, 209
Astronomy, 154
Athens, 100
Atlantis, 10-14, 124-129, 142, 150, 153-158 passim, 193-197, 204-205, 209, 213, 218, 219, 220-224, 244

Aton, 211
Auphanim, 154
Authorised Version, 216
Automatic writing, 30-31, 32-37, 65
Avalon, 205, 208
Avatar, 155
Avenging Angel, 173
Aztecs, 124
Azure, 228

Babylon, 9, 155, 218, 238
Babylonian Fragments, 9, 240-244
Balder, 224
Ballad form, 67, 226
Bannockburn, Battle of, 112
Bards, 227
Bayswater, 7
Bayswater Road, 26
Bean sidhe, 91, 128
Beauty, 212
Bells, 223
Bemerside, 112-113
Berkshire, 124
Besant, Mrs. 122
Bethesda, Pool of, 101
Bethlehem, Star of, 155
Bible, 101, 205, 216-220
Binah, 150, 158, 172, 202
Birnam wood, 112
Black serpent, 212
Blackwood, Algernon, 8
Blake, William, 107
Blithe Spirit, 3
Bluebells, 228
Blue Ray, 228
Boat of Ra, 179
Bond, Bligh, 14
Book of the Dead, Egyptian, 176
Bookman, The, 82
Both Sides of the Door, 4, 8, 20-64, 65, 71, 225, 236, 237, 244

Brazil, 16
Britain, 104, 153, 155, 195, 206, 209, 227
Britons, 153
Brittany, 128, 196
Brownies, 92
Bruce, Robert, 110
Bunyan, John, 131
Butler, W.E., 72

Caduceus, 212, 215
Calvary, 34
Cambridge professor, 231
Canada, 101
Candlemass, 146
Cap of Winds, The, 239-241
Cardinal points, 158, 167
Carmelite, 109
Cattle, 181
Caucasus, 11
Celtic Group-soul, 104
Celtic symbols, 116
Celts, 90, 91, 92, 101, 141
Centaurs, 99-100
Ceremonial magic, 109-110
Chakras, 123
Chaldea, 155, 195, 218, 219
Chanson, 39
Chanting, 64, 222, 224, 227
Chapel of the Grail, 205, 208
Charon, 32-37, 43-47, 51-52, 65
  See also Wilde, Oscar
Chastelard, Pierre de, 237
Chastelard to the Queen, 237-238
Chesed, 172
China, 123, 155, 223
Chokmah, 158, 172
Christ, 33, 116, 122, 155, 156
Christian era, 116, 117, 136
Christian Grail, 152
Christianity, 33, 101, 155, 158, 207-208
Christian Mysteries, 209

INDEX

Church of the Grail, 208
Circuit of force, 152
Clairvoyance, 15, 46, 72, 104-107, 127
Claverhouse, 233-234
Coleridge, 229
Company of Avalon, 205
Conan Doyle, Sir Arthur, 71
Concreter of Seven Spheres, 178
Connaught Mansions, 65
Copper, 109
Cornish Sea, The, 244
Cornwall, 92, 94, 128, 140, 196, 197
Correspondences, 12
Cosmic archetypes, 172
Cosmic Christ, 207
Cosmic Doctrine, The, 186, 213-214
Cosmic forces, 168
Cosmic vibratory laws, 224
Cosmos, 194
Coward, Noel, 3
Coué, 107-108
Creation, 208
Creator of the World, 157
Cretan forms, 123
Cross, sign of the, 56, 62
Crowley, Aleiter, 105
Crusades, 155, 199-200
Cummins, Geraldine, 16
Cup, 206
Cybele, 103
Cycle of Creation, 154

Daath-Yesod circuit, 183
Damascus, 204
Dana, 92, 103
Dancing, 138, 141
Daughter, Mysteries of the, 187-193 passim
Daughter Goddess, 189
Dauphin, 237

Dauphiness, 25
David, King, 231
Dead languages, 224
Dead Sea, 200
Death, 165
Delirium tremens, 62, 63
Delphic Club, 72
Delphic Oracle, 111, 135, 2227
Delville, Jean, 104
Demeter, 103, 187-193
Demoniac obsession, 219
Devas, 89, 94, 128, 141, 142, 164-165, 170, 232
Devic force, 164
Devon, 197
Devotion, 211, 215
Devotional Aspect, 214
Dionysian force, 135
Dionysus, 99, 209, 231
Discs of light, 43, 49, 69, 120
Disk of the Sun in his Boat, 179-180
Divine Right of Kings, 127
Doctors, 40, 50
Dominions, 103
Dorking, 81
Dozmary Pool, 94
Drama, 164
Drama, Greek, 103
Dreams, 73-89
　Clear, 74-75
　Realistic, 80-84
　Symbolic, 76-80
　Transcendental, 84-89
Druids, 124, 153, 155, 195, 227
Drum, 223
Dryads, 99, 140
Dryburgh, 111
Dublin Review, The, 229
Duff tartan, 77
Duke of Fife, 77
Duncan, Isadora, 232
Dunsinane, 112

Ear, 220
Earl of Huntingdon, 198
Earl of March, 110, 116
Earlston, 110, 113, 117
Earth, 174, 192, 213, 219
Earth, Element of, 138, 148, 152, 159, 163
Earth forces, 135, 136, 179
Earth Mysteries, 210
Eastern countries, 219
Edgware Road, 23, 25
Edinburgh, 110
Edward, 21, 56, 60, 69
Edward I, 110
Ego, 228
Egypt, 14, 103, 104, 207, 209, 217
Egyptian forces, 120
Egyptian pantheon, 174-183
Egyptian priesthood, 217
Eildon Hills, 110, 115, 116
Elder-Tree Mother, The, 96
Electricity, 47, 69, 221
Elemental Creatures, 152
Elemental Cross, 140
Elemental forces, 105, 144, 152
Elemental Kingdoms, 116, 145
Elemental Kings, 139, 145, 168
Elemental music, 223
Elemental Other World, 89-110
Elementals, 70, 102, 133, 137163' passim, 164, 168
Elemental Tides, 148
Eleusis, Mysteries of, 187-193
Elfland, 115, 116
Elijah, 220
Elisha, 202, 205
Elohim, 219
Emanations of God, 173
Empress Elizabeth of Austria, 91
England, 197
English language, 224

Enoch, 219
Epidaurus, 109
Equinoxes, 136
Eric, King of Sweden, 239
Eros, 106
Erskine Macdonald, 9, 232
Esoteric geography, 124
Essenes, 199, 201-205, 209
Essential Self, 122
Eternal Fire, 156
Etheric, 217, 219, 220
Etheric body, 123, 226
Evil, 156
Evil Genius, 128
Evil spirits, 119
Excalibur, 94
Exeter, 15

Faeries, 157
Faery alchemy, 152, 160, 162
Faery contacts, 160
Faery Song, A, 143
Fairyland, 115, 116
Fairy Queen, 110, 114-116
Fairy Tree, 113
Faith, 122
Familiar spirit, 217
Fate, 180
Fate of Colonel Fawcett, The, 16-17
Father of MLB, 4-5, 55
Fawns, 99
Fawcett, Brian, 16
Fawcett, Colonel P.H., 10-17, 225
Fawcett, John, 15
Fawcett, Nina, 15-16
Feminine power, 202
Femme fatale, 238
Fielding & Collins, 1
Financial Chronicle, The, 9, 232
Fire, 153-158
Fire, Element of, 148, 153-158, 159, 163

INDEX

Fire Race, 157
First World War, 113
Flaming Wheels, 154, 157
Flash of light, 47
Flood, 218
Flowers, 63, 69, 94, 97-8, 158
Forest Order, 199
Fortune, Dion, 1, 14, 17, 158-159, 170
Fountain fairies, 141
France, 102, 206
Frankincense, 158
Fraternity of the Inner Light, 135
French court, 237
French language, 224
Friar Tuck, 199
Fustiness, 22, 63, 66, 71
Fyvie Wood, 112

Gabriel, 166, 169-170, 171
Galawater, 110
Gambling, 58
Gardiner, Colonel, 78
Gavel, 223
Geburah, 173
Gems, 36
Genesis, 218
Genetics, 126
George III, 4
Germany, 82, 206
Gethsemane, 34
Ghoulish/grotesque figures, 43, 44, 47, 51, 57, 66
Giants, 158
Glasgow Herald, The, 9, 232, 234
Glastonbury, 10, 14, 99, 149, 158, 159, 230
    Chalice Hill, 149
    Chalice Orchard, 158
    Chalice Well, 149-50, 159
    Tor, 149, 159
    Wearyall Hill, 159
Gnostics, 203, 209-211

God Himself, 157
God, 158
Goddess, dark side of, 217
Gods, 102-110, 130, 134
Goethe, 232
Golden Dawn, 158
Golden Gates, City of the, 128, 193
Gong, 223
Good, 156
Gordons of Gight, 91
Gow, David, 72
Graham, John, 233
Grail, 155, 157, 197, 203, 205-211 passim
Graves' disease, 83-4
Gray, Thomas, 231
Great Banquet, 204
Great Goddess, 114
Great Lodges, 11
Great Mother, 122, 161, 195
Great Names, 204
Great White Lodge, 172
Greece, 100, 109, 131, 156, 207, 223
Greek key-pattern, 226
Greek language, 224
Greek forms, 106
Greeks, 90, 99, 209
Green Master, 183
Green Ray, 183-187, 197, 211, 212
Gremlins, 102
Grimm, Brothers, 96
Group entity, 90
Group Soul, 119, 164, 165, 183, 185-186

Hades, 115-116
Haggard, Rider, 10
Haig, Field Marshal, 113
Haigs of Bermerside, 113
Hamilton, H.O., 64, 225

Hampstead Heath, 43
Hapsburg, House of, 91
Hapsburg ravens, 90
Harmony, 223
Hathor, 178-183
Haunted house, 18, 20-72 *passim*
Hawthorn, 113
Hay, Irene, 4, 8, 18, 232
Hebrew prophets, 117
Healing, 101, 117-123
Healing magnetism, 123
Heat, 47, 57, 69
Heather, 158
Hebrew words, 219
Hell, 35, 115-116
Hellas, 184
　Earth Mysteries of, 187-193 *passim*
Heloise, 239
Henley, W.E., 82
Henry, 21, 28, 56, 60, 69, 244
Herd of Heaven, 181
Hermes, 104, 106, 178, 212-215
Hermetic Ray, 213
Herne the Hunter, 104
Herons of Gight, 90
Hieroglyphs, 177
Higher Intelligences, 133
Higher Self, 132, 134, 149, 160, 162, 228
Highest, 219
Hilarion, 148
Hod, 173
Holy Grail, see Grail
Holy Land, 199
Holy Living Creatures, Four, 162
Horus, 175-178
Hosea, 202, 205
Hyde Park, 41
Hysteria, 46-47, 49, 50

Illumination, 214
Imhotep, 120

India, 107, 155
Indians, South American, 15
Initiates, 193
Initiation, 131
In Memoriam, 226
Inner Planes, 201
Inner Temple, 202
Innes, Brodie, 98
Innisfree, 90
Intellect, 212
Intentions, 79
International Psychic Gazette, The, 71
Ireland, 144, 196
Irish, 107
Ishtar, 238
Isiac force, 131
Isis, 173-178 passim, 181, 188, 218
Islam, 200
Israel, 216-220 *passim*
Israel, Secret Tradition of, 201, 204
Israel, Temple of, 196
Italy, 206

Jacobite, cause, 235
Jacobite rising, 78
James II, 229
James VI of Scotland, 112
Japanese artist, 231
Jester, The, 230
Jerusalem, 34, 204
Jesus of Nazareth, 201, 203
Jesus the Christ, 209
Jewish mysticism, 164, 166, 173
Jewish traditions, 218
Joan of Arc, 198
Josephine, 27
Joseph of Arimathea, 99
Judaic tradition, 200

"Kathleen Trent", 19, 20-64

INDEX

Keats, 232
Kelpie, 100
Kephera, 177
Kerry Mountains, 128
Kether, 158, 172
Killiecrankie, 233
King Arthur, 94, 126, 152, 205
King, Robert, 72
   See also "Merton"
Knight, Gareth, 159, 170
Knockers, 92
Kore, 189, 192
Krishna, 230
Kubla Khan, 229

Lady of the Lake, 152
Lance, 206
Land-Under-Waves, 124
Land's End, 128
Language, 67-69, 220-232
Larynx, 222
Latin, 224
Lazarus, 218
Leaderhaughs, 110
Learmont, Thomas, see Thomas the Rhymer
Left Hand Path, 120
Leicestershire, 83
Lemuria, 156, 219
Le Panneau, 80
Leprechauns, 92
Les Ballons, 80
Lesser Mysteries, 136
Liberal Catholic Church, 72
Library World, 9, 232
Life of the Earth, Mysteries of, 188
Light, 153, 156
Light, 71, 72
Lilith, 238
Lion, 209
Litany of the Sun, The, 4, 9, 232, 233

Little John, 199
Little People, the, 148
Living Fire, 105
London blitz, 108
London, City of, 7
Lord Jesus, 152, 206, 211, 217, 219
Lordly Ones, 114
Lord of Dreams, 171
Lord of the Elemental Nature, 153
Lord of the Four Elements, 170
Lord of the Personality, 153
Lord of Truth, 105
Lourdes, 101, 120-122
Lottery, 83
Love, 211
Lyonnesse, 128
Lyre of Orpheus, 104, 184-185, 223

Macbeth, 112
Macleod, Fiona, see Sharp, William
Macrocosm, 215
Madame Arcati, 3
Magi, 153-157
Magical knowledge, 216-220
Magicians, 137, 144
Maid Marian, 198
Maida Vale, 8
Malkuth, 170
Mantra, 67, 221, 224, 225
Manus, 153, 202
Marble Arch, 4, 25, 31, 43, 65
Mark the Evangelist, 209
Marlowe, 232
Marriage of Heaven and Earth, 183
Mars, 108
Martial force, 179
Mary, Queen of Scots, 24, 25, 28, 54, 60, 237

Master Magician, 148
Master of Knowledge, 212
Master of Masters, 152
Master of the Temple, 202
Masters, 130, 134, 148, 165
May day eve, 146
Melchizedek, 203-205, 206
Melrose, 110
Mercury, 104
Merlin, 104, 111, 126, 152, 153
"Merton", 57-59
    see also King, Robert
Mesopotamia, 195
Messire de Boduel, 54
Metatron, 172
Metre, 226
Mexico, 91, 124
Mexico, Gulf of, 128
Michael, 166, 167, 168, 173
Microcosm, 215
Middle Pillar, 172
Midsummer Night's Eve, 55
Milk of Paradise, 36
Milton, 232
Mithra, 156
Montreal, 101
Montsalvat, 205, 208
Moon, 169-170, 179, 192
Moon consciousness, 171
Moonlight, 145
Morgan, 17
Morgan le Fay, 152
Moses, 216-217
Mother, Mysteries of the, 187-193
    passim
Mother of Birth, 194
Mother of Death, 194
Mother of MLB, 4-7, 55-56
Mountain of the West, 180
Mount Carmel, 202, 205
Murder, 58
Muse, 227

Music, 138, 142, 221, 224
Myrrh, 158
Mystery language, 210
Mystical Qabalah, The, 170
Mystic Announcer, 171
Mystic Cults, 172

Naiads, 99
Napoleon, 27, 46
Narada, 153
National Angels, 164
Nature Beings, 164
Nature forces, 139, 156, 183
Nature mystic, 137, 148
Nature spirits, 93-102, 134
Negative Force, 178
Netzach, 140, 161, 173, 183
New Age, 155
New Dimensions, 2, 73
New Thought, 65
New Year's Eve, 146
New Zealand, 15
Nixie of the Millpond, The, 96
Nixies, 145
Noah, 218
Non-human entities, 135
Normans, 197
Norsemen, 92, 197
Northamptonshire, 4
Northern England, 197
Nostradamus, 117
Notting Hill Gate, 7

Obsession, 46, 64, 66, 219
Occult communities, 10, 11
Occult Hierarchy, 10, 11
Occult Review, The, 10, 64, 73, 225
Occult Side of Poetry, The, 64
Odin, 104
Ogilvies, 95
Old French, 54
Old Testament, 217, 219

INDEX 259

Om, Ohm, 12
One God, 103
Opium, 53, 58, 69
Orion, 32
Orpheus, 104, 183-187, 223
Orphic myths/philosophy, 184
Orphic Path, 185
Osiris, 111, 173-178 passim, 186, 188, 195, 209, 217
Ostend, 56
Other Woman, The, 238-9
Ouija board, 125, 128, 129
Our Lady, 101
Outer Greater Mysteries, 194
Overlords of Hell, 116
Oversouls, 96, 101, 140, 145, 150
Ovid, 5, 9
Oxford Street, 31

Pagan times, 136
Palestine, 155, 199
Palomides, 157
Pan, 99, 105-106, 138, 199
Past Incarnations, 134
Paul of Tarsus, 203, 204
Pecksniff, 95
Pentecost, 218
Perceval, 157
Persephone, 103, 114, 115, 179, 192-193
Persephone in Hades, 30
Persia, 153-157
Personality, 149, 153
Peters, Vont, 13
Pharaoh, 211
Pillars of Glory, 172
Pilgrim's Progress, 131
Pindar, 231
Pine-cone, 212
Pipes of Pan, 138
Pisces, 155
Piskies, 92
Pixies, 140

Place memories, 3, 18
Plantagenets, 197
Pleiades, 32
Pluto, 189
Poltergeist phenomena, 37, 46, 48, 50, 66, 69, 70-71
Poetic forms, 67
Poetry, 32, 33, 46, 67-69, 164, 225-246
Points of flame, 44
Post-mortem condition, 34-35
Powell, Ellis T., 71
Power, 211, 212, 215
Power Aspect, 214
Power Ray, 212
Powers, 103
Practical Guide to Qabalistic Symbolism, A, 170
Prana, 118
Prestonpans, 78
Priest of Osiris, 217
Primal Fire, 155
Prince of the Grail, 207
Prince of the Sun, 157
Principalities, 103
Prophets, 218
Publishers' Circular, The, 9, 232
Puritans, 232
Psychical research, 72
Psychic, as an abused term, 19
Psychic disturbances, 18-72 *passim*, 119
Psychic experiments, 18
Psychic phenomena, 34
Psychic Upheaval, A, 64-71
Psychological devices, 107-109
Psychometry, 58, 70, 72
Purchas's Pilgrimage, 229
Purple Ray, 211
Pythagoras, 184
Pythian power, 130-137

Qabalah, 124, 200

Quarter tones, 53
Queen of Elfland, 111, 114-116
Queensborough Terrace, 17
Quest of the Grail, 206
Quiberon, 128

Ra, 177, 179
Rakoczi, 148
Raising the dead, 217
Raphael, 117-118, 166, 172, 173-174
Realisation, 211-213
Recitation, 226, 227
Redeemers, 118
Red Indians, 90, 101
Reformation, 197, 224
Religion racial, 224
Religious services, 224
Renaissance, 125
Resurrection, 116
Rhombus, 154
Rhythm, 226
Richard I, 199
Richmond Green, 124, 128
"Ricks", 37-38, 48-63 passim
Righteousness, road to, 115
Rimell, Raleigh, 15
Ring Chaos, 160
Rio de Janeiro, 14
Rite of Nature, 142
Ritual, 222, 224
Rivers, 100-101
    Avon, 101
    Boyne, 101
    Highland, 100
    Huntly Burn, 113
    Pawsayle Burn, 112
    Severn, 101
    St. Lawrence, 101
    Thames, 100
    Tiber, 100
    Till, 101
    Tweed, 110, 111-112

Robin Hood, 197-199
Roman Catholic Church, 33, 77, 196, 229
Roman Empire, 156
Romans, 99
Rome, 104, 156
Root of Water, 150
Root Race, Fifth, 155
Rose of all the World, 139
Rose of Life, 142
Roses, 79, 85, 98
Rosicrucian, 204
Round Table, 202
Royal Geographical Society, 15
Russell, George, 107, 228, 230
Russians, 90
Ruta, 153, 193, 195
"Ruth", 8, 19, 20-64 passim
Rhymer's Tower, 113

Sacrificed gods, 118, 158
Sacrificed Daughter, 192
Sacrificed Maiden, 189, 192
Saladin, 199
Sandalphon, 170-171
San Francisco, 15
Sappho, 9, 228
Satyrs, 99
Savage countries, 219
Savage tribes, 223
Saxon, 122, 197
Saxon Royal House, 104
Scandinavian, 90, 108
Scarabs, 79
Scatcherd, Miss, 72
Scilly Isles, 128
Scotland, 92, 112, 113, 116, 144, 237
Scots faeryland, 9
Scotsman, The, 9, 232
Scottish families, 110
Scottish Lowlands, 111
Sea Cult, 193-197

INDEX

Sea System, 197
Secret Tradition in Arthurian Legend, The, 159
Sephiroth, 170-174
Sept, 179, 181
Serpent of Wisdom, 212
Sex, 161
Shah of Persia, 56
Shakespeare, 112
Sharp, William, 107, 229, 230
Sherwood, 199
Side Pillars, 172
Silenus, 99
Silver Cup, 152
Sister of MLB, 6, 8, 70
    See also "Theo Trent"
Snake, 217
Society of the Inner Light, 1, 2, 3, 17, 130, 170
Soho, 21
Solar disc, 211
Solar festivals, 136
Solar Fire, 156
Solar Logos, 233
Solar power, 179, 195
Solar system, 197
Solomon, 195
Solstices, 136, 149
Somerset, 197
Sonnet form, 67, 226
Sounds, 12-13, 67-69, 220-232
Sothis, 179, 182
South America, 14
Space, 193
Spain, 206
Spatial Air, 160
Speaking with tongues, 218
Spectator, The, 9, 232
Sphere of Manifestation, 184
Sphinx, 226
Spirit, 212
Spirit of God, 216
Spirit of Living Fire, 158
Spirit of the Atom, 170
Spirits of Motion, 232
Spiritualism, 14, 27, 40, 65, 119, 217, 218
St. Jude, 125
St. Michael, 94
St. Michael's Mount, 94
St. Theresa of Avila, 228
St. Therese of Lisieux, 109
St. Winifred's Well, 101, 141
Staff of Power, 212
Staff of Wisdom, 215
Stars, teachings of, 219
Stead, W.T., 31, 34
Steiner, Rudolf, 123, 228, 232
Stellar forces, 203
Stellar System, 197
Stockwell, Arthur H., 19
Stone, 206
Stopes, Dr Marie, 10
Story of Dion Fortune, The, 1
Stuart, House of, 9, 128
Subconscious, 40, 220, 224, 231
Summer Solstice, 17
Sun, 156, 174
Sun behind the Sun, 210
Sunday Dispatch, The, 15
Sun force, 136
Sun Temple, 194, 196
Sun worship, 193-197
Supernals, 158
Supreme Table, 204
Swinburne, 46, 227, 232
Sword, 206
Sybils, 135
Symbols, religious, 61, 70
Symphony in Yellow, 80
Syria, 179, 199, 201, 206

Table of Melchizedek, 204
Table of Merlin, 204
Table turning, 28, 50, 65

Tannhauser, 99
Tasso, 232
Teaching Fraternities, 125
Telepathy, 16
Television experience, 16
Templars, 199, 202, 203, 209
Temple of Jerusalem, 202
Temple of the Grail, 208
Temple of the Sun, 153
Temple Sleep, 131
Teneriffe, 128
Tennyson, 226, 227, 231
Teutonic tribes, 104
Theban Hills, 181, 182
Thebes, 178
Theosophy, 14, 28, 33, 65, 72, 94, 104, 120, 121, 122
"Theo Trent", 19, 20-64 *passim*
Thirteenth Path, 183
Thomas the Rhymer, 91, 110-117
Thomas of Erceldoune, see Thomas the Rhymer
Thoth, 104, 105
Thrace, 184
Three Rays, 215
Thrones, 103
Tide of Destruction, 149
Tide of Purgation, 149
Tides, Elemental, 148
Times Literary Supplement, The, 9, 232
Tiphareth, 158, 172
To a Grey Cat, 245-6
Tobias, 166
To Lais, 30
Toltecs, 124
Toothache, 225
Tranchell-Hayes, Maiya, 158
Tree of Life, 118, 133, 140, 170-174, 183, 200, 204
Trees, 97
Trinity, Name of the, 62, 70, 120

True Thomas, see Thomas the Rhymer
Tuatha da Danaan, 92
Tudor, 197
Tunis, 15
Turner, 113
Tyburn, 25, 58, 65, 120
Tyre, 195

Under-Earth forces, 131
Understanding, 211-213
Underworld, 179, 213
Universe, 204
Urwelt, 89-110

Valkyrie, 108
Veil, 221
Venus, 109, 110, 173, 238
Vibrations, 221
Villanelle form, 67
Virgin Mary, 114, 125, 171
Viscount Dundee, 233
Vision, 169
Vision of the Grail, 206
Voice production, 26-27
Vowel sounds, 67-69, 226

Wales, 92, 93, 101, 196, 197
Wallace, William, 110
Water, Element of, 146, 148-153, 159, 163
Water forces, 135
Water Tide, 149
Weather, 102
Weigher of Hearts, 105
Wesley, Charles, 117
Western Tradition, 204, 215
Wheel, 154, 221
Whitby, 81
White bull, 78
White cow, 180
White Emperor, 127
White serpent, 212
Wickedness, road to, 115

Wilde, Oscar, 65, 79, 226
  See also Charon
William of Orange, 112, 233
Will Scarlet, 199
Wine, 231
Wisdom Aspect, 211-216
Wise Men, 158
Witchcraft, 217
Witch cult, 113
Witches coven, 104
Witch of Endor, 217
Withdrawn Temple, 193, 194, 196
Wizardry, 217
Woden, 104
Words, 36
Wotan, 104

Yarrow, 110
Yeats, W.B., 107, 143, 227, 230, 231
Yesod, 172
Ys, 128, 196

Zeus, 213
Zeppelin, 84
Zoroaster, 153, 158

Other titles from Thoth Publications

AN INTRODUCTION TO RITUAL MAGIC
By Dion Fortune & Gareth Knight

At the time this was something of a unique event in esoteric publishing - a new book by the legendary Dion Fortune. Especially with its teachings on the theory and practice of ritual or ceremonial magic, by one who, like the heroine of two of her other novels, was undoubtedly "a mistress of that art".

In this work Dion Fortune deals in successive chapters with Types of Mind Working; Mind Training; The Use of Ritual; Psychic Perception; Ritual Initiation; The Reality of the Subtle Planes; Focusing the Magic Mirror; Channelling the Forces; The Form of the Ceremony; and The Purpose of Magic - with appendices on Talisman Magic and Astral Forms.

Each chapter is supplemented and expanded by a companion chapter on the same subject by Gareth Knight. In Dion Fortune's day the conventions of occult secrecy prevented her from being too explicit on the practical details of magic, except in works of fiction. These veils of secrecy having now been drawn back, Gareth Knight has taken the opportunity to fill in much practical information that Dion Fortune might well have included had she been writing today.

In short, in this unique collaboration of two magical practitioners and teachers, we are presented with a valuable and up-to-date text on the practice of ritual or ceremonial magic "as it is". That is to say, as a practical, spiritual, and psychic discipline, far removed from the lurid superstition and speculation that are the hall mark of its treatment in sensational journalism and channels of popular entertainment.

ISBN 978-1870450263

PRACTICAL OCCULTISM
By Dion Fortune supplemented by Gareth Knight

This book contains the complete text of Dion Fortune's *Practical Occultism in Dialy Life* which she wrote to explain, simply and practically, enough of the occult doctrines and methods to enable any reasonably intelligent and well balanced person to make practical use of them in the circumstances of daily life. She gives sound advice on remembering past incarntions, working out karma, disination, the use and abuse of mind power and much more.

Gareth Knight has delved into the Dion Fortune archive to provide additional material not available before outside Dion Fortune's immediate circle. It includes instruction on astral magic, the discipline of the mysteries, inner plane commmunicators, black magic and mental trespassing, nature contracts and elemental shrines.

In addition, Dion Fortune's review of *The Literature of Illuminism* describes the books she found most useful in her own quest, ranging from books for beginners to those on initiation, Qabalah, occult fiction, the old gods of England, Atlantis, wirchcraft and yoga. In conclusion there is an interpretation by Dion Fortune's close friend Netta Fornario of *The Imortal Hour*, that haunting work of faery magic by Fiona Macleod, first performed at Glasonbury.

ISBN 978-1870450478

SPIRITUALISM AND OCCULTISM
By Dion Fortune with commentary edited by Gareth Knight

As well as being an accultist of the first rank, Dion Fortune was an accomplished medium. Thus she is able to explain the methods, technicalities and practical problems of trance mediumship from first hand experience. She describes exactly what it feels like to go into trance and the different types of being one may meet with beyond the usual spirit guides.

For most of her life her mediumistic abilities were known only to her immediate circle until, in the war years, she responded to the call to try to make a united front of occultists and spiritualists against the forces of materialism in the post-war world. At this point she wrote various articles for the spiritualist press and appeared as a speaker on several spiritualist platforms

This book contains her original work *Spiritualism in the Light of Occult Science* with commentaries by Gareth Knight that quote extensively from now largely unobtainable material that she wrote on the subject during her life, including transcripts from her own trance work and rare articles from old magazines and journals.

This book represents the fourth collaborative work between the two, *An Introduction to Ritual Magic, The Curcuit of Force,* and *Principles of Hermetic Philosophy* being already published in this series.

ISBN 978-1870450386

THE GRAIL SEEKER'S COMPANION
By John Matthews & Marian Green

There have been many books about the Grail, written from many differing standpoints. Some have been practical, some purely historical, others literary, but this is the first Grail book which sets out to help the esoterically inclined seeker through the maze of symbolism, character and myth which surrounds the central point of the Grail.

In today's frantic world when many people have their material needs met some still seek spiritual fulfilment. They are drawn to explore the old philosophies and traditions, particularly that of our Western Celtic Heritage. It is here they encounter the quest for the Holy Grail, that mysterious object which will bring hope and healing to all. Some have come to recognise that they dwell in a spiritual wasteland and now search that symbol of the grail which may be the only remedy. Here is the guide book for the modern seeker, explaining the history and pointing clearly towards the Aquarian grail of the future.

John Matthews and Marian Green have each been involved in the study of the mysteries of Britain and the Grail myth for over thirty-five years. In THE GRAIL SEEKER'S COMPANION they have provided a guidebook not just to places, but to people, stories and theories surrounding the Grail. A reference book of Grail-ology, including history, ritual, meditation, advice and instruction. In short, everything you are likely to need before you set out on the most important adventure of your life.

This is the only book that points the way to the Holy Grail Quest in the 21st. century.

ISBN978-1870450492

THE FORGOTTEN MAGE

The Magical Lectures of Colonel C.R.F. Seymour.
Edited by Dolores Ashcroft-Nowicki

Charles Seymour was a man of many talents and considerable occult skills. The friend and confidant of Dion Fortune, he worked with her and his magical partner, Christine Hartley, for many productive years.

As one of the Inner Circle of Dion Fortune's Society of the Inner Light, Seymour was a High Priest in every sense of the word, but he was also one of the finest teachers of the occult art to emerge this century.

In the past, little of Seymour's work has been widely available, but in this volume Dolores Ashcroft-Nowicki, Director of Studies of the Servants of the Light School of Occult Science, has gathered together a selection of the best of Seymour's work. His complex scholarship and broad background knowledge of the Pagan traditions shine through in articles which include: The Meaning of Initiation; Magic in the Ancient Mystery Religions; The Esoteric Aspect of Religion; Meditations for Temple Novices; The Old Gods; The Ancient Nature Worship and The Children of the Great Mother.

ISBN 978-1870450393

THE WESTERN MYSTERY TRADITION
By Christine Hartley

A reissue of a classic work, by a pupil of Dion Fortune, on the mythical and historical roots of Western occultism.

Christine Hartley's aim was to demonstrate that we in the West, far from being dependent upon Eastern esoteric teachings, possess a rich and potent mystery tradition of our own, evoked and defined in myth, legend, folklore and song, and embodied in the legacy of Druidic culture.

More importantly, she provides practical guidelines for modern students of the ancient mysteries, 'The Western Mystery Tradition,' in Christine Hartley's view, 'is the basis of the Western religious feeling, the foundation of our spiritual life, the matrix of our religious formulae, whither we are aware of it or not. To it we owe the life and force of our spiritual life.'

ISBN 978-1870450249

*   *   *   *   *

A MODERN MAGICIAN'S HANDBOOK
By Marian Green

This book presents the ancient arts of magic, ritual and practical occult arts as used by modern ceremonial magicians and witches in a way that everyone can master, bringing them into the Age of Aquarius. Drawing on over three decades of practical experience, Marian Green offers a simple approach to the various skills and techniques that are needed to turn an interest into a working knowledge of magic.

Each section offers explanations, guidance and practical exercises in meditation, inner journeying, preparation for ritual, the arts of divination and many more of today's esoteric practices. No student is too young or too old to benefit from the material set out for them in this book, and its simple language may help even experienced magicians and witches understand their arts in greater depth.

ISBN 978-1870450430

PRACTICAL MAGIC AND THE WESTERN MYSTERY TRADITION
Unpublished Essays and Articles by W. E. Butler.

W. E. Butler, a devoted friend and colleague of the celebrated occultist Dion Fortune, was among those who helped build the Society of the Inner Light into the foremost Mystery School of its day. He then went on to found his own school, the Servants of the Light, which still continues under the guidance of Dolores Ashcroft-Nowicki, herself an occultist and author of note and the editor and compiler of this volume.

PRACTICAL MAGIC AND THE WESTERN TRADITION is a collection of previously unpublished articles, training papers, and lectures covering many aspects of practical magic in the context of western occultism that show W. E. Butler not only as a leading figure in the magical tradition of the West, but also as one of its greatest teachers.

Subjects covered include:

    What makes an Occultist
    Ritual Training
    Inner Plane Contacts and Rays
    The Witch Cult
    Keys in Practical Magic
    Telesmatic Images
    Words of Power
    An Explanation of Some Psychic Phenomena

ISBN 978-1870450324

PRINCIPLES OF HERMETIC PHILOSOPHY
By Dion Fortune & Gareth Knight

Principles of Hermetic Philosophy was the last known work written by Dion Fortune. It appeared in her Monthly letters to members and associates of the Society of the Inner Light between November 1942 and March 1944.

Her intention in this work is summed up in her own words: "The observations in these pages are an attempt to gather together the fragments of a forgotten wisdom and explain and expand them in the light of personal observation."

She was uniquely equipped to make highly significant personal observations in these matters as one of the leading practical occultists of her time. What is more, in these later works she feels less constrained by traditions of occult secrecy and takes an altogether more practical approach than in her earlier, well known textbooks.

Gareth Knight takes the opportunity to amplify her explanations and practical exercises with a series of full page illustrations, and provides a commentary on her work

978-1870450348

*   *   *   *   *

THE STORY OF DION FORTUNE
As told to Charles Fielding and Carr Collins.

Dion Fortune and Aleister Crowley stand as the twentieth century's most influential leaders of the Western Esoteric Tradition. They were very different in their backgrounds, scholarship and style.

But, for many, Dion Fortune is the chosen exemplar of the Tradition - with no drugs, no homosexuality and no kinks. This book tells of her formative years and of her development.

At the end, she remains a complex and enigmatic figure, who can only be understood in the light of the system she evolved and worked to great effect.

There can be no definitive "Story of Dion Fortune". This book must remain incompete and full of errors. However, readers may find themselves led into an experience of initiation as envisaged by this fearless and dedicated woman.

ISBN 978-1870450331

www.ingramcontent.com/pod-product-compliance
Ingram Content Group UK Ltd.
Pitfield, Milton Keynes, MK11 3LW, UK
UKHW041313120125
4067UKWH00025B/125